EVERY LOVING GIFT

Every Loving Gift

How a Family's Courage
Saved a Special Child

Judy Polikoff
as told to
Michele Sherman

G. P. Putnam's Sons   New York

This is a work of nonfiction. The Polikoff family and their struggle and victory are real. However, most of the names used in the book are not the true names of the people involved in this story. This is due, for the most part, to a simple desire to provide privacy for so many who gave so much to Andy and his family.

All hospital names have been changed. Also, all names of doctors, lawyers, programmers, and friends. However, there is one group of men whose real names have been used: Dr. Robert Doman, Mr. John Unruh, and Dr. Carl Delacato, all of the Centre for Neurological Rehabilitation.

Library of Congress Cataloging in Publication Data

Polikoff, Judy.
Every loving gift.

1. Brain-damaged children—United States—Biography.
2. Polikoff, Andy. I. Sherman, Michele. II. Title.
RJ496.B7P64   1983   362.3′092′4   82-18045
ISBN 0-399-12783-6

To Scott and Todd, whose emotional pain and suffering were never underestimated, and whose love and support helped make the family what we are today— I'm proud of you.

And to Jack, who always believed—the root of all the best and longest-lasting dreams of my life. I love you.
                                        Judy

To my husband, Harold, keeper of the faith, who is everything, absolutely. Always.

And to our son, Jason.
                                        Michele

Contents

Acknowledgments

There are an awesome number of people to thank, and though nothing would please us more than to name every individual personally, space requirements wreak havoc with requirements of the heart.

Our deepest thanks go to every soul who passed through the door during those programming years. Every pair of helping hands. Every giving heart. And . . .

To all those others who, though they could not physically take part in the programming, nevertheless contributed to the making of Andy by doing telephone duty, devising schedules, and undertaking a wealth of unsung, everyday, vital activities. And . . .

To all the merchants who were patient and generous. And . . .

To the media, which responded to the story of a little boy with interest and coverage.

We want to personally thank Carl Lopatin, who became a dear friend through many hard hours, the members of the Delco Stanton Lodge, and Bernie Magid and the Wolf Baron Lodge, Max Duretz Foundation. Also, Marcie and Bill Samuelson, who never said no, whatever the request. And Bill Stewart.

And, of course, the family. To the Sokoloffs—Judy's parents, and to Ned, her brother. To Sadie Polikoff—Jack's mother, and to Jack's late father—the source of some very special values. And to all the rest—aunts, cousins—especially

Phyllis and Larry Miller, who were there at all hours and in all situations.

To all of these, and to anyone who might, inadvertently, have been misplaced in the crush of hundreds and hundreds of people—a lifetime of thanks for an unrepayable gift. This is to acknowledge all of you—the life-givers.

Finally, we have another group of contributors to thank. Dr. Robert Doman, who was kind enough to include me in his Parents' Orientation, and to offer any aid or information I might need. John Unruh, who spent a great deal of his very valuable time giving me a better understanding of the work of the Centre for Neurological Rehabilitation. John E. Gordon, Ph.D., Director of the Neuropsychology Laboratory at the University of Pennsylvania's School of Medicine, Department of Psychiatry, who provided detailed information on Andy's psychological profile.

And last, but definitely not least, our deepest regard and thanks to Dr. Carl Delacato, who not only encouraged the writing of this book, but brought the entire world of Andy Polikoff into a rare perspective through his own great enthusiasm in dealing with children.

Michele Sherman
Philadelphia
Spring 1982

Preface

This is the story of a family. Of a challenge. Of great obstacles. It's a story of immense courage.

Judy Polikoff lived this story, through tears and triumphs, solidly supported by friends, neighbors, even strangers, yet never able to relate her own feelings to the written accounts of other women faced with similar crises. The emotional support she sought was lacking in the majority of these published accounts, which failed to mirror the terrors and the tremulous hope that Judy herself experienced.

This, then, was the purpose for writing this book. To provide a different frame of reference. To say, in effect, that all emotions are allowed. That no feeling, no matter how mean or unhappy or momentarily hating, is out of line. That all the ordinary emotions of life are normal and natural and also shared. That above all else—shared.

This is the story of a community. A family. A woman.

EVERY LOVING GIFT

I
THE BIRTH

1

The room was semi-private, moderate in size, bright and quiet. It was pleasant enough, as hospital rooms go. Only past experience was to blame for Judy's wariness. Jack had been with her from late afternoon on, talking and reminiscing and making plans for the new baby. He hadn't given her time to be alone or to indulge in last-minute anxieties.

The corridor outside the room was unnaturally still. That seemed odd, in maternity, especially during visiting hours. But Franklin Central was closing down its maternity ward, and most of the rooms stood empty. Judy's baby was to be the last. Then, the redecorating could get started.

It was one more odd thing—having the last baby.

Jack, sprawled in the chair by the bed, glanced at the small clock on the night table then stood up, stretching. It was the moment Judy had been dreading. Something of her nervousness communicated itself to him. From his vantage point of six foot two, he gazed down at her.

"It's okay, Judy?"

He was frowning again. The crease between his eyes had grown distressingly familiar. She wanted desperately to be reassured herself, so she put her heart into reassuring him.

"Everything's fine," she grinned up from her easy pose against the flat pillow. "And anyway, if you were thinking maybe you'd change your mind, you should have thought of that about nine months ago. Besides," she placed her hands flat on either side of the mound of her stomach, "it's the little girl we've always wanted. You can bet on it. Nurse Stoner told me."

17

He laughed, then bent and took her face between his hands, and she threw her arms around his neck and clung to him, just for a moment. Then, she kissed him with gusto and shoved him roughly away.

"Get yourself out of here, Daddy, and go to bed. You need all the rest you can get."

"I'm right next door," Jack reminded her, quite unnecessarily. "If you want anything, or if you just want to talk . . ." he hesitated. "You know everything's great, don't you, Judy? All those things you were worrying about before— none of that's important. We can always make the money stretch, and the rest of it . . ." He shrugged. "That was just fate. Tubal ligations never were foolproof."

She opened her eyes very wide, in mock surprise. "Look who you're telling," she said lightly. "Now get out of here and let me get some sleep. I am having a baby in the morning!"

It comforted her to know he was sleeping nearby. With the ward so empty, the hospital people hadn't minded. She'd had serious complications at the birth of their second child. She wanted him close. It seemed like protection somehow.

When she was alone, she dropped back flat on her cushionless pillow, wriggling around to find a comfortable position. She wanted the surgery over. Her entire pregnancy had filled her with unending trepidation. She heard soft footsteps out in the hall, then the night nurse passed her open door, and the strange silence of a nearly empty ward descended over everything.

"Well," she said, *"we're* here, so who else counts?" She tickled her fingertips over the flesh of her stomach, then tapped lightly at her navel. "You asleep in there?" she asked, then placed both hands delicately, lovingly, at the sides of the mound, marveling over the quietness of this baby. Her unborn child kept its own counsel, even in the womb. Not so her other children. Scott had shown a definite pre-birth toss-and-turn persistence, and Todd, two weeks late, was a big league kicker from his earliest days.

But then, nothing about this third child had followed a

18

planned, understood pattern. She'd tried to explain how uneasy that made her feel the day they'd taken Todd to the zoo, but it was impossible. It was trying to explain a woman's "feelings" to a non-woman.

"Do you want to keep it a secret?" Jack had asked as they roamed the zoo paths that sunny May day.

It was the middle of the week and the zoo was deserted. Jack was on the swing shift at Century Steel. This week, his days were his own. His nights belonged to the company.

Judy wasn't really surprised that he knew. He'd known the last time, too, when she was pregnant.

"I didn't want to worry you until I was sure," she said, reaching up a hand to tickle Todd, riding on Jack's shoulders.

"Why would I worry over you being pregnant?"

Judy made a face. "Right. We won't mention that little bit of surgery I had done after Todd was born, okay?"

"We knew that wasn't guaranteed, and besides, why would I worry?" Jack persisted. "I'd be surprised, maybe," he grinned. "I am surprised." He looked at her. "I'm not sorry, Judy."

She knew that. Jack would have loved a dozen children. For herself—well, this wasn't something she'd hoped for. Todd was eighteen months old. Scott was almost ten. One pre-adolescent and one baby were more than enough to handle.

"It's about two months, isn't it?" Jack asked. "Why don't you go and have the test done and make sure? Then we can start to plan."

She already had an appointment for later in the week. She felt nervous about it and unhappy. Jack studied her expression and absorbed something of what she felt. He shifted Todd and put an arm around her.

"What's wrong, babe?"

She looked up into his eyes. "It just doesn't feel right." She swallowed, not knowing how to make him understand what she didn't fully understand herself. "I have a bad feeling. About having had a tubal ligation and getting pregnant, anyway. I wasn't supposed to get pregnant. I'm frightened."

19

It was a fear that hadn't abated. Not when she'd learned she really was pregnant—she'd felt a stifling sense of terror when Dr. Albertson called to confirm it. Not during all the long months after, bringing her, finally, to that last night at Franklin Central.

Lying very still, breathing softly, she listened. There was no sense of communication with her baby. No movement from the womb. No kick against her flattened palms. She stretched herself out, gently stroking her belly.

"A little pre-birth dialogue might be nice about now—just the two of us," she whispered, thinking herself past herself, inside herself to the child still unknown. Maybe it *was* a girl— dresses and frills and delicate little blouses. Tiny sandals in summer . . . She grinned to herself.

And drifted slowly into a light sleep.

Her sleep was fitful. She came half-awake time after time, sweating and disoriented. Finally, on the last such awakening, she turned her head sleepily to the clock. The hands pointed to three o'clock.

There was no sound from the hospital corridor. There was no movement from the womb. After a long while, she drifted back to sleep, vaguely uneasy, not trying to pursue the cause for this unrest beyond the natural anxieties of giving birth.

Her unborn child was very still inside her.

The operating room was quiet. Conversation was minimal. It was eight A.M. and the first of two surgeries was a delivery by Cesarean section. Those present were the surgeon—Paul Albertson, his partner, two nurses, and the anesthetist. The pediatrician, Myron Kohn, was present also. This was standard procedure at Franklin Central in cases of Cesarean delivery.

"It's crying," said the scrub nurse some little time later. The cord was clipped twice, the cut made neatly. The newest member of the Polikoff family made a howling entry—not the daughter Nurse Stoner had predicted, but a tiny baby boy. The child was placed on his mother's stomach and stroked, then laid on a blanket and given into Dr. Kohn's care, to be whisked from the operating room.

Dr. Albertson turned back to his patient for the second stage of the surgery.

Waking should have ended the anxieties of her pregnancy, but she was far too sick to indulge in self-congratulations. She rejected an intensity of pain she couldn't tolerate, and fell into unconsciousness.

Some time later, in midafternoon, she tried it again, surfacing to test the waters. With consciousness came a single thought: Wrong! Something's wrong!

She went away again.

When she came around for the third time, it was late. She had lost her bearings. She thought it must be the same day. After all, why wouldn't it be? After a while, she became aware of light pressure on her hand and she turned her head without thinking. The abrupt motion hurt her neck, chest, abdomen, but there was Jack stroking her fingers, in the chair by the bed.

She wet her lips. He saw her try to speak.

"Everything's fine, babe," he assured her quickly. "We have a beautiful little boy. No dresses and bows this time around, either, but think of all the hand-me-downs from Todd . . ." He smiled down at her with overpowering love.

Her mouth was too dry, her tongue felt swollen and thick. She couldn't make a sound. When Jack bent to kiss her forehead, she barely felt the brush of his lips.

"Shhh," he admonished her. "Let me get you something to drink."

Her tongue was plastered to the back of her throat. The straw appeared magically, conveniently bent. She gulped and ice water trickled over her tongue to hit her stomach in a solid block. Jack was fast. When she vomited, he already had the small basin under her chin.

Long minutes passed.

"Jack," she finally managed, weakly.

21

"Shhh," he said again. "Everything's fine, the baby's fine, you're doing fine, you're just weak. The nurse'll be back in a little while to give you a shot, everything's fine, we have another little boy. Andrew Polikoff."

"Jack," she moaned.

He looked into her dazed eyes, then traced both cheekbones with his thumbs, softly, wanting to hug her tight, knowing he must not.

"The baby," she whispered, through lips that wouldn't flex. The nauseousness was rising again, but slower this time so she could monitor it. "My baby . . ."

Her skin was cold to Jack's touch. Only minutes before she'd been feverish. Her hair lay lank over the hospital sheet, its rich red-brown looking anemic. Her eyes, normally a vibrant blue, were unfocused and glittered like slate and she was whiter than the sheet . . .

Jack was scared to death.

"I love you, Judy," he moaned. "I love you so much." He lowered himself toward her to hold her without lifting her, to cradle her without hurting her. "I'm right with you, baby, I'll be here when you wake up, I want you to try to sleep now, baby, everything's good, everything's right . . ."

Her heart was leaping into her throat. Dumb animal panic. Instinct. Everything was not all right. There was no reason behind this knowledge—she just knew and that was that! In one desperate surge of strength, she gripped Jack's arm and hauled herself half up.

"What's wrong with my baby?"

It blasted out, louder than she'd meant, stronger than she'd thought. It was expelled on a wave of apprehension and sickness compounded by the terrible jarring she gave herself as she tried to pull erect. Nurse Stoner was suddenly beside her, where Jack had been a second before.

Nurse put her to sleep.

She woke at dawn the next morning, Tuesday, December 11, to vomit again. Jack was there, as he'd promised.

22

"What's wrong with me?"

"There's nothing wrong, Judy."

"Don't lie to me."

"I wouldn't lie to you, babe."

"I shouldn't hurt like this, not from having a baby. I've had babies before, Jack, there wasn't pain like this—what's wrong?"

"You never had a baby by Cesarean before," Jack said reasonably.

"Jack!" She'd been white as death seconds before. Now she looked flushed. "Where's the baby, Jack, did I lose the baby?"

He gripped her hand hard. "The baby's fine, Judy, a beautiful little boy. You'll see him yourself just as soon as you're strong enough."

She lay flat on her back, panting. After a while, she lifted her eyes to his face.

"Why do I feel like this, Jack? What did they do to me down there?"

So he told her. Because whatever she'd imagine would be worse than the truth. That's what he told himself.

"They did a hysterectomy instead of another tubal ligation, Judy. Albertson felt it was best."

She merely stared at him. There was no comprehension of what he'd said. The words penetrated and dissolved without leaving a trace. She didn't know why Jack should have become alarmed, but apparently he was. Nurse Stoner appeared again, and Judy slept.

It was noon, that same day. Judy lay very still, getting her bearings, eyes closed, mind wandering, words and phrases swimming in and out and, among them, Jack's words. They still meant nothing. There was a numb barrier between the words and her ability to comprehend their enormity. It wasn't that Albertson never mentioned the possibility of a hysterectomy. She had a history of difficult deliveries and a lifelong problem with her menstrual cycles, coupled with the desire to insure her own sterility. But she'd gone to sleep expecting another tubal ligation. Not a hysterectomy. A hysterectomy had always been ranked as a last option. She'd never believed the option would be exercised.

Finally, with great care, she opened her eyes and the ceiling swam, then steadied, and she thought, I can bear this now, the pain's less, I can bear this.

There was a movement by her left side. She thought it was Jack. It wasn't. The cool hand touching her head had a familiar scent. She eased her cheek around, and stared.

"Mom?" Her voice was a hoarse croak.

"Jack called last night. He was worried about you. I came right up. Dad's at home, waiting to hear from me. I wanted to see you awake before I called."

Judy closed her eyes again, trying to think of Jack calling her mother. Of her mother coming right on up, as if it were a turnpike jaunt, instead of a flight from Florida to Philadelphia.

Ceil Sokoloff definitely expected a more vibrant sign of life. She prodded her daughter.

"Judy. Listen to me. You have to get up!"

Judy's eyes flew open and her breath choked in her throat at the thought of trying to stand on her own two feet, then the dry little sound turned to a dismal hiccoughing and she started to cry helplessly, all the while holding every single muscle absolutely still.

"Judy!" Her mother's voice grew more strident to insure being heard over the choking sobs. "I want you to get up! You don't have time to indulge yourself! You have a responsibility to your new little boy. Do you think I'd ask this of you if it wasn't vitally important? You have to come look at the baby!"

She had to be told to rise from her deathbed to admire her newest offspring. She really should have thought of that herself.

"His color's bad," Ceil whispered frantically. "Please try. Try to get up. There's no time to waste. Jack and I—we'll help you!"

The nursery was nearly empty. There were two babies there, neither of them her boy. Her new son lay in an isolette in a

24

small section at the back, without infant company. She stared, dazed, at this tiny wizened wrinkle, the smallest infant she'd ever produced. His mouth was a twist, his face fretful, his limbs small . . .

She wished she could see his hands and feet but the blanket covered most of him. She rubbed at her own face vaguely and couldn't feel the knuckles against her skin.

Behind her, wheeling the chair, was Jack. He stood silent, staring at their new son with her.

"He's yellow," her mother was saying urgently. "Look at his little face. Look how tiny he is. Even Jack can see there's something wrong. That's why he called me last night and why I came right up. Can't you see he's yellow, Judy?"

If this was really Tuesday, then Andrew was one day old. Judy thought that out carefully. His one-day-old birthday. It made her inexplicably giddy. She felt weak and sick and wondered what medication they were giving her.

"Judy?"

Yellow. Yellow? What had her mother just said about yellow? She knew it was important. Her mother wouldn't ask otherwise. She closed her eyes and swallowed, then opened them again, squinting, and tried bravely to determine if her baby was off-color.

The chair squeaked and wheezed as Jack wheeled her back along the quiet corridor. Nurse Stoner was there to help her onto the bed.

"Judy," Ceil's hand was light on her daughter's arm. "Let Dad and me get a second opinion. That's all I want."

Second? There was a buzzing in her head. The trip to the nursery had set her back, all the agony of her wounds was heightening again. Her mother's voice reverberated through a rising hum of chaos and she tried to think—second? Had she ever had a first opinion? Her head ached and she tried desperately to comprehend why she needed either a first or a second opinion.

"Let us pay for it, Jack," she heard her mother say. That was too much, Judy couldn't have that, and she heard her own voice struggling to form an appropriate comeback but her breath had gone shallow. She couldn't make the sounds. Her mother's voice went on and on. She knew she was in trouble when the helpless tears started trickling down her cheeks, ice-cold droplets. She wasn't aware of both fists beating weak against the mattress, but there were voices, a meaningless drone, and then a sharp, pinching prick.

All things faded swiftly. She felt blessed.

Wednesday was better. The pain remained, but in bearable form, and her mother had been momentarily vanquished.

"Well now, I'm very sorry you're upset, Mrs. Sokoloff," Nurse Stoner stood planted in the hospital room door. "But my patient's my first responsibility, not your feelings, and Mrs. Polikoff's got to get her strength up and visits only seem to upset her. I've asked Dr. Albertson to forbid all visitors except, of course, her husband, and the doctor's agreed, at least for today, and possibly for tomorrow."

Ceil Sokoloff knew defeat when she was bludgeoned by it. She retreated, but only temporarily, to the cafeteria.

At ten-thirty that morning, Dr. Kohn came to visit. He'd been in before, but Judy had been sleeping. He'd already answered Jack's questions, and those of Ceil, and he spent twenty minutes now repeating his reassurances about Andy to Judy.

"So you're saying," Judy finally asked, pleating the sheet, "that Andy's not just a little bit—yellow?"

No, Andy wasn't yellow. If he had shown signs of jaundice, he would be treated for it. That was obvious, wasn't it? And his position in the nursery was indicative of nothing. The nursery was empty—the maternity ward was being phased out. The isolette was nothing more than a heated crib; all the new babies were placed in heated cribs to maintain a constant temperature. There was nothing to worry about, no nightmares to dredge up.

When Dr. Albertson visited later that morning, he said essentially the same thing.

26

So Judy rested. She slept. She woke again to find the pain receding even more; she could feel normal things again.

Everything was fine. The doctors said.

The chill glare of December would have made the room dismal whatever the emotional environment. Judy, fighting depression, felt gripped by a desperate lethargy that began with Kohn's visit early that Friday morning. Jack stood with his back to her as she lay on the bed. He'd been standing like that for the longest time. She didn't know what he was thinking.

"My mother still wants that second opinion," Judy finally ventured. "Especially now."

Jack turned his head and looked at her expectantly.

"Today's Friday," Judy continued. "I told Kohn I thought Andy's color was bad right here, myself, when he stopped in on Wednesday. You told him before that. Mom told him. You'd think it's sort of late for him to be deciding Andy has jaundice!"

Jack faced her fully, leaning against the windowsill, his arms folded across his chest. He looked tired and just a little bit impatient. The days had been terribly long, his fears for Judy and the baby increasingly debilitating. He wanted very much to believe that any problems were already being handled.

"Kohn's treating the jaundice," he said reasonably. "He said he started the treatment last night. Since he's admitted there's jaundice, and he's treating Andy for it, I'm not sure what your mother wants a second opinion on. Kohn stressed there's nothing to worry about. He's getting lab tests done twice a day to check on the level of jaundice."

"Nothing?" Judy whispered.

"Jaundice isn't uncommon," Jack said, a bit shortly.

Judy was silent for a little while. Then, "Would you trust Kohn as Andy's pediatrician?"

Jack considered that. "Why don't we wait and see how he handles all this? We can decide if we want to change pediatricians when we're home with the baby."

"They brought me Andy last night, after you left," Judy

27

rubbed her face despondently. "I guess Kohn must have decided to start the treatment right after. I don't understand," she stared at Jack. "I didn't know he made evening rounds. What decided him?"

"One of the nurses called him. Something like that," Jack shrugged. "We can find out later, if you're interested. But what matters is that Andy's being taken care of. Now it's time for you to take care of yourself."

She wasn't listening. "He's still making those screeching sounds," she tried to grin. "Andy, not Kohn."

Jack was perfectly aware of what sounds she meant. This wasn't the ordinary pitch of baby howling. Andy's cries were sharp, hard, breathless shrieks. It was terrifying.

"And I laid him down on the sheet and watched the way he holds his hands. His arms—you know, when he's on his back. And there's something . . . He's still rigid, Jack. I held him against me and he didn't cuddle, he's never cuddly, Jack."

Jack sat down abruptly on the side of the bed and put a hand very gently over her stomach.

"I want you to get well, Judy," he said. "I want it more than anything. Andy's being taken care of now, and all those problems will clear up. Please! Don't get worked up. It's not good for you and you've got to start thinking about yourself."

She looked up into his eyes. She was very unhappy. Part of it was Andy, of course, but a great deal of it involved her own surgery. She couldn't seem to come to grips with the reality of the hysterectomy. She was astonished by her own weakness. She'd imagined herself tougher.

Thirty-one, she thought. Thirty-one and wasted. She closed her eyes to hide swift tears and felt Jack's strong hand in her hair, and let him pet her gently.

On the twenty-second of December, a brilliant, flawless day, Jack took them home. Judy was exhausted and despondent. The child in her arms was rigid. Never once had he loosened up, not even after the jaundice was gone and the problem apparently treated.

28

Ceil Sokoloff stayed to help out over Christmas week, then had to return to Florida. January, 1974, found Judy on her own. Just herself and her family. Weeks after surgery, life waited to be faced, and she didn't know how to cope with it.

She was still not herself.

There was still something wrong with Andy.

2

Judy was afraid of Andy. She was overwhelmed by that knowledge from the very start, back in Franklin Central, with her new child a rigid, shrieking bundle in her arms, but she denied her fear to herself and mentioned it to no one else. It was terrible to be afraid of her own baby!

Her early visits to the pediatrician weren't satisfying. His answers seemed to skate around the major issues, so her fears were never laid to rest, and she asked the same questions over and over.

The sound of his cry?

The sound of Andy's cry was only Andy's particular way of expressing himself. Was she going to worry over every individual trait of this child?

The jaundice. Couldn't the jaundice have caused other problems?

But they'd treated the jaundice, Dr. Kohn reminded her. And reminded her. With great patience, he told her that he'd had to be sure. That he'd had to observe. That he'd had to take care.

"That's not what you said in the hospital," Judy reminded him. "You said everything was fine. That Andy was fine. That there was no reason to worry."

But he hadn't wanted to alarm her before he was sure. She'd been sick, very sick from her surgery.

And his hands . . .? The position of his hands . . .?
Andy, it appeared, was double-jointed.

Twelve weeks went by. Andy was three months old. Judy had spent three months watching a child who broke all the known rules, taking him to Dr. Kohn with more frequency than was required, then coming home torn between the fear that this man was inept and the even greater fear of going elsewhere and finding she was right and that her baby was indeed damaged.

Her lethargy and lingering postoperative pain made her feel considerable anxiety about her own condition, thus providing some balance for her fears about Andy.

For the first time in her married life, she was afraid to be intimate with Jack. In all this time, these three long months, there had been no normal closeness between them. There was a shyness now that touched on actual fear. She was certain she'd been mutilated. She didn't want to learn she could no longer feel physical love, but more than that—far more than that—she couldn't fail Jack.

They were in their bedroom. The three boys were all asleep. Judy was gathering up her night things preparatory to fleeing into the bathroom where Jack wouldn't be able to see her undressed.

"Kohn said he'll be able to do some simple tests on Andy the next time we come," she said. "He would've done them today, but Andy had his polio vaccine and he shrieked the whole time we were there anyway.

"I think we'll wait just that long. See what these 'tests' are, and what the results are like. After that, if the best he can come up with is 'double-jointed,' we'll go to somebody else.

"I don't understand a single thing that's happened to me since I found out I was pregnant!" Judy blurted suddenly. Then she stopped, because they'd been over it before and it was pointless.

She turned toward the door.

"I love you, Judy. I'd never hurt you. You know that, don't you? How much I want you?"

Her throat constricted and she couldn't answer him. She couldn't have formulated an answer in any circumstance, nor could she find the courage to turn and face him. She stood halfway between bed and door, clutching her night clothes in her hands, and stared miserably at the floor.

"I just want to hold you and love you," Jack said wistfully.

She sensed he was about to rise from the bed and that brought her close to panic. She couldn't let him see the surgical scar, couldn't make him understand the other, deeper scar that came with her realization of the baby's problems. There *was* something wrong with Andy, and she was his mother. The pleasure of physical love under these circumstances seemed heartless and unnatural.

She realized she'd begun to cry only when the room blurred and, with it, Jack's face. He rose swiftly and came to her, enfolding her in his arms. When he finally led her over to the bed she wasn't afraid, not like before, because the bed was safe as long as he held her like this—like a child. The blanket sheltered them both.

The visit to Dr. Kohn at the end of March provided no answers to their long-standing questions. Andy was sick, feverish and vomiting, congested and tormented by diarrhea. This was not the time for testing. Kohn diagnosed an upper respiratory infection, prescribed skim milk and Kaopectate, and restricted Andy's diet.

Judy stood watch for the next six nights. The congestion characterizing this infection wasn't new. It was an extension of a problem already noted and reported on every successive visit to the pediatrician. There was always a thick dribbling of mucus from the baby's mouth and nose. Judy had started checking him periodically through the night, fearful of his choking.

Don't worry so much, Kohn said, exasperated. He's got a head cold.

Spring arrived and brought with it Ceil Sokoloff, up for her spring visit to her daughter's family. By the time she left, one

31

week later, her flat pronouncements on Andy's total lack of normal development had goaded Judy out of whatever state of protective procrastination she'd been living in.

She felt hounded by her mother's words and angry and scared to death.

"Why don't you call Uncle Murray?" Jack suggested.

She'd thought about calling him for weeks. "He's not a pediatrician," she countered lamely.

"He's our family doctor," Jack answered flatly. "Who would you trust more? He's a second opinion."

This produced a brief silence between them. Such silences were becoming more and more frequent.

Two days after Ceil's return to Florida, the call to Uncle Murray still hadn't been made. Needing a diversion from the constant anxiety, Judy played hostess to two old friends, her first social function since Andy's birth.

She moved wearily around her kitchen while her friends sat gossiping in the living room. Each time she passed the phone, hanging by the door, her mind flew to Andy, lying in his playpen under the watchful eyes of her friends.

Coffee and small talk. She put out cups for the coffee. The sugar bowl. The ceramic pitcher for the milk. She arranged these things, and a coffee cake, and some rolls and butter on a large tray, along with napkins, spoons, and forks. She went back for the cake and butter knives, legs heavy with exhaustion, wondering why she never felt any better and why the small art of making conversation was so difficult this morning.

She paused in the kitchen doorway, momentarily invisible to her friends around the angle of the dining room wall and, leaning there, she heard their voices pitched suspiciously low and made the mistake of listening in on them.

"How can I say a thing like that to Judy?"

That was Carol, speaking to Jenny Blackman. Judy had known them both since grade school.

"You *are* her closest friend, Carol," Jenny retorted. "What are close friends supposed to be for? You can't just wiggle out of it because it's painful and embarrassing. Think of Judy, not yourself! It has to be the worst thing a mother ever has to face, and she's got to be made to talk it out with somebody she cares for so it doesn't eat her up alive!"

"Her mother was just up."

"That's different and you know it!"

"I can't just bring it up out of the blue, Jenny. If she needed me, or wanted to talk to me, she'd say something herself. You can't seriously expect me to intrude on her most private business like that!"

"She's not about to bring it up herself, and you know it. She's trying to pretend it'll all work out all right. Wouldn't you? She's trying to convince herself everything'll be fine if she just leaves it for another week, or another month. And it won't be fine, Carol. And she's got to face up to that fact!"

"I can't do it!" Carol said, her voice still soft, though it carried farther than a shout. "I can't hurt her like that. I can't tell her Andy's retarded!"

Jack stood in the kitchen doorway, that same doorway, hours later, watching Judy get dinner. The boys were in the living room, Scott wrestling Todd around on the floor, Andy on his stomach in his playpen.

"What happened today?" Jack asked.

She didn't answer him.

He eyed her back shrewdly. "Was it Andy?"

She turned to stare at him, trying to formulate the words, giving it up as useless. She couldn't tell him what she'd overheard. It was somehow obscene. The rest of that visit passed in slow-motion dread while she sat and sipped coffee and listened to the chatter of her friends and waited for one or the other to say something unmentionable.

Neither had.

"Andy?" she said. "Why would you think anything happened with Andy?" Her voice went grim. "Nothing ever happens with Andy."

33

She moved past him to place a platter of chicken on the dining room table. When she returned for the vegetables, Jack was leaning against the refrigerator, his face concerned.

"What's wrong, then?"

"Nothing's wrong."

Jack seemed, at least for the moment, to accept this.

"Did you ask Carol for the name of her new pediatrician? It was today she was coming over, wasn't it?"

"I didn't ask her." Judy turned to the vegetable pan and stirred the mixture inside gently. "I forgot. I'll call her."

"Would you rather give Kohn that chance to do the tests? Andy hasn't been so cranky and congested the past few days. Do you want to consider sticking it out another month?"

She didn't comment, intent on spooning the vegetables into a serving bowl.

"It's a big move, changing doctors," Jack persisted. "And he did take good care of Scott and Todd before all this business started."

"He took good care of them?" She was jolted out of her silence. "Exactly what did we ever need him to do that would have shown him up as incompetent? We took Todd to him, and Scott to him, and there wasn't anything wrong with Todd or Scott—thank God!—so he had two healthy, normal boys to look after and he managed not to screw either of them up. He gave them their shots and he listened to their chests and he smiled. He smiles a lot, Jack!"

"Judy . . ."

"It's different now, with Andy."

But Jack really didn't want to hear that it was different with Andy. Feeling it, in his heart, was one thing. Hearing it stated in Judy's certain tones was another. Jack was afraid.

"Kohn said he'll do the tests, and if there's anything wrong . . ."

"Do you think he'll wait as long to decide if anything's wrong as he waited to treat the jaundice?"

They glared at each other.

34

"I should have insisted on getting a second opinion the day after Andy was born," Judy's voice was harsh. "There's no possible excuse for failing to do that. I'll never be able to live with the guilt of that!"

"For God's sake, Judy, we were in a hospital, we had a whole floor of second opinions! Albertson was there, he visited constantly, and the nurses, all the nurses on the floor are trained to observe just that sort of thing, aren't they? And Kohn himself! He explained why he waited. He needed to be sure. He *did* treat the jaundice, Judy! And it went away. You know that! So what were we supposed to get a second opinion *on,* anyway?"

"What if his delay in treating the jaundice caused new problems?" Judy asked, then bit her lip and stared at Jack wildly.

There was a deadly silence.

When Jack finally spoke, his face looked gray and old.

"Everything'll be all right, Judy."

She didn't even bother to comment.

Dinner was a dismal meal. Scott eyed his silent parents and fell silent himself, pushing his vegetables around until they'd gone stone-cold. Todd stuffed his mouth until he choked, watching first his mother, then his father, from beneath furrowed brows, waiting in vain to be reprimanded.

Judy cleared the table and stood in the kitchen, staring pensively at the dirty dishes littering the sink, when Jack came in to put the milk back in the refrigerator. The older boys had thundered upstairs, and shrieks sounded from the back bedroom. Andy still lay in the playpen, being—well, being Andy.

She felt Jack there, at her back. Finally, she turned to glance at him. He was hanging by the refrigerator, looking belligerent and vaguely ashamed and it hurt her. She turned back to the sink and started the dishes.

"I'm sorry, Jack."

Behind her, Jack shuffled. The apology made him very unhappy. If there was one thing he knew quite surely it was that Judy shouldn't be apologizing. Judy was worried sick about the baby, as was he, himself. Pretending he didn't believe she was

35

right about Kohn wouldn't make the threat of what she said any less potent.

"I'm just being silly," he heard her murmur, heard the slight catch in her voice and knew she was crying. It seemed, these days, she was always crying.

And this was impossible. He wouldn't let her say it. Judy was never silly about the kids.

He crossed the small kitchen to put his arms protectively around her, standing behind her, his chin resting against the top of her head. He would have given a great deal to know some magic solution that would ease away the worry they'd shared since Franklin Central. To make her happy again. He adored her.

But he was tired, and cold, and the warm press of her body reminded him of other, better nights. He wondered what she was thinking.

What she was thinking was that she was terribly sad. That it was hard to draw a complete breath. That breathing seemed like too much trouble. She would have given everything to be able to believe what Dr. Kohn said. That Andy was simply developing at his own speed. That the harsh crying was the way he expressed himself. That his lack of response when he was cuddled was—well—what? The doctor hadn't really said.

She shivered, though the dish water was hot against her wrists, and there was a frigid chill around her heart. She made her mind a blank.

There followed a long and bitter time of aloneness, days of indecision, while she sat behind her locked door admitting no one to her house. The phone would ring and go unanswered. She wanted to talk to no one. The days stretched out, into first one week, then the start of another, and during that time she stared at her baby and made herself think only positive thoughts.

Finally, she couldn't bear it. Not for another day. Certainly not for weeks or months or years—it seemed it might be that long if they left it to Dr. Kohn to decide whether or not to proceed with his tests. In a terrible trembling hurry now that she'd made her decision, she gathered up her family and drove to Uncle Murray's.

The office was old and painted bright pink. Judy sat holding Andy in her lap, staring at the cheery walls, trying not to anticipate anything. When the last of his scheduled patients had gone, Dr. Murray Gross brought his unexpected visitors into the inner office.

"Well now, little fellow."

Andy was tiny and vulnerable on the examining table. Uncle Murray tickled, patted, prodded, then finally held out his fingers for the baby to grasp, helping the tiny right hand to close around his index finger, and encouraging the child to grip with the left hand.

Uncle Murray pulled up gently.

The baby's fingers clung for a second, then lost their tenuous grip and dropped, and Andy began his harsh, ragged shrieking.

Judy sat staring blankly at her child and at the white coat of her uncle, bending forward, obscuring the table. Long minutes passed and she felt dizzy and unwell, her throat dry, blood pounding in her ears.

Finally, Uncle Murray straightened. He turned and his eyes were sorry. She saw the helpless sorrow, and that was when she started dying. For all the after years, she remembered.

"I want you to take Andy over to Pediatric Hospital. Right now. I'm going to call and arrange it for you. I'll let them know you're on your way and why you're coming.

"Now, I have a house call to make," he tried to smile. "But I'll be in touch with you, if not later today, then certainly tonight. I don't want you to worry. It's not time to worry yet."

Judy came to her feet. Jack's grip steadied her.

"Is he retarded?" she finally asked. Her lips were stiff. The words were barely audible.

Uncle Murray looked directly at her. "I think we'd better find out."

37

Pediatric kept Andy for testing. Judy stayed with him, while Jack went home to be with the older boys. After three days, they sat in another doctor's office, this time at Pediatric, a cluttered, dusty, over-used little space.

The doctor was middle-aged and heavily lined around the eyes and mouth. His manner was abrupt, but this was only because he was harried.

And sad. Perhaps that.

"Take your little boy home and love him."

Judy and Jack Polikoff sat and stared.

"He has cerebral palsy."

3

The van pulled up to a spot three houses down the block and Jack, standing by the front door, watching for it, noted its jerky attempts to back into a space too small for it. After a minute, he half-turned his head.

"It's them," he announced. There was no expression in his voice.

The living room behind him was brightly lit. Judy had turned all the lights on, to try to dispel the shadow that seemed to fall just behind her eyes, blurring her sight. It was a reaction she'd experienced for the past five days, every time she thought of this upcoming visit.

The Cerebral Palsy Association people. Arranged through a social worker at Pediatric Hospital.

"It's a van," Jack said. His tone was conversational. He might have been describing a slightly boring fourth-inning play in the middle of baseball season.

Judy sat hugging herself for warmth, though the evening was mild, a lovely May night. She was dead-center on the couch.

"They're getting out."

She didn't need the play-by-play. She didn't need this visit at all, but the social worker was insistent, determined to help.

"Some people will come out to your house to talk to you, probably a representative from Cerebral Palsy and a family willing to tell you about their problems and what they've done to alleviate the worst of them and rehabilitate their child."

She didn't want to know about anyone else's problems. Nobody shared her problems. She had no problems. The term cerebral palsy belonged to other people, sad unfortunate people you read about or saw in documentaries on television. Not your relatives or your friends. Not yourself.

The screen door was opening. She couldn't see who entered. Jack's broad back blocked her view of the entrance and besides, she'd gone blind in that same second. Blind, and nearly deaf as well—the normal sounds of greetings were a rumbling buzz.

Then, a man was coming through the foyer, past Jack, smiling, carrying a black plastic briefcase. She blinked as her vision cleared, then another man entered—the father? Behind him—it was a regular procession—came a woman who smiled gently toward Judy, then proudly down at the child whose hand she held. The child was a girl, perhaps six years old. She entered the Polikoff house, head bobbing, walking on the insides of her ankles.

In the very act of rising to perform her function as hostess to this doubtful gathering, Judy froze. She sat rigid, staring at the child. She could not make the room go blessedly blank again, not a single degree of clarity was lost. All the textures all around took on an added sharpness. Every line and crease. Every feature on the little girl's face—the slackness of her mouth, the deep frown between her eyes, the awkward angle of her head—stood out brilliantly.

Jack was staring towards the couch. Judy saw him turn his head. Jack's mouth moved, making introductions. Silent words

39

flashed back and forth through the air while she sat, in their midst, wholly unable to rise or make a sound. She continued to stare at the child as her throat constricted and her stomach ached—awful, empty ache, and her mind tried to formulate the appropriate hostess phrases: Won't you sit down? Would you like something to drink? What an adorable child!

But they were already sitting without any help from her. Jack must have asked them to sit. Jack, himself, was coming to sit beside her on the couch, and everyone smiled at everyone else. The mother reached for her daughter and put both arms tight around the child. Then the child's mouth shifted. Judy stared helplessly, then realized the child was smiling at her sweetly.

For the full half hour of that meeting, while the representative talked and the family nodded and nodded, while an occasional rumble from Jack told her he was asking questions or making comments, while this small group of well-meaning people buzzed around her, her head grew heavier and heavier. She knew she was in shock, literally, and was helpless to fight the sensation or snap herself out of it, come awake, alive, tell them they had to get out of her house . . .

". . . actually guarantee anything, of course . . ."

These were the words she finally heard through the fog, penetrating with a force that made her back muscles jerk, the tightness in her neck dissolve, a certain normalcy return with a suddenness as disconcerting as the leaden shock.

"Guarantee?" It was her own voice.

All the adults in the room were startled. The little girl's mother looked pleased, perhaps gratified that Judy had finally managed to snap herself out of her own thoughts.

"Well, no," the woman said gently. "It can't be guaranteed. No one could possibly make such a statement, not with each case being so different. It can't be guaranteed that your success with your little boy would be the same as ours with our daughter," she gently stroked her child's head.

Judy saw that her eyes were moist with pride. That she truly felt this thing—that she and her husband had been uncommonly successful in rehabilitating their child.

"But if you and your husband work very hard, and give it your entire heart, if you make it your entire life," the woman promised her gravely, "your little boy can someday be like our daughter."

She was thirty-one years old and had believed she was totally average, a living testimonial to normalcy. All the past experiences of her life had led her to a certain level of expectation as to the consequences of her actions.

Things were either likely to happen, or unlikely. It was likely, for example, that her marriage to Jack would succeed and last. It had been unlikely that her first marriage to Scott's father would fail, but fact was fact. It was likely she'd have two children—having two children was average enough for the most center-of-the-road mentality—and that they would grow and thrive and be deeply loved. All the rest, from the moment of suspecting she was pregnant after the tubal ligation, all the rest was not likely, and this deviation from the norm was embodied in the third child.

Whole weeks of languid summer days passed her by. Judy viewed herself in a void and was amazed at how well she was taking this. She'd accepted the judgment without flinching, without cracking. Without screaming. Without dying.

But there were things she could not bear to consider. One of these things was her behavior with the people from Cerebral Palsy. Surely that was allowed her? It did no good for Jack to assure her she hadn't offended them. She knew she'd been awful. Unresponsive. Ungrateful. She would have felt immeasurably better if she could have called them up to tell them how much she appreciated their coming, their attempt to share their optimism. But she couldn't do that because she *didn't* appreciate it. She *couldn't* equate Andy with that little girl!

*   *   *

41

They'd been discussing options. Jack tried to encourage her, to make her feel hope.

There was only one problem. There was a dearth of options fo Andy.

"We'll find something as long as we don't give up. Don't you see, there must be a hundred things we could do that we just don't know about yet."

"Tell me one," she suggested.

He couldn't.

"What do we do, Jack? Sit here while Andy gets bigger and bigger, making no progress whatsoever, with the breathing problems getting worse and worse and nobody coming up with anything saner than taking him to a little room somewhere, once a week, and rolling him on the floor as therapy?"

Jack didn't reply. He seemed to have other things on his mind. He stared at her, and she saw that he was angry and perhaps hurt.

"You called Uncle Murray again."

She faced him fully. Her eyes had gone flat, slate gray. She didn't know how dangerous and chill it looked, or how much it upset him when she looked that way.

"Why not? I call Uncle Murray a lot. I always did, didn't I? He's a doctor. He's always listened to any questions I had about the kids, normal questions. About colds and the flu and Scott and Todd and even about me and you."

She was getting angry herself, and hearing the harshness of her own tone, tried desperately to make a joke out of it.

"You're jealous all of a sudden of a bald, sixty-year-old man?"

Jack refused to be placated. "He said you were crying," he accused her. "He said you call him every day and you cry every time you call. He said you told him you're scared to death about Andy and what's to become of Andy and you have nobody else to talk to so you call him." His voice shook.

"What does that mean, Judy? That you have nobody else to talk to? Don't you want me?" he cried, appalled. "Can't we

42

share this? Can't you tell me what you're feeling, cry if you want to . . ."

But that brought Judy's anger up in a choking wave. There were so many times, days long past, when she'd argued with him, fought with him—little, unimportant spats. Other times when she'd needed a good screaming match, but Jack wasn't a screamer, Jack soothed and petted and if that failed, Jack simply left the room or even the house. There were times she'd followed, refusing to be balked, needing a really good and unimportant battle, then the gentle joy of making up.

Too many of those times he'd gone for a walk, leaving her alone, the sequence of her anger stunted.

She stood in the doorway and stared at her husband and told herself she felt nothing. There was a damaged child in the next room and to feel was to ache, and to ache would be deadly.

But Jack was watching her and there was a hot flush of panic around his eyes. Judy's head felt light as she hung there, in the doorway, trying to cope with this poisonous bite of life—that either Jack got hurt, or she did. She was quite sure that didn't make sense, but she was too afraid to unravel it.

And she couldn't afford to let Jack see. If Jack thought she was weak, he'd come to her, hold her, and her resolve would melt in a desperate clutching of need. And then she'd be vulnerable.

So she never did answer his cry for help. She never did tell him what she was feeling. She didn't cry for him, either. She turned and fled to plunge blindly into the bathroom.

She slammed the door. She locked it.

He didn't try to follow her. She waited and waited for an eternity. She didn't quite believe it even after it was crystal clear. He hadn't even tried the door. He'd simply left her there.

When eleven o'clock passed, she stopped waiting. Jack must have gone to work while she was still in the bathroom.

She sat in her living room, hugging her elbows to her sides, sitting upright in the least comfortable of the chairs with her knees held tight. She was thinking about Scott, and what he'd said, staring down at Andy, childish confusion and disappointment on his thin, intelligent face.

"When does he *do* something?" he'd asked, innocently.

She looked at him, her eyes going that cold slate color.

"Go to your room," she finally said.

"Huh?"

"Do what I tell you!" she'd screamed, and he'd fled, and she'd settled herself then, calmly watching the baby. The baby hadn't moved at all, not even when she'd screeched wildly at Scott.

She felt a total separation, that night, from every male member of her family. If she sat it out long enough, she thought, if she could manage to catalog Jack's sins with total efficiency, if she tore out enough of her own heart, she might eventually be able to live through this.

Sometime during the course of those endless hours, with her mind harking back and back, immersed in the absolute silence of her misery, she saw, complete and in full color, those days in the hospital when Andy had jaundice. She sat up even straighter in her chair, and started asking herself specific questions.

What if?

She stared at the walls of her living room and forced herself to think clearly and unemotionally.

What if the treatment wasn't suited to the extent of the problem? What if more serious jaundice resulted? What if the jaundice, itself, was caused by something Albertson had failed to do, or had done incorrectly?

Because no one, no one at all, had yet ventured a guess as to why Andy was cerebral palsied.

Who was to blame, then? Were the doctors incompetent?

Her pregnancy had progressed in a normal way, according to the manner in which Albertson handled it.

There was no history of cerebral palsy in her own or Jack's family.

And why had the tubal ligation failed? Fate?

Around and around and around. She always came back to the jaundice. Days passing without an admission it was even there, days without any treatment . . .

The harsh cry . . .

The rigid limbs : . .

The position of the hands, thumbs . . .

There's nothing wrong with your new baby, Judy, baby Andy's fine, just fine . . .

Take him home and love him. He has cerebral palsy . . .

Just what *had* been done to Andy?

4

Downtown Philadelphia was steaming. The crowds moved more slowly than usual. The temperature—Judy preferred not thinking about the temperature. The perspiration under her arms had soaked through the thin fabric of her blouse.

The office in which she sat gave an impression of opulence. Perhaps it was due to the generous proportions, or the carpet, or the treatment of the walls. The air conditioning was on full-force but the sweat still poured from her and she felt disheveled, depressed, and at a definite disadvantage with the man behind the desk.

"I don't know what I'm doing here," she heard herself say. But that wasn't really so. She was here because Alexander Thorpe was a litigation lawyer, and she'd understood, the night before, sitting deep in thought, alone, that there was some mystery surrounding Andy's birth, some question about those days in the hospital. Consulting a good lawyer seemed the right step to take next. And she'd been luckier than she knew. Thorpe had just settled a case out of court. His calendar was momentarily clear. He could see her that very day.

"I want to tell you everything that happened from the minute I suspected I was pregnant with my third child. Even before that. It really started with the birth of my second child," she said haltingly, "and with the tubal ligation that was performed right after."

And suddenly the words were all there, pushing and jostling for position. She called up all the images of the months before, all the questions she'd asked herself, all her doubts.

The atmosphere of Thorpe's office was curiously comforting. All its shelves and surfaces were piled and stuffed with books and papers and folders and reports. It had a lived-in look. She could speak here, not in whispers of dread or shame. She could tell her story to this stranger and somehow not feel demeaned.

She ran it all through for him while he listened in attentive silence. She moved from the tubal ligation to the unexpected pregnancy and on to her RH-negative factor. She described her confinement with Andy. She mentioned that the actual delivery took place two weeks earlier than the estimated date, and that the only reason given was that the baby was ready, so why wait? It was a Cesarean, anyway. She detailed the operation, the hysterectomy. It was a mass of bits and pieces she now perceived as the puzzle surrounding Andy's defect.

She found the courage to tell him something of her talks with her obstetrician during the pregnancy. She'd been afraid, she admitted it freely. Albertson told her everything was proceeding normally, though the baby's quietness in the womb disturbed her. She described her mother's anxiety over the health of the newborn baby, her own growing certainty that something was wrong and that the pediatrician was doing nothing to handle it. Then, the admission that there was jaundice, but that everything was under control.

She told Thorpe about the next seven months at home. This with a fading spirit. And about Pediatric.

She did not tell him about the people from Cerebral Palsy who'd come to her house. She couldn't.

She talked and talked until her throat went dry. She remembered the cup of coffee she'd been offered and took great gulping swallows and was surprised to find it cold. Her brain felt soft, she'd been filled with rage for so long. Now, she'd talked herself out and the rage, even the terrible fear, was temporarily gone.

Behind the desk, Thorpe still watched her, noncommittal, cool and distant. His face gave no clues as to his thoughts. He made no comments throughout her long narrative.

She finished all the coffee in the cup and set it down carefully, then fished in her bag for a handkerchief and wiped her lips because they were trembling and because she felt suddenly wretched and ill.

When Thorpe finally spoke, his comment was unexpected and seemingly out in left field. A feeling of unreality descended upon her.

"He told me about an institute. A place in Morton, called the Centre for Neurological Rehabilitation—CNR. He gave me their number. He also gave me the number of a pediatric neurosurgeon. He wants us to have more tests done on Andy by this doctor—Robert Carr. He's got an office on Elm Square. The tests would be a complete evaluation, to make sure of the problem."

She blinked, staring at Jack, who was listening to her intently, his eyes wide with surprise. She'd gone to Thorpe without talking it over first. That wasn't how they handled family matters.

"Dr. Carr would tell us if he wants the tests done at CNR. He'll give us the complete evaluation when the tests are done. Then Thorpe wants us to authorize Carr to send him a copy of the evaluation. After that . . . well, we'll see. Depending on the results. Dr. Carr might want us to enter into programming. Thorpe couldn't say, of course.

"What Thorpe decides to do for us will depend on Carr's diagnosis and suggested treatment. I tried to ask him . . ." she faltered again. "About a trial, things like that."

She looked into Jack's eyes.

"He said, 'First Carr. Then we'll talk some more.'"

The call to Carr turned out to be little more than a formality, for Thorpe's office had already been in touch to recommend an immediate consultation. The appointment was for the following Wednesday.

It was a terrible weekend, holding, as it did, the aspect of waiting for some awful judgment. There was no backing out now, no safe haven to run to. Judy went into mental hiding on Sunday, sank deep into depression on Monday, got the shakes on Tuesday, and woke unnaturally calm on Wednesday morning.

They drove to CNR together—Judy, the baby, and Jack. Scott and Todd were being looked after by a neighbor. It was a very short drive from Overbrook to Morton. Most of the people with appointments like theirs had traveled from vast distances, at enormous expense, after considerable soul-searching.

She hadn't expected such rows and rows of people. The three waiting rooms were fairly large, yet every space was filled—chairs, aisles. Parents sat and stood and leaned and paced. She could ignore the parents. But the children, like the little girl who'd been brought to the house—the children were unspeakable.

There were ungainly, unwieldy children slouching, slumping, jerking in the chairs. There were children who lay on tables in coma. Who writhed on the floor. Who were strapped into special chairs to hold them upright or to protect passersby from their biting teeth and slashing nails. There were children in crash helmets, children who spit when anything approached them. There were children who keened and squawked and wailed.

Andy leaned passively first in Judy's lap, then in Jack's, until finally it was his turn to be carried away. Then they waited, she and her spouse, side by side as if they still shared. And the greatest pain throughout that waiting period was that Jack never tried to take her hand. Every atom of her being cried out for the comfort of his arms and she nearly touched him—a tentative, frightened touch—then gripped her hands together in her lap and averted her eyes.

Being loved by Jack meant giving love to him—totally. She couldn't give anything to Jack until she knew what she had to give to Andy.

When they finally had their turn in an inner office with the pediatric neurosurgeon conducting preliminary tests, Judy understood how desperately she was counting on him to end her terror. Dr. Carr was well known and admired within his profession. Sitting stiffly in one of the chairs before his desk, Judy realized how totally she'd imbued him with final responsibility. Coming here had seemed the end of a long, unmarked tunnel to nowhere.

When they finally heard what they'd waited to hear, when the evaluation Thorpe had sent them for was spelled out in detail, Judy understood nothing, shrinking back into a dark, safe place. It was up to Jack to repeat it all for her later. It was Jack who was actually cool enough to hear what Carr had said.

"It's worse than we thought." The statement was flat, but there was compassion in his voice. "We believe there's pressure on the brain."

There was no way on earth to comprehend such a judgment on her child!

"I want you to listen carefully to what I'm going to tell you. I want to do more tests, in Midtown Hospital. One of these tests will be to determine if there's any blockage to the brain. I'll be

49

testing to see if there is a build-up of fluids—if so, it may be necessary to shunt your son in order to drain off these fluids. I will do nothing that is unnecessary.

"Right now, I want to explain just a little to you about the situation. When I know more about that situation, we can talk again. It's vitally important that you try to understand what I'm saying. I believe your son needs these tests. I believe there is no alternative solution for you.

"If what I believe to be true *is* true, your little boy can become very sick. He's already experiencing those breathing problems common to children with extensive brain damage. It's imperative that we waste no time. That you come to a decision as quickly as possible.

"When you've made up your minds about entering Midtown Hospital, get back to me immediately."

There was a silent crowd occupying her house. She stopped in the tiny foyer, confused, and looked helplessly up at Jack, but it was only the family and some close friends.

It didn't matter. Nothing mattered.

The curtains were closed tight throughout the downstairs of the house. She hadn't the slightest idea why. It made the rooms brooding and dark, almost funereal.

Hot tears smarted behind her eyelids and the ache in her throat made it impossible to swallow. She grabbed Jack's arm and heard a whispered clucking as they climbed the stairs. In the bedroom, she stood frozen while Jack placed Andy in his crib, then followed her.

He closed and locked the bedroom door, then he came to her. He gathered her to his heart, his darling, his love, and the protective ice Judy had built around herself shattered. She clutched him, finally, forgetting for a time her new aversion to being smiled at, kissed, handled.

It was a desperate relief to shelter against Jack.

The bedroom was sanctuary. There were only the smallest

intrusive sounds of life. Cars passing on the street. Water running. The clock ticking.

She sank down on the side of the bed, Jack's side, and stared up at him blankly, and he knelt and put his arms around her again, hating the staring agony in her eyes, helpless to take the pain onto himself. He was already stifling with the pain.

Her arms gripped him tight. Her face was wet against his neck. He could feel the heavy thud of her heart.

"T–tell me," she finally choked, huddling, not looking up.

He moved back an inch to take her face between his hands and smooth the tears away with his thumbs. Her eyes were bleached out, almost colorless and swimming with fresh tears, and a muscle was jumping under her right cheek. Jack stroked her cheek, then sighed, then stood to turn on the bedside light.

"Don't you already know?" he asked.

"No!" It came out hoarse and terrified. "No, we have to talk about it. We have to consider everything—everything, Jack! We have to decide this together.

"It's his whole life!" she wailed.

Jack made a movement toward her, then stopped. He saw her straining desperately to get a grip on herself. Her mouth set and her eyes went dry, taking back that steely glint. And he finally understood, just a little. She had to find the strength, inside herself, to live through this.

"I love him so," she suddenly moaned, then gasped, and the tears gushed again, helpless tears of pain and terror and rage. "He's always seemed so helpless and sad. I feel I've failed him . . .

"He could die," she said very clearly and flatly.

"Is he living now?" Jack's voice was too calm. She couldn't imagine such calm. Indeed, she felt her own hysteria mounting in resistance to such control.

"They don't *know* anything, Jack," she said. "It's just a guess. An educated guess. They want to test our baby and maybe open up his head, on a guess!"

51

"You're talking about the shunt. We don't know anything about shunts. We don't even have to know anything now. Carr doesn't even know if shunting, or any other surgery, is even necessary. The tests are to determine that.

"But there are things that are better than just guesses. Things they feel they know. Like the fact that he's six weeks developed while he's eight-and-a-half months old. And there have to be reasons for that, Judy, and if there is pressure on the brain, something has to be done to alleviate it.

"We have to know! We can't hide from the truth. That won't help anyone. If Andy's brain-damaged . . ."

She jerked away as if to bolt, and Jack gripped her shoulders, shaking her a little.

"If he's brain-damaged, we have to know that too, Judy! What do you want to do, play around with this thing forever? Watch him lying there, getting bigger and bigger—you were the one who was sure something was wrong, weren't you? You were the one who felt we had to do something! Well, you were absolutely right, and we've waited too long already. We can't afford to wait any longer!"

A curious calm enveloped her. She'd known the truth all along, and now she was vindicated. Jack had finally admitted that a problem did exist. And out of that vindication, she'd find the strength to make the right decisions for her child.

Not that there was any choice. Jack was right about that—there was only one way to go.

Midtown Hospital. Dr. Carr had told them, in intricate detail, about the options open to them. It hadn't taken long—there were very few options. They could sit and wait, hoping for a miracle, or they could take the offensive and thereby face whatever dangers ensued from their actions.

Two days later, on Wednesday, September 11, 1974, Judy Polikoff and her youngest son entered Midtown Hospital. They were given no discharge date, which was fortunate since Andy developed a respiratory infection that evening and the tests were held up indefinitely.

*　　*　　*

They stayed for nearly a month, in residence at Midtown Hospital. During that time, autumn arrived, a discovery Judy made on those nights Jack brought the older boys to take her out to dinner. Three nights a week when she left Andy there and pretended life still held some normalcies.

Whatever her earlier feelings had been for hospitals, supercharged by her latest, disastrous stay at Franklin Central, however morbid she might feel, surrounded by illness and unhappiness, there had never been any past experience in her life to prepare her for the fourth floor of Midtown.

The fourth floor was devoted totally to Carr's brain-damaged patients. Judy and Andy were alone in a room at the end of the shorter of two corridors. The room was freshly painted and papered with airplane motifs and was cheerful enough, even cute, with enough bright light from the windows.

But the patient was her child. The other patients were apparently children too—at least most of them. The entire concept of a floor full of dangerously sick children felt alien and terrible. It filled her with apprehension to realize that her own son was one of them.

A narrow bed had been provided for her. It was pushed into a corner, and Andy's small crib snuggled into another. There was a dresser and a mirror. She avoided the mirror.

The smells of the floor were the usual hospital smells, yet they seriously offended a stomach that stayed tight and sore. She had no appetite, only an unyielding thirst, and that first day, and the second, she could not force herself to venture into the hall.

Years after, during periods of sad remembering, she'd recall the sounds and half-sounds from around the corner that finally pulled her from hiding. They were normal enough—women's voices, a child's cry, yet her knowledge of the nature of the problems on this floor gave every sound the touch of abnormality. When she knew her imagination was growing worse than any reality, she took her first walk. That was when she

53

learned the schedule and saw for herself the dual atmosphere of the floor.

There were visiting hours, that was one atmosphere, when the mothers not in residence came to feed their children. Lunch—eleven to two. Dinner—four to seven. During those hours the halls were filled with noise and bustle and activity. It made for an impression of full life. Hours she would anticipate. A parody of normalcy.

Then, there were the non-visiting hours. The other atmosphere. For all those hours she was confined, by hospital rule, to the room she and Andy shared. And these hours were characterized by silence. Heavy, stifling silence. Silence spasmodically broken by distant, odd shufflings. Shattered by an occasional screech.

Impressions of a half-life. The stuff of nightmares.

She walked her own short corridor to the tiny lobby by the elevator where all the other mothers sat exchanging tales of life, laughing, chiding, cuddling their children, coaxing, stroking, and loving them. She nodded a cool, detached greeting, moving on blindly, sensing their concern but blocking it, denying it, resenting their implied right to consider her one of them—she wasn't.

She avoided the faces of the feeding children. Andy simply could not belong in a place filled with these children. The mothers' faces, on a level with her own, refused to be banished so easily. Smiles. Smiles filled the corridors: tired smiles, honest smiles, grimly determined smiles. Even the occasional tears were accompanied by sorry smiles.

She thought she might have felt less sick if one of these women wasn't smiling.

She returned toward her room, her mouth grim. Her head was swimming. The room was sanctuary, she found herself at the far wall and, filled with terror for her child, with guilt that she might have failed him, she gripped her hair in both hands and wrenched, needing to hurt something and having only herself, wrenched until a scream welled. The tears, so prevalent through all those earlier days, refused to come, would not fall, and she turned and beat her fists into her pillow. When that didn't work either she beat at the mattress, both fists balled, hitting and hitting, teeth clenched, tears frozen, her breath coming shorter and sharper until the room swam.

Finally, appalled by her own furious frustration and fear, she sank down on the bed, turned her face to the wall, closed her eyes and tried to rest.

There was a girl. A new arrival. A beautiful girl, about eighteen years old, with wide, wary eyes.

For Judy, she represented normalcy, despite the fact that she was a fourth-floor patient, admitted for testing. Such a lovely, natural, sweet girl didn't belong here any more than Andy.

Her name was Lisa and she wanted to be an actress, she revealed with shy confidence. Judy took to stopping by her room each day.

The days began to pass slowly and the routine Judy developed became her new normalcy. Reading through the hours alone. Napping. Staring at Andy. Making herself robustly cheerful. Bustling around. Humming little snatches of tunes and having endless monologues with her child. She even got around to planning the vacation they'd have when Midtown was a memory.

When the other mothers arrived at visiting hours she was ready for the illusion of company. She chose to walk in the hall. To nod at people as if they were vacation acquaintances. To remain aloof since there was no possible basis for a relationship.

Andy wasn't like these children. Andy wasn't one of them. Of the entire in-house population on the floor, only Lisa was normal. It became a desperate necessity to have her daily chat with Lisa.

The first week finally ended. The hours were growing longer, especially the night hours. Nervous apprehension and forced inactivity had given her insomnia. What she needed was a strong, warm body to snuggle against. A sympathetic ear to

55

confide in. A touch of optimism. Even a confirmed skeptic, to challenge her, to make her angry instead of frightened.

When two of the mothers invited her out for coffee she went. The hour passed quickly as they told her their stories, to which she nodded and exclaimed without absorbing anything. She couldn't afford to feel their hurt. She couldn't even manage her own misery. She didn't want to be forced to share their personal tragedies.

Later, much later, she realized that the last thing either woman wanted was her pity. The realization came to her afterward, when her own need was great, that what they'd done was to try to impart to her the courage to go on.

She began going to lunch with small groups of mothers, to inexpensive places in the deteriorated neighborhood around the hospital. She discovered a battered bookstore just around the corner and bought the three books they carried on brain-damaged children. She brought her purchase back and wriggled into the rocker in her room, reading first one, then another, then the third, all of them cover to cover. When the last was done, the day after she'd bought them, she called Jack and asked him to go to the library for her. Armed with a fresh supply of books every dinner-out night thereafter, she read away the lengthening, endless hours.

She made a study of these ghastly stories, most of them dipped in saccharin. No real person accepted hell so sweetly. What she sought was the story of one mother who felt as she felt, who shared her grief, frustration, rage, and hate. Not these stories of godly love, faith, hope, and charity that turned her stomach and made her wonder about herself.

Andy's respiratory infection finally cleared up and the tests began. She concluded they must be terrible: There was no other explanation for the state Andy was in when he returned to the room. Carr, on a visit, assured her this wasn't the case.

"The scan we did today, for example." he said. "We injected

dye, then followed its path to see if it would reach all parts of the brain without running into a blockage.

"This isn't an agonizing process," he assured her gently. "But Andy is just a little baby, he doesn't understand anything that's being done to him or for him, and even an adult would hate being poked and prodded and injected.

"Try not to imagine horrors."

The days continued to pass and she began to recognize the children on the floor. To know their names, unwillingly. To feel something akin to liking for some of them, a feeling of definite awe for one in particular—a child in a wheelchair. Benny was twelve and lived strapped to his chair so he wouldn't take a tumble and do damage to himself. This was necessary because Benny danced. Constantly. Without end. Judy would have called it convulsive jerking if she hadn't seen the grin on Benny's face. The grin wasn't witless. Benny was aware. Benny's eyes burned with life. There was no ugliness in Benny.

Judy didn't at all understand Benny's joy, nor did she understand the pride in his mother's tired face. But she did recognize that the emotion was genuine and that helped her, finally, to face the other children.

By the end of her second week at Midtown, she was familiar with the other women, though still aloof and cool. She could look every one of them in the eye now. She could stare directly at their children. And she stopped every afternoon to say hello to Lisa.

On the day life kicked her once again, she had no premonition. No "feelings." No woman's instinct.

There were no visitors in Lisa's room that day. There never were visitors. Judy hadn't asked Lisa why—they never discussed personal things. The room was dim. No lights were lit. The window was covered. Judy came halfway into the room, glancing toward the bed.

Lisa lay there on her back, under the sheet, not moving, not

57

speaking. This was unusual. The bed looked old, criblike, and it took Judy some time to realize there were foam bumpers around the sides. But Lisa looked even more odd: She was wearing a crash helmet. She lay still, and stared ahead at Judy, through Judy, through the wall behind Judy . . .

"Lisa?"

She didn't understand at all the hideous thing Lisa began doing. She didn't understand why Lisa's body arched, flying up from the mattress, lifting the sheet grotesquely. She didn't understand why Lisa's face contorted, the slapping sounds, the guttural grunting. She looked at once-pretty Lisa and understood—nothing.

Then she was backing out the door, her only clear thought: Her arms are tied! Clutching blindly at the doorframe, stumbling and nearly falling, turning and trying to run, legs glue, caught in a slow motion paralysis of terror, pitching down the corridor while the hall bleached and tilted around and the faces of the women swooped up, surrounding, and she heard a terrible screaming.

And thought, That's disgusting, letting people screech like that in a hospital.

Then tripped, and nearly plunged headlong into the nurses' station at the turn of the corridor.

She was lowered, gagging, into a chair, while a telephone at the station kept ringing and ringing. The screaming had stopped, to be replaced by an animal whimpering. One of the mothers she'd joined for lunch pressed close, an arm offering protection, while a nurse's face swam before her eyes.

"That's what Lisa's here for, dear. I thought you understood. She's just having a seizure. Sometimes she has them one right after another, continuously."

The whimpering choked to horror then the horror blossomed into rage and formed words, harsh and explosive, bottled up inside since her heart had been broken by Pediatric's diagnosis on Andy. She felt the words burst between stiff lips, heard them spit between clenched teeth, through gasping sobs.

It was she, herself, flung down in grief unable to find control. "Not me!" threatened a voice only vaguely like her own. "Not my baby!" Her teeth ground. "Not like that, freaks . . .!" her voice nearly screamed. "Pretending! Like it doesn't matter! Pretending it doesn't rip your hearts out! Pretending you feel the same for them you'd feel if they were normal! I can't . . . can't . . . my God!" she gasped, "don't you see what it *is*? Don't you see what they *are*? Don't you care what they *have*? They live a half-life, they're not alive, do you honestly expect anybody to believe they *live?*"

A rasping sob tore her throat.

"I'll see him dead first! I'll kill him myself, first! They can't say my Andy's like that, they can't make him be like that, I can't I can't I can't . . .!"

Someone stroked her hair and she gasped, then wailed.

"I'm sorry." She was sobbing in earnest, unaware of the soothing murmurs.

"I'm sorry," she kept saying, over and over, though no one required apologies.

"Cry it all out," someone else murmured and, of course, so advised, she found her sobs dying abruptly.

Benny's mother took her to her room, and stopped in the doorway. She looked thoughtfully at Judy, then straightened and with firmness in her voice said, "You're a good strong girl, Judy, but you've been trying to keep all this inside. Now that you've had your cry, you'll get yourself straight and handle your life. Because it never goes away."

She looked into Judy's swollen eyes. "It never gets better, I'm telling you the truth, but you do learn to live with it. You find a place for it. You make your life work!"

Judy passed a very peaceful night, then rose at dawn to look at her child. She thought, I can learn to handle this, I can moderate how much I care, I can put it in a box somewhere outside my heart and be good and gentle without having to hurt this way.

59

But they took Andy for testing later that day and all her fear and anxiety resurfaced.

If I could give him my own heart to make him better, I would! she argued her anguish through. But if I can't, if there's nothing I can do, then maybe he *should* die, not live a half-life! She spent what felt like an eternity of bitter loss and guilt, wondering if there'd been something more to do.

Make a stand then, she advised herself, gritting her teeth. Isn't it really just that simple? Admit you care terribly and take it from there, or else give it all up and stop pretending to Jack and your friends and yourself. Stop hoping for miracles that won't happen. Put him in an institution and stop loving him.

Can you do it? Can you?

Andy's tests were over. Judy spent the night holding her baby, crooning to him, laying him down, standing staring into the crib. When dawn finally touched the tiny room, the exhausted child, the sad brave airplanes, the corridors—still empty for a little while—when dawn came and stirred her mind, she finally understood the mystery of the smilers. The mystery of the fourth floor of Midtown Hospital.

You had to make a commitment. To yourself. Nobody else mattered. You had to start early, you had to get the ball rolling. You had to build up enough initial steam to carry you through your purgatory.

Because it wouldn't go away. It wouldn't get better. But you could make up your mind to learn to live through it and get on with the business of life.

And it was all right to hate. Sometimes. To despair. Sometimes. To cry and scream and *be* hateful as long as you tried to find balance. It was all right because it was human, and the women of the fourth floor of Midtown Hospital were nothing if not human.

Dr. Carr called to see her the next morning at six A.M., when the floor was very quiet. After he'd left, she wandered out to the phone at the nurses' station, stared blankly at the hall wall,

60

dialed a number. Her cousin's number.

"Phyllis? I know it's early, I'm sorry, you're asleep, but I need to talk to somebody." Her voice was absurdly steady.

"Judy? Are you okay?" Phyllis, still half-asleep, was rousing rapidly, stirred by apprehension. "Is it Andy? The tests? Judy?"

"He needs intensive programming," Judy said, her throat suddenly dry. "He has severe brain damage and he needs five hundred people to program him."

There was a tiny silence and she panicked.

"Phyllis? Where can I possibly find five hundred volunteers to program Andy?"

Phyllis came through. Of course. That was why she'd remembered no number but Phyllis's at 6:20 in the morning on yet another most terrible day of her life.

"Leave everything to me," said her cousin, the organizer.

She did.

They were to go home as soon as Andy was fully recovered from the effects of the testing, and in the days that remained she formed solid friendships. It was as if the masks had suddenly been dropped. Not masks the women had donned themselves, but masks Judy had imagined for them. Behind the sameness of features and the smiles she saw the reality of their personalities and trial and trauma and resolve.

And though she couldn't know it yet, they'd become a part of her. Even the majority she'd never see again had somehow grafted on. Tiny pieces of personality. They'd survived their ordeals. She could hope to survive. They'd stayed human, warm, and real, genuine in their love for their children. She, too, could hope to achieve these things. She could find a place for this tragedy, eventually, and go on from there.

On a lovely autumn Sunday in October, 1974, they let her take her baby home. Carr's report still sounded quite terrible in her mind. But she'd internalized lesson number one, learned from the mothers at Midtown Hospital.

She met Jack smiling.

61

ROBERT CARR, M.D.
Elm Square Clinic
Elm Street at Dale Road
Philadelphia, Pa.

TO: Alexander Thorpe, Esquire
FROM: Robert Carr, M.D.
SUBJECT: Andrew Polikoff

In accordance with your request, and under authorization of Mr. and Mrs. Jack Polikoff, parents of the above-named patient, the enclosed is a summary of our evaluation of the patient.

Andy has been our patient since 9/4/74, at which time a thorough neurological evaluation was carried out at the Centre for Neurological Rehabilitation, in Morton, Pennsylvania. Following this evaluation, Andy was admitted to Midtown Hospital, in Philadelphia, for contrast studies. He was discharged from Midtown Hospital on 10/6/74.

This ten month old child was previously diagnosed as Cerebral Palsied. No specific diagnostic testing was done in depth to justify this diagnosis.

Studies at CNR demonstrate a child seriously behind in all areas of motor development, visual motor perception, coordination, etc. There is a marked responsiveness, however, to the environment. The percussion note to the skull is slightly elevated, but the coronal suture lines are wide open. X-rays of the skull show suture lines are wider than desirable. There are, however, no digital markings. Echoencephalogram demonstrates ventricles larger than they should be. Brain scan suggests an abnormality which is not specific. There remains the possibility of a subdural collection. There is no specific seizuring, however, on the EEG.

The mother's comments include observations that at the third or fourth month of the patient's development, there was marked retardation, particularly with baby sounds, activity and general behavior, as compared with that observed earlier in her two older children.

The results of the hospital testing are being sent under separate cover.
In summary: Hospital tests included the following:

Indium Scan: The study revealed rapid excretion, suggesting an abnormal study with no uptake at all. It was felt that the significance of this was likely negative at this time.

Pneumoencephalogram: This was later carried under Ketamine general anesthesia. The pneumoencephalogram demonstrated Grade III to Grade IV cortical atrophy with marked dilatation of the subarachnoid spaces. The ventricles showed minimal enlargement.

In our experience, when this situation is found on the air study, along with early motor function retardation, the prognosis with rehabilitation is essentially far better than if there were also an accompanying markedly enlarged ventricular system.

In view of these findings, the patient will be started immediately on a very intensive rehabilitation training program, and will be carefully watched in follow-up at the clinic.

It is felt that there is no evidence of any surgical lesion at this time.

Final diagnosis:
1. Chronic encephalopathy;
2. Brain and cortical atrophy;
3. Severe psychomotor retardation.

5

They went to see Alexander Thorpe together—Judy and Jack. To report on what they'd learned from Dr. Carr, and to try to get some feeling for Thorpe's view of their case, now that they had their diagnosis and recommendation for programming.

Later, driving home, they discussed the lawyer's brisk, impersonal comments on the situation.

They would go to the parents' orientation at CNR. Thorpe was quite sure of it. It would be absurd, having come this far, to lack the courage to take the next step. They would go and listen to Dr. Robert Doman, they would learn about the philosophy and overall method of the Centre, they would even meet the physical therapist who'd program Andy if they decided to try the programming, and when they'd done all these preliminary things, they would report back to Thorpe on the specifics of Andy's rehabilitation.

And fees? There was no need to worry about fees. Thorpe's fee and whatever costs would be incurred in the preparation of the case would be settled as a percentage of whatever settlement would be won if their case ever did go to trial. Until that time, that distant, hypothetical time, there would be no fees. If they lost, he would get nothing.

The trip from Thorpe's office to the house was short. Judy sank numbly onto the couch, knees locked, hands clasped in her lap—her habitual new posture. In this position she remained, robotlike, watching Jack.

"If Carr recommended this programming," Jack was saying, "he obviously expects it to have a good chance of success. He can't promise us results, every case is different, but some degree of success is implied through the simple act of his asking us to

64

go out to CNR and learn about their methods.

"You see that, don't you, Judy? You see there's really hope for Andy to improve or even to get completely better?"

She didn't remind him people don't get better from brain damage.

Jack sat in his chair and talked enthusiastically to the walls, to the floor, to the tables, to the couch. But he did not talk to her. Surely not. It was ridiculous for him to pretend to make the attempt. She hadn't the will to hear him, the heart to give him his cues, the desire to pick up her lines. She could pretend, but even the pretense was tiring. It took every last ounce of her courage to stay pleasant-faced and upright.

"And we know now," he said, sounding momentarily pleased. "We can handle this, Judy, we can handle anything once we're given the chance to know!"

She decided then and there that Jack was crazy. Cracked, from all the strain. Talking about "knowing" as if it actually mattered to know. As if knowing automatically corrected the error nature had made.

You made a mistake in the household accounts but you *knew* so you erased it and reworked it. Or you found holes in your socks but you *knew*, so you got out your needle and thread and sewed them up. Mercurochrome on cuts and scratches. Ace bandages on sprains, ice on swellings, a silence on misery you couldn't express.

How did you bandage a damaged brain?

She had a brain-damaged child.

She made herself repeat it, inside her head, to herself, unflinching. She'd been making herself do that, every day, since this latest diagnosis. So she could make no mistake, have no easy escape from believing it. It was necessary to believe it in order to deal with it.

They had a brain-damaged child, herself and Jack, and Jack was rattling on about "knowing."

"The parents' orientation's this weekend," he continued.

"They'll explain it then, how the programming and this 'patterning' business work. We'll meet other parents in our situation . . ."

There was no one else in the world in their situation, not even the family of women she'd discovered at Midtown Hospital. She hadn't yet earned the right to join them in their optimism.

"You won't feel so alone."

Alone. Yes. Alone in a nightmare, not knowing how it started, staring perplexed and helpless at Andy.

"It all seems incomprehensible now because we have so much to learn . . ."

Not incomprehensible. Not even complicated. Simple. Andy had dead brain cells. Andy was living in twilight. Here, in the house, away from the fourth floor companionship, her courage was rapidly deserting her.

"Once we learn the specifics about the programming, everything will become more personal, more directly geared to us, more hopeful . . . We'll meet the doctors who actually worked up this method. My God, Judy! That's luck! To have those men right here, and to have found out about this program while Andy's still so little!"

Luck. To have a child who couldn't sit up. Who couldn't jargon, or play, or think, or get into normal children's mischief. To watch that child and to realize he didn't know she was his Mommy.

That broke her heart. Ten months old now and unaware of that simple fact.

"We'll work it all out. You'll see."

She didn't contradict him. She was confused and terribly sad. Right now she would have given years off her life for a long hard crushing embrace from Jack.

She looked up, dazed, her tired eyes filled with tears, and Jack finally stopped talking and came to her.

6

It was parents' orientation night at the Centre. The lecture room in which they sat for hours was bitterly cold and uncomfortable. The chairs were hard and unyielding as stone. It was an ordeal to be gotten over.

But Judy had determined to stay calm and unemotional. She was on top of everything, positive in her attitude, and knowledgeable in her choice of questions. Not once did her nerves betray her, her mind hide in a dark place, tears fill her eyes, though there was an ache in her throat constantly.

"Mr. and Mrs. Polikoff—do you mind if I talk a little about Andy?"

It was a question she'd been dreading. Dr. Doman had already asked it of two other couples present. How could you say, Yes, I mind!

"Mr. and Mrs. Polikoff are here tonight as the end result of much the same process that brought Mr. and Mrs. Andetti and so many of the rest of you. This process centers around our mothers and plays a large part in our admissions. You all know what I'm talking about, ladies."

Judy didn't want to know, not if it involved her child. She shrank from hearing Andy's name spoken here, in this context.

"Mother-instinct."

This jerked her back to full awareness.

"Instinct? No. Mother-*knowing!* Despite disclaimers from family doctors, who should certainly know what they're saying. Despite the attempts of our families, themselves, our closest friends, those who truly love us, to soothe us into inactivity . . ."

Her eyes widened at that and Doman, perceiving every reaction throughout the room, noted her instant identification with the atmosphere he painted.

67

"Am I right, Mrs. Polikoff? In spite of all this clucking and petting and trying to soothe maternal anxieties away, Mrs. Polikoff *knew*. Mrs. Polikoff, like so many of our mothers, knew in that special way mothers always do know when something's wrong with their babies."

The repeated use of her name inured her to the raw discomfort of hearing it. The nodding agreement of other women's heads gave her a sense of oneness with the group. Robert Doman, physiatrist, contributor to the Doman-Delacato-Doman Profile so constantly alluded to in so many of the books Judy had just read, member of the team that originated this entire method of rehabilitation for the brain-damaged, saw her glance hesitantly around and smiled at her encouragingly.

"Andy Polikoff had some problems following his birth. The symptoms of these problems were noted by his mother and, eventually, tests were performed and treatment carried out. The problems, however, apparently persisted. Little was done to determine the exact nature of those problems until tests were performed this past spring and a diagnosis made of cerebral palsy."

There was a murmur of sympathy throughout the room.

"In attempting to more closely pinpoint the problem to try to find some way of dealing with it aggressively, the Polikoffs brought their son to Dr. Carr and further tests were carried out, this time at Midtown Hospital."

Andy's latest diagnosis became group property.

"The brain damage is diffuse. That means it's not limited to any one specific portion of the brain. It also appears that no single section of the brain is completely damaged. This is, obviously, a very positive, hopeful aspect of the diagnosis.

"The tests Andy underwent at Midtown seemed to negate any need at this time for surgery. They also indicated, along with other medical observations, a very good case for the rehabilitative treatment we use here.

"And so, Mr. and Mrs. Polikoff, like the rest of you, are here tonight because you've all found it necessary to look one step further than anybody told you it was sane to look. You've all arrived here despite almost surely being told that our methods are not the usual methods . . ."

Around the second hour, Judy started to ask questions. A great number of questions. Her success in the spotlight made her less hypersensitive and more eager to participate. She found all that reading she'd done in Midtown stood her in good stead. She'd retained an impressive amount of semi-technical material. The time began to pass more swiftly. She began to feel a little less helpless, a little less like a victim.

The atmosphere in the room helped. There was never anything less than a sense of personal warmth and commitment at orientation due, in large part, to the honest caring and great warmth of Robert Doman himself.

"We don't treat the paralyzed limb or the deaf ear or the blind eye as such. We are audacious enough to deal with the very top. Literally. With the brain itself. The human brain! But why do we treat the brain, when it may be the legs that can't move properly, or the ears that can't hear, or the skin that can't feel heat or pain? We treat the brain because the brain is the location of the injury. It's just that simple. The brain is where whatever went wrong went wrong."

The room was full, but not packed. There was a couple from California, sitting on Jack's left—their daughter a near-drowning victim. They'd brought pictures of a grinning, toothy ten-year-old, and one latest shot of a slouching child in a wheelchair.

There was a couple from Maine, sitting in the back row, hands tightly clasped throughout the night—their child lay in coma at Midtown Hospital.

The woman from North Carolina sat beside a nurse. No airline would let her son board a plane without such medical support. The woman's husband had deserted her.

The older couple in the middle row represented another aspect of this medical problem. The husband was a stroke victim. Not all CNR's patients were children.

69

Then, there was the woman who kept crying, not intrusively but worse—quietly. In the far corner of the back row, her husband shifting and sighing and blowing his nose. It was the woman who'd been driving when the brakes of the car failed on a hill to pitch car, mother, father, baby daughter, over the edge to the rocks below.

"There has always been a great lack of understanding of these problems. Our brain damaged have traditionally been isolated. Do you know what they call these people in England?" Doman glanced around the room. "Cabbages. Just as, I'm sure, you've heard them referred to as vegetables here at home."

Judy's neck went stiff with embarrassment. She herself had used the term. But then, they'd shared this once, all the people in the room—the normalcy of unconcern.

"We don't isolate our patients," Dr. Doman said. "We've learned that in some cases so-called 'traditional' methods of therapy have resulted in so limiting the intensity of sensory input as to essentially condemn the patient forever.

"Tomorrow morning, you'll be meeting with our physical therapists. At that time, you'll be learning some of the specifics of the actual programming, as it would apply to each of you individually should you decide to try our program. I don't propose to go into any of that now, except to stress the fact that our rehabilitative techniques rest strongly on the absolute belief that in order to survive and function adequately, an organism must react successfully to the stimuli it receives constantly from the environment. Adaptation to the environment depends on successful neurological organization—and that's a term you've all heard in the past day or so, and one on which I won't lecture tonight. You can read up on it with far better results, when you're not tired," he smiled, "in Carl Delacato's book, *Neurological Organization and Reading,* and if there's anything you then don't understand you can simply ask Dr. Delacato himself, since he is, as you know, a member of our team.

"What I want you to bear in mind when you meet with our therapists is simply this: The nervous system is the focal point

70

in dealing with injuries to the brain, because it's the nervous system we strive to stimulate, with all sorts of sensory inputs, to try to bridge the area of injury and form a new, healthy, working linkage in the brain."

When the lecture was finally over, when they were free to climb into their coats and into their car, when she could finally ease the smile off her lips, she sneaked a peek at Jack. At his hands on the wheel. At his beloved features, posture, shoulders, strong jaw. Jack looked tired but relaxed. And what did he feel? That she no longer knew.

She couldn't afford to think about needing Jack. She considered the orientation instead. She felt she'd done well. She'd remembered what she'd read and when Dr. Doman called for responses, she'd known the answers—every one. She'd answered question after question until hers was the primary responsive voice, then she'd asked some intelligent questions of her own, always cool, always alert.

And she'd made an important transition during the last of the coffee breaks, with three other mothers hanging on her every word. She'd come a good bit of the way toward fully joining the sisterhood of Midtown Hospital.

She'd determined to accept this new role. To be strong and an inspiration for whoever needed her. To be all things for Andy, unwavering and untiring. To make what had been the cool act of this night the reality of her life.

For all the years that followed, after the initial strangeness and pervasive anxiety and anguish had worn down to something mellow that could be defined, Judy remembered John Unruh as he was the next morning, back at CNR. Unruh was the physical therapist who would handle Andy's programming if they made that final decision to try CNR.

After the all-night orientation session, she and Jack returned to the Centre at nine A.M. the next day. To hear the rest of the pitch, though that was hardly an accurate or fair phrase, as Unruh himself pointed out.

"We don't need you, you know. You need us."

He was tall, taller even than Jack, with football-player shoulders and hair that was obviously prematurely white, for he couldn't have been out of his thirties.

"You figure this was all a pep talk, don't you? The whole session with Bob?"

Judy flushed, though she couldn't imagine why. After all, what difference did it make what little judgments she made? She respected a really good pep talk.

"Well, I'm afraid now *I* get to give you another little pep talk," Unruh grinned broadly. "You're falling asleep and I can't have you getting bored.

"This program," he plunged in with relish, "is harder than anything you've ever imagined. You're supposed to suspect that from your ordeal last night. There was a definite point to that, beyond the simple need to say a great deal in a limited number of hours. Perseverance was involved. Your group showed an amazing amount of perseverance. Nobody falling asleep or out of his chair. And from what I gather, you did your best to put Bob through an ordeal of his own. It was his longest single session.

"Also, it's apparent from what I heard from my first appointment this morning, that at least part of that over-run was due to your participation.

"'Mrs. Polikoff was so wonderful.' I heard that from the lady who just left. 'Mrs. Polikoff was so well-informed.' I have the feeling I'll be hearing that all day.

"You're a hit!"

He had a definite trick of appearing to mimic without the least trace of mockery so that other people's voices came real and vibrant into the room. He was so full of energy himself that it was impossible to fade out even after a long night without sleep.

"You're making fun of me," Judy said quietly, without anger.

"No, I wouldn't do that," he corrected her earnestly. "I never make fun of our mothers. There's no group of individuals I think more highly of than the mothers here at CNR. It's the mothers who make our program work. Without you, there's nothing. You give it the spinal support. We could dream up the best and newest and most innovative programs known to the human race, but without your full-hearted, staunch support, none of it would matter a bit!

"Look, you already know enough about the program to understand that it's conducted by you, in your home, not by us. That puts the burden squarely on you yourselves. We give you all the support we can, we teach you to do the program, we update the program, we maintain a careful watch on the results—all that, of course. But the burden, and it is a tremendous burden, falls directly on the family.

"Anything as demanding as what we're discussing has to cause changes in the style and quality of your life. There's just no way a family could live normally and still keep up. This is especially true in a case like your little boy's, where the damage is severe and the program intense.

"So what we come down to is the prospect of sacrificing everything you consider your normal routine. Of giving up every aspect of your outside life."

He paused. Judy was listening intently. Beside her, Jack sat easy and relaxed, his eyes on the therapist.

"I'll sell my soul, right?" Judy finally asked politely.

If Unruh noted the use of the singular, the only sign he made was a swift glance at Jack. Jack met his gaze blandly.

"Your soul," Unruh agreed pleasantly, "your home, car, oldest child . . ." A charming smile flickered across his mouth.

"You'll find that if you enter into our program you'll become hypercompulsive. You'll do anything to keep your son to his schedule. To other people you'll look, to be frank, like a nut.

You'll refuse to miss or cut short a single session. You'll refuse to take a day off. You'll work as many jobs as you have to to afford what you need to afford, and you'll go without sleep, if necessary, for impossible lengths of time, to adequately provide for the child.

"You'll do all these really terrible things not because you're so much better as people or so much more wonderful as parents or so much less selfish than anybody else, but because you'll come to a point very quickly in the programming where you know you've gone too far to quit and not far enough to back out.

"And that's a life that's hard to contemplate, even after a decent night's rest!" he admitted. "So we like to think you'll consider it as fully as it's possible to consider a nightmare before you make any decision to go ahead."

There was a momentary silence.

"And if we decided we couldn't imagine doing all that?" Judy interjected. "Then what?"

Unruh didn't answer. There was no answer. *This* was the last resort. The other options added up to unacceptables. She'd read up on the CP route; she had an image in her mind of treating all the wrong parts. Exercises in nullification. Exercises in doing zip, waiting, trusting to the same God who'd let it happen in the first place. Trusting in time to make it come right.

She felt a terrible nervous excitement, yet the outer shell of supreme calm was so glossy, so snug, that she was quite sure none of the other feeling leaked out.

"We can stop the pep talk," she suggested. "Tell us about this horrendous program."

In her lowest, most depressed states she'd never imagined such a schedule.

Nine in the morning until ten at night, seven days a week, no let-up. Four volunteers an hour, to move Andy's limbs, to put him through his paces, with the program repeating every fifteen minutes in the beginning weeks or months, then, hopefully, rounding out from fifteen minutes to an hour, the hour to repeat over and over.

Patterning. The damage was diffuse; they'd have to start at the very beginning with the basic movements leading to crawling. These first patterns would involve turning Andy's head, lifting the shoulder and hip, lowering them.

A breath mask—this was to be used as part of the program, to increase the volume of blood flow to the brain and, consequently, the amount of oxygen available. It would also, ultimately, increase Andy's chest capacity and alleviate the breathing problems that had plagued him since birth.

Tactile stimulation—Andy was to be brushed over every inch of his body. Head to toe, even his tongue, to awaken his senses to the environment.

Rolling—this on the floor. First in one direction, then the other.

Hanging upside down—blood to the brain.

At the end of each session, hugging, loving, and cuddling.

There were other things—it took her time to absorb all of them. Every sense was to be assaulted. Specific tastes to be repeated over and over. A pocket flashlight in a dark room to stimulate sight. The list seemed unending.

And that was only the start. They'd return to CNR in a matter of weeks to see if these beginning moves had accomplished anything. If they had, if there was improvement, Unruh would upgrade the program. That would mean, in time, they could go on to more complex patterns. The pattern for crawling. Then the pattern for creeping. Finally, the pattern for walking.

Every new upgrade would depend entirely on the success of the past programming.

*   *   *

The Centre for Neurological Rehabilitation
32 South Morton Avenue
Morton, Penna. 19070

Patient Record

Name of Patient: Andrew Polikoff
Age: 10 months
Date of Admission:
Today's Date: 10/13/74

Recording Therapist: J.U.

Initial impression of a brain-injured youngster with severe developmental lag. Signs of rigidity in all four limbs including tight hips. Visually, demonstrates an alternating divergent strabismus. Fine and gross coordination poor. Visual, tactile and auditory responsiveness below expected chronological level. Still shows signs of tonic neck reflex at ten months. Lacks complete range of motion in extremities and can't crawl. Sitting balance could not be demonstrated and functional speech level at about the ten week level. Could not demonstrate cortical opposition with either hand and was somewhat unresponsive to tactility, including pain.

Prescribed a full program of neurological rehabilitation, to include wide variety of sensory stimulation techniques, developmental motor activities, vision exercises, breathing exercises and prescribed activities designed to provide better environmental opportunity for neurological development.

7

The radio station was tiny. It took Judy and her cousin Phyllis an hour and a half that Tuesday to find it. They had an hour to make their appeal on the air, an appeal for volunteers to program Andy.

What they got was one hour of phone calls expressing horror, sympathy, religious fervor, and a single five-dollar pledge that sent both Judy and Phyllis into a wave of hysteria. They giggled all the way home over the utter terribleness of it.

But it didn't bring in any of the five hundred necessary volunteers, so they tried something else Wednesday.

Phyllis composed an open letter and took it around to all the community newspapers in the Philadelphia area:

A HOPE LINE FOR ANDY

His name is Andy. He's ten months old. He appears to be a healthy, happy baby, and when he smiles he smiles with the love of all the world. But Andy is not a healthy baby. Andy has BRAIN DAMAGE. And Andy needs YOU!

He needs five hundred volunteers to program him. He needs therapy eleven hours a day, seven days a week, and for this, he wants YOU to give ONE HOUR PER WEEK of your own time.

That's not so very much to ask for a child who needs you so desperately.

With your help, and God's, someday Andy may be a healthy, normal child.

Please call Phyllis Levin or Betty Conti at Andy's Hope

Line. His program begins in early November. Remember, it's only ONE HOUR PER WEEK for you. It means a whole lifetime for Andy!

ANDY'S HOPE LINE   Phyllis: 555-8310
                                    Betty: 555-2246

The letter appeared in every community newspaper at the end of that week, and was picked up by the two major newspapers in Philadelphia on Saturday. Then the calls started coming in. From all over the city—the Great Northeast, downtown, the suburbs, even Bucks County. Long lists started forming under the flying pencils of Phyllis and her neighbor and friend, Betty Conti.

On Monday, October 21, Judy and Jack again sat in Alexander Thorpe's office. It felt more natural this time, sitting and having coffee, telling the lawyer the latest news about Andy.

Thorpe had seen the Hope Line article. He'd liked the tone and impact of it. Judy felt gratified. She was coming to need Thorpe's approval. It seemed to give added support to her actions.

"He thinks about a trial as a collection of bits of ammunition, doesn't he?" she said, staring thoughtfully out her window as Jack drove toward home.

"No," he said. "Not really. Just a bunch of puzzle pieces. It takes time to collect the pieces. You heard what he said about keeping him informed about everything. Every single report gets sent to him. Every bill, every medical expenditure. His office will keep an accounting of our debt. We have to consult with him about everything we do for Andy."

Judy's face seemed to shrink into the underlying bone. She stared at him.

"Our debt," she repeated.

"We have to be realistic," Jack concluded, a bit shortly.

They had to be realistic. Andy's medical bills were going to be astronomical. Every visit to Carr would be a major expense. There'd be equipment to buy for the CNR programming. Medications. Vitamins. Things Judy and Jack had no concept of. Yet.

8

It was to be a vast project, a massive undertaking, the goal being the making of Andy. The challenge inherent in this goal was so enormous she couldn't grasp it, but projects were something Judy understood.

Two weeks before the programming was set to start, she bought some things at the drugstore around the corner. She came home and laid these purchases out. Posterboard. A twelve-inch ruler. Two felt-tipped pens, one red, one black. A regular graphite pencil from the kitchen drawer completed her supplies.

The house was quiet. Scott was in school and Jack was upstairs with Todd and Andy. She sat down at the dining room table and eyed her materials, then pulled the blank posterboard toward her. She took a breath and picked up her pencil.

There was something soothing about the cream-white of the paper. She drew neat lines and from the lines she made perfect squares. She made letters in the squares, drawing them precisely.

This exacting process took thirty-three minutes to complete.

Finally, with the muscles in her neck starting to hurt and a dull headache forming behind both eyes, she had her heading:

Concise and simple. She didn't ask herself why she was agonizing over the poster, or why she'd decided to make it at all. The idea had come to her on a sleepless night, a manageable miniproject that she grasped at eagerly because it gave her immediate direction.

She eyed her heading, tongue caught between her teeth, chose the black marker and went over all the letters, then highlighted them with the red marker.

The rules, in neat little rows beneath the heading, half its height, took quite a bit longer to write out:

1. This is not a social hour.
2. Please remove shoes in basement.
3. No eating or drinking in the house.
4. Come on time and leave promptly when you finish your program.
5. Please use basement lavatory.
6. Please notify us as early as possible if you can't make your scheduled program.

When these rules were done, neatly penciled in, she wrote in script a large black THANK YOU.

Judy took the sign and propped it on the back of the couch, surveying her handiwork with satisfaction. The words came up sharp against the cream background—one small, easily completed project.

Phylls called late that afternoon to say she already had two hundred fifteen of the needed five hundred volunteers.

"I can't believe how good I'm starting to feel about people in general," Phyllis said. "I mean, it's actually like what you read about places like New York, and blackouts and things. People can come through in a pinch. Maybe it's human nature to cooperate when the need's great enough. If you could be sitting here,

Judy, taking some of these messages—I'm keeping notes, I'll show them to you later.

"We've actually got four Girl Scouts coming together as one team, all the way from Bucks County. One of the mothers will drive them, and she'll be available for that same hour as an extra pair of hands. We've got over twenty people signed up from Chester County. I haven't counted how many from downtown.

"I've also been getting calls from churches and synagogues. And people asking where to send donations, to help pay for equipment and medicines and things like that. And three different doctors called today to offer equipment, if you need it—breathing masks, like that."

"We're coming along great!"

They were coming along great. Judy hung up distractedly, wondering where to mount her sign.

Scott walked in from school minutes later and showed a mild enthusiasm that smacked of condescension when she displayed her work, but then, Scott was ten and wrapped up in himself. Jack came downstairs when he heard Scott and was effusive about the poster, which made Judy sure he was humoring her. Todd, only three, was too young to be put on the spot, and Andy lay in his playpen, staring at the ceiling and grinning at some private joke.

She took her sign to the basement and taped it to the wall. From that position it would proceed to fall, no matter how securely she taped it—slow slips, fast slides, she'd find it face down and trampled over and over for the next two and a half years, desperately hard years that would seem an eternity.

Late that night, when Jack had left for work, she made her bedtime rounds. Scott was asleep on his back. Todd slept too, curled on his side. Andy stared at her from his crib with a sleepless frown and she lifted him to her breast and hugged him tight.

"Don't worry, lovey," she crooned. "Daddy and Mommy

81

and five hundred strangers are gonna see that everything works out right."

She stroked the fine hair on the tiny head and tried to turn the child from her breast, but he clung to her arm, rigid.

"Well, well," she whispered hoarsely, startled but not yet alarmed. "Trying to get out of going to sleep?"

He was coiled around her arm, tight as a boa.

"It's not nice to attack Mommy," her breath shortened.

She tried to pry him off and down into the crib. He still clung to her arm. She heard herself moan with breathless terror, and tried to swallow the sound so as not to make matters worse by waking Todd.

"Oh, God . . ."

It was horrible!

She knew she was about to lose control and the thought drove her from the room. Across the hall and into the master bedroom. She kicked the door shut with her heel, stumbled to the bed, and yanked the phone off the hook. With her free hand, she dialed a familiar number.

"Put him down on the bed," Uncle Murray said.

"I c-c-can't," she stammered, tears streaming down her face.

"Lie down on the bed holding him," Uncle Murray's voice was calm.

"I can't get him off my arm!" she cried, shuddering with fear.

"He's having a seizure. You were warned of the possibility. There's nothing you can do except to lie down and hold him gently until he relaxes."

Hours and hours of night. She'd been warned of the possibilities. The seizures were a possibility. So she lay and held her frightening baby close.

Seizures. Silent seizures. Like if he cried and couldn't get enough oxygen. Or for other reasons. There was a long list of possibilities. Seizures and breathing problems and chest complications due to an underdeveloped chest capacity.

And of course there wasn't any guarantee that any of it would come right. Not even with the programming. The very decision to go with CNR had made the family a target for a far different attitude than that Phyllis was encountering.

"You're Judy Polikoff, aren't you?"

The woman stood behind her in the supermarket checkout line. "My cousin pointed you out to me. You're the one going against God's will. You'll be punished, mark my words, putting your sweet little baby through the devil's own torture!"

That had shocked and hurt her and she'd made the mistake of trying to explain. No explanations were acceptable.

There'd been other, similar ugly confrontations. The rehabilitative method, because it was rigorous and had failed to gain AMA support, was highly controversial, and Judy soon found herself in the middle of a battle zone.

"God forgive you," an acquaintance of seven years had stared up into her face and prayed. "I always liked you, Judy, but I'm forced to say you don't deserve to have children!"

The voices would follow her through the years.

She shifted, finally, and looked down at Andy's sleeping face. He was nearly eleven months old now and didn't know she was his mother. Didn't know what a "Mommy" was. But it didn't matter. She knew. She knew he was her child. She knew this meant she owed him things. Chances. Choices. Life.

Later, much later, she'd wonder why she had ever imagined she herself had any choices.

She closed her eyes, chilled and too tired to move, afraid to move anyway, afraid to wake Andy, afraid that if he woke he'd have another seizure, afraid—afraid of practically everything.

She slept.

At the end of the second week before the start of the programming, Phyllis had a list of names she could organize into time slots. She and Betty and another friend, Arlene Cohen, started making return phone calls. Checking on availability and flexibility. They were handling the impossible task of getting

83

the needed volunteers and, through the Hope Line, of making a scheduled reality out of a nightmare. They were also trying for a little character analysis, some indication of who would stick, who would not. Everyone sounded kind and dependable. There was no way to prepare for future dropouts.

A frenetic activity had invaded Judy's house. All normal functions speeded up and then, when chores were completed too quickly, everything had to be done again.

There was too much time to think.

Judy scoured and rescoured the house in a compulsive effort at exhausting herself and preventing herself from sinking into fearful depression. Jack lost count of the scourings.

The basement, point of entry for the volunteers and site of most of the programming exercises, she cleaned until it seemed bleached. She cleared out the old bookshelf standing in the corner of the basement closest to the steps, and placed another, much smaller sign on top:

PLEASE LEAVE SHOES HERE DURING
PROGRAMMING

Saving on the rugs. Saving on dirt. She was proud of herself for thinking of that small expediency.

Andy lay motionless while she bustled about.

She bought herself a notepad. A schedule-keeper. A list-compiler. Such activities provided a businesslike atmosphere, a backdrop of manageable security. On the first page of the notepad was a schedule for using the washer and dryer, both of which were closeted discreetly behind folding doors in the basement. Such a schedule was vitally necessary, for she had no intention of doing her dirty laundry in public. There were things you didn't compromise. There were standards you kept if you had self-respect. You might beg for the hands and warm bodies to move your child's rigid limbs, but you never ever aired your privacies.

Other families fell apart. Hers would be forcibly adhesive-

84

taped together and made stronger by the very act of surviving.

The second page had her schedule of housework. The housework could not be permitted to pile up. The house had to remain as spotless as she'd always kept it, regardless of how many strangers invaded.

Judy Polikoff had yet to experience the reality of hundreds of shoeless feet parading through the endless hours of endless days of weeks of months of years.

There were other lists on her notepad. Long, comprehensive shopping lists, for example. All for her own use. In none of her calculations did she have an actual category of skills or chores designated for Jack. It wasn't a conscious omission. It was simply that asking for help made her feel more vulnerable, and vulnerability lessened her resolve.

The equipment had been arriving. The patterning table stood near the living room/dining room arch. It wouldn't fit in the basement. It had a solid, strictly business look that made her want to block it out, so she got her dust cloth and carefully dusted both dining room table and patterning table, trying to relegate the new arrival to some essence of normalcy.

It didn't work. She felt a definite aversion to the patterning table.

Other equipment sat in the basement, not all of it needed now. Some of it had been built by Jack's Brith Sholom Lodge. A crawl box. A hanging bar. Judy gazed at these things and felt a painful tightening in her throat at the wish, dearest wish, that her child might someday progress that far.

There was a pile of breathing masks donated by doctors for the masking that would remain a constant throughout the programming.

On the last evening but one before the start of the programming, the chores had been done to death. Jack was in the living room, reading. Judy entered the room at a determined bustle and confiscated the section of newspaper Jack had just dropped. It was gone before he could mourn it, stuffed into the heavy-

85

duty trash bag she was dragging along. Jack stared at her in thoughtful silence. This was how Judy coped. He imagined it was how she'd survived the death of her father, even as a small girl. The death of her first marriage. The death of anything that hadn't gone the way she'd wanted. Perhaps her mother's remarriage. Her stepfather's severe stroke. Jack himself endured intolerable pain until it diminished with time. He found it very difficult to understand Judy's aggressive dance with life.

For now, it was necessary to endure the equipment springing up all over the house. The growing accumulation of medications that seemed silent proof of bills already starting piles. It made him curiously unable to draw a complete breath. He felt, often, as if he was stifling. He thought about his own physical self for the first time in his adult life. He thought, endlessly, about his job at Century Steel, and Century's own financial problems. The long-threatened layoffs. His own vulnerability. It was this lengthening shadow of a medical unknown that made him vulnerable.

Then there were the children—his boys. He'd probably only imagined the strangeness about his boys. Scott, who'd been his since the tender age of six, whose every expression and mood he knew so well, looking confused these days, and unnaturally excited. Todd, sucking his thumb in the bathroom—he'd been sure he saw that, though a second glance found Todd's face bland and his little hands loose at his sides.

Jack had a sudden, unwanted picture of his wife, creeping around the silent, sleeping house, unable to sleep, nervous and overwrought, washing and rewashing the windowsills, the picture frames, dusting the invisible undersides of tables, chairs, couch. Making endless nocturnal trips to the basement bathroom to rewash the toilet bowl rim, trying to exhaust herself, trying to numb her fears and thoughts.

It exhausted him, watching Judy.

If only she'd ask him to help—but she didn't. He would have felt less apathetic if she'd asked. He couldn't get up the energy to volunteer and be turned down, but he would have given himself gladly if she'd asked.

He stirred.

"Judy?"

She was plumping the pillows on the couch.

"The programming doesn't start this second, Judy," he said, but without hope. "Can't you just sit down with me for a while and talk?"

She gazed at him for a long minute, and her shoulders seemed to sag. Then she straightened, jaw set, and that steely light was back, flattening the look in her eyes.

"What do we talk about?" she asked, genuinely curious.

Jack was silent, overwhelmed by her remark.

"About the programming?" Judy asked him. "About Andy? About how scared I am?" But she sheered away from this, and smiled lightly. "Or about how much all this is going to cost? Or about how long it might be before we even know if it'll work?"

Jack seemed to slouch deeper into his chair. Judy shrugged.

"Don't you think," she asked, "it might be better if we don't talk?"

Phyllis called that evening at ten after ten, tired but cheerful. She had, after all, taken a total impossibility and turned it into a living achievement: real people, donating real time. And the list kept growing.

There was a total, now, of nearly four hundred names.

Thirteen hours a day. Four people an hour. That was fifty-two volunteers a day. Times seven days a week. That made it three hundred sixty-four. Beyond that, you needed all the extra names you could get. People would cancel, drop out, have other last-minute appointments. There would be those who couldn't come each and every week. Their slots would have to be filled by somebody else. The total of five hundred was a ball-park figure. The reality of nearly four hundred on call meant the programming could, indeed, get started on schedule.

"We've got senior citizens and teenagers and everything in between," Phyllis exulted. "We could start our own United Nations. I had several calls from people who could barely speak English. People who don't want to volunteer want to know where to send donations, or if there's anything at all they could do besides actually come and help with the programming.

"I've had women call and ask how old their children would have to be to help program. I've signed up at least twenty women with teenagers, whose kids will be coming with them as additional programmers. In fact, the response from high school age kids is really remarkable. A lot of them really are idealistic and unselfish enough to put themselves out for somebody else.

"I feel tremendous about all this, Judy. It's terrible that it takes something disastrous to make the point, but people really can be wonderful!"

She finally hung up. Judy stared at the phone thoughtfully. She wanted Phyllis to be right. She wanted to receive this gift from the programming. A lasting closeness with other people that had nothing to do with lifelong friendships. And it was an incredible number—nearly four hundred volunteers!

No one could know or wanted to know that only sixty-seven would stay until the very end.

It was Saturday. The last day before the programming. Jack had just made a cautious suggestion. He and Judy were folding clothes from the dryer.

"We *should* take the rest of today, just to be together as a family. We need the time. The kids need our full attention."

Judy placed a bath towel on the already folded pile.

"I have to make sure everything's clean. I don't think I can count on doing any straightening up tomorrow."

"You've cleaned everything in the house a hundred times!" Jack protested. "What's the matter with you? These people are coming to manipulate Andy's arms and legs. They're not coming to admire your housekeeping!"

"No?" she smiled cryptically.

"Now look, Judy," he tried to ignore the smile, which was cool and sarcastic, "the house looks fine, nothing needs doing in the house, but there are other things that could stand some attention before everything gets hectic tomorrow."

She folded the last washcloth and piled all the clean things in the basket to take upstairs.

"I leave things undone that should be done, Jack?"

Too late, he wished he'd avoided this.

"The boys . . ." but he stopped.

"What about the boys?"

"If you have to fill up every minute, maybe you could take a few to tell them about the strangers about to overrun the house."

Judy stared at him. There was a moment's silence.

"Do you honestly think," she finally asked him quietly, "I haven't tried?"

He didn't answer her. He didn't know if she'd tried.

"Scott doesn't listen after the first two sentences," Judy said flatly. "And Todd's a little young to understand. Exactly what would you have me tell them anyway? That their little brother's brain-damaged?"

"I don't know exactly what they should be told, Judy," Jack admitted. "I just think it's important to sit down as a family and make them see they're part of all this, so they don't feel neglected."

"They know I'm counting on them," she said mulishly. "They know this is a family affair. Especially Scott. Scott's a big boy. He's always known I need him there."

"Don't you think," Jack persisted, "that it might be a good idea to impress on them both that all the attention Andy's about to get won't in any way detract from the love they'll always have from their parents?"

But she couldn't afford to indulge in discussions of love. She couldn't allow soft emotions to touch her. She was the mother of a brain-damaged child. That was all the reason she needed for any other temporary omissions.

"You talk to them," she suggested. "You're their father. Have a man-to-man talk with them."

"Judy . . ."

"I don't have the time right now," she said desperately. "My God, Jack!" her eyes flashed, "don't you understand? I can't think of anything tonight but the programming!"

He turned away. It wasn't only tonight. She'd been elusive since the diagnosis. He desperately needed to talk to her about it, to hold her, to tell her of *his* fears. Her remoteness hurt him. He didn't think he'd ever let her know how *much* it hurt.

He got his coat and left the house.

She'd bought a diary—her first. Even as a young girl, when all her friends were sporting small fat books with fake leather covers and tiny goldtone keyholes, she'd never felt the desire or the need for one.

The diary was small enough to slide easily into her drawer under her night things. Large enough to rest comfortably on her knee. Thin enough to fill from cover to cover if she was studious. Thick enough to be its own challenge.

She had no idea at all how unnerving Jack was finding her hyper-response to challenges.

The diary was, of course, for Andy. That's what she told herself when she bought it, on impulse.

The house was much too quiet with Jack gone. She got the diary from her bureau, sat down on the bed, and turned on the light. She stared for a long while at the blank white page, her mind jumping from this thought to that.

Saturday, November 2, 1974

This is a momentous occasion. Tomorrow morning is the start of Andrew Polikoff's CNR programming. This diary will be a record of the results, however long the programming takes, or however quickly we see our miracle.

I know I won't sleep tonight. I'm so excited and nervous. It would have been smart to leave something really big needing to be done, but I didn't, the house is spotless. Scott and Todd are playing out front. Jack's out walking.

So here I sit, alone and thinking, and I guess it's natural to find myself rehashing things. And even being scared, wondering how it all happened and if I'll be able to handle this. Wondering exactly what we'll end up accomplishing by the end of the programming.

This diary is for positive thinking. It is officially for Andrew Polikoff. It's something for him to read when he's older and better and into reading, and will naturally be thrilled to find a little book all about a little boy named Andy.

She was finishing the first entry in her diary, sitting on the side of the bed with the book open on her knee, when Jack returned from his walk. She didn't hear him. Indeed, he took pains that she shouldn't.

A faded sun had lit his walk. Shadows encumbered the living room. Chill winter sat in the marrow of his bones and he minded. He minded desperately.

He stood staring blankly at the empty playpen—Andy was upstairs in his crib. He listened half fearfully for some sign of Judy. When he heard a sudden creak from the floorboard near the bed he moved with suspicious speed, into the kitchen, to take her little memo pad from its magnet on the refrigerator. He scribbled a swift note, tore off the page, and took it back to the living room. He left the note on the table by the playpen.

Then he was gone again, soundlessly, out the front door to gather up the two older boys and hustle them into the car.

"Let's get hamburgers," he said conspiratorially.

He thought Scott looked worried. But he couldn't go up and

91

ask Judy to come with them. Judy would refuse, make excuses about taking the baby to a restaurant, and besides, he didn't want to interfere with her housekeeping.

The Burger King was crowded, and the crush of people in and out, added to the circus of children bunched around the nearby tables, held Todd's attention while Jack and Scott talked.

"Do I know them?" Scott asked.

"The volunteers? Some of them. A lot of them. There are four hundred of them, maybe even more by now. I don't think you could possibly know all of them."

"Are they your friends?" Scott persisted. "You and Mom?"

Jack sat back and considered this thoughtfully. "I guess they're friends of the family now," he decided. "After all, look what they're willing to do for Andy."

The boy was silent, staring at the food he'd hardly touched.

"Everything's gonna work out, son," Jack finally said.

Scott lifted grave eyes and gazed at him doubtfully.

"I know this is bothering you," Jack pressed, gently. "Talk to me, Scott. Tell me what you've been thinking about."

Todd had turned his attention to his dinner. He was in the process of dissecting his sandwich. He'd placed the roll, in two halves, neatly on his open napkin, and was busy peeling the cheese from the burger. Scott sat and watched this process with the same grave attention he awarded everything.

"Scott?" Jack finally prodded.

"We should've brought Mom," the boy said quietly, turning the full force of that stare once more to his father's face. "It was wrong to leave her."

Jack studied him for a long minute.

"I know," he admitted.

They finished their meal in silence.

II
PATTERNS

9

Sunday, November 3, 1974

Today, at long last, is a landmark day for the Polikoff family! We officially started Andy's programming! There was such a feeling of excitement in the house this morning, waiting for the arrival of the first programmers.

Phyllis gave me a list of names to date. We have a total of four hundred twenty-seven scheduled. How's that for a start? And the calls are still coming in from every part of the city and suburbs. Phyllis also has mail. Three crucifixes, by special post. Seventeen printed prayers, each different, from every religious denomination imaginable

I had such crazy mixed feelings when I first read over the list. So many of the names are those of friends or neighbors or acquaintances. I don't know which seemed more strange—the names I knew or the names I didn't.

Every set of programmers was complete today. Every set was exactly on time or else a few minutes early. Every single person followed the rules. Most of today's programmers were women.

And Andy, star of the show, was amazing!

We started at nine on the button and continued to eight-twenty this evening. Until I actually saw it accomplished, I don't think I really believed it was possible. Andy's goodness itself is our first success in this programming!

Toward the end, he got a little cranky. So sue him—right? Not bad at all, considering the state of utter exhaustion of his Mommy! But for the first time since this nightmare with Andy began, I have some hope for the future. Not because there was any noticeable effect of the programming on this first day, which there wasn't. But because we're finally doing something positive for Andy! And Andy will still fool them all. I know it!

The boys—all three—were in bed. The last volunteers were gone. The nine-to-ten set was canceled, since Andy had fallen asleep and it seemed stupid to Judy to try to wake him for just one more hour. He was exhausted. Judy herself was utterly drained. Her heart ached with misery for the unhappiness of her child. She'd been forced to stand and hear him wailing through the endless hours. The day had been long, slower than she'd dreamed possible. The front walk of the house became a refuge to which she'd fled every hour on the hour to escape Andy's sobbing. It was torment, listening to that throat-catching crying. Andy, fretting through the entire day, crying nonstop through the afternoon hours. Screaming as if he was being maimed at the start of every new set. That wasn't exactly how she'd put it in the diary, but the diary was meant for Andy to read someday, so she'd naturally tried to slant the facts and make this first day sound positive and happy.

As Judy got ready for bed, Jack was preparing to leave for work. He glanced at the night table, at the closed diary.

"Why did you decide to keep a diary?"

Judy blinked, hesitated, then shrugged, not really sure she knew all the reasons.

"It was just—it seemed, *felt* like a good idea."

Jack was silent.

"I can keep everything recorded."

There was a stubborn look to Jack's face. "Instead of talking to me," he said, "you'll talk to your diary?"

It was too close to the truth to deny. She said nothing.

"At least," Jack said sourly, "it might come in handy. For Thorpe."

96

Her anger flared. It was growing too easy to lose her temper. Recognizing this, she controlled herself with an effort. She wasn't interested in having her personal diary handy for Thorpe. The diary was for Andy. If there were other reasons for noting down her thoughts, it wasn't necessary to try to figure them out for Jack. It was simply that a diary, a journal, was a logical extension of her strategy. Paperwork. She could view it like that. A business operation, with records kept for posterity.

"He called," she murmured, walking over to the dresser and handling her hairbrush. "His office. Thorpe."

Jack sat on the side of the bed to pull on a clean sock.

"For what?"

"To remind me I can't do anything without letting him know first. Bills for treatment and medicines. Copies of all the medical reports. Everything."

She hesitated, glancing at Jack's bent head.

"He didn't even bother to say 'good luck' on the first day of programming."

Jack heard the bitter edge in her voice and looked up, amused.

"Why should he?"

She turned away, exasperated.

Behind her, her husband bent to tie his shoes. A pulse was hammering in his throat. This "I" business she'd adopted had taken the place of the "we" they'd always used so naturally. It was her studious habit since the hospital. It was her way of making herself a freestanding, invulnerable entity. It made him wonder exactly what she'd internalized on the fourth floor of Midtown Hospital months ago, alone with Andy, away from him and the boys, with nothing but a bunch of depressed women for company. Some of whom had lost their own husbands. Some of whom had destroyed their own happiness. For a single obsession which must now become Judy's and his obsession—the care and feeding of a damaged child.

Judy's little tricks. There was a whole bag of them recently.

97

He didn't mind the other crutches she was using, but the "I" he minded greatly. Life was difficult for him too lately.

"It was a hard day," he said, standing. "You must be tired."

He gazed down at her, his compassion full and quick, for she looked so deadly weary. Reaching out, he curled the end of a long length of vivid hair around his index finger. He touched her cheek with his fingertips, then pulled her to him.

Judy looked vaguely past him and disengaged herself carefully.

There was a small silence between them.

He didn't explode. He didn't even ask her why she pulled away. It wasn't his way to ask questions like that. He didn't yell or rage or even tell her how much he needed a good hug. He didn't press himself on her. Judy would come back when there was something left over to share. When she could manage love.

He made himself believe this. It was necessary to his existence.

He went off to work, leaving her in her own misery.

Monday, November 4, 1974

Day Number Two of the programming! It was dull and drizzly this morning. Andy didn't do quite as well as he did yesterday, poor little baby, he cried a lot today and fell asleep at 6:00 this evening.

I didn't wake him.

It would have boosted my spirits, which for some reason were sort of low, to have seen him go the full distance. But I've never in my life had cause to doubt my instincts and I knew today, as I knew last night, that his capacity for this will develop.

Jack never had these instincts. Jack goes by the book. It makes him see things in stark black and white. I'm starting to think we have totally different outlooks. And I won't waste the time or the space writing what he had to say about stopping the programming early for the second day.

Tomorrow will be a much better day for Andy!

Tuesday, November 5, 1974

I had to stop the program at 4:30 today. And when I say I *had* to, I mean just that! If I'm going to talk about instinct, which I'm not, all I'll say is that if I'd really followed my maternal instincts we'd have stopped at noon, but I didn't let myself do that. And every day I'll try to brave it through that little longer until we've built to the whole program. You simply don't jump right in at the top. You work up, gradually. But Jack doesn't want to face that. I can't figure him out. How can he seriously expect a little baby to endure being yanked and tugged and bullied without letup, if there's no learning period first to accustom him to the schedule?

I think I'm a little depressed tonight. I guess that's natural. I spent so much time anticipating the start of the programming that now the actual schedule has started, the slowness of the process is a let-down. I know that's silly, but I'm allowed a little silliness, aren't I?

I have to school myself to the idea that we're lucky if it's one step forward, two steps back. I have to be super patient. I'll make this a success only if I am patient. Andy can't fail if *I* don't give up!

Wednesday, November 6, 1974

Andy showed absolutely no progress today. He was up sick most of last night, which proves I was right to stop the program early yesterday.

Jack tried to explain to me how he feels about going the full distance each time. He thinks Andy might eventually figure out he can avoid doing these things if he's cranky enough to force a stop to the programming. I can understand Jack feeling like this, but I also refuse to believe that Andy's capable, at this point in his life, of the kind of rational thinking that could work all that out. If he cries it's because he's exhausted or in pain or furious because he's being pushed and pulled throughout the day, but not because he's sly and conniving at getting an hour's rest.

And I won't give in on this! I won't have Andy programmed when he's so exhausted that he's in very real danger of having a seizure from all that screaming and gasping and crying.

What I am trying to force myself to do is wait the very longest I can. Not to just stop the programming without giving it a chance. Today I let it go on nearly to the end, and this despite the attitude of several of the programmers, who felt I should stop, and who seemed surprised, then shocked, and even disgusted with me when I insisted on trying to go on.

They truly care about the baby. They don't only move his limbs, they give him unbounded love. I don't feel the same about all of them, but that's only natural, isn't it? They have a wide range of personalities, like any other group of people. Some of them would have been instant friends if I'd met them in other circumstances. A lot of them *are* my old friends. And others . . .

If I should start to gripe about personalities, just ignore me. It's a normal part of human relationships.

But it hurts to think they believe I'd mistreat my own baby by forcing him to work when he's crying and feverish—I *have* to keep him to the program, at least as much as humanly possible! They don't understand the commitment I undertook, or even the real thrust of the programming.

Then again, how could they?

Thursday, November 7, 1974

Andy seems to be coming down with something. He had a low-grade fever today. I kept him in programming until after seven, but he was much warmer by then and I put him to bed early.

Friday, November 8, 1974

Andy's sick, with a fever of 101. No programming.

Saturday, November 9, 1974

Andy's temperature's up to 102. No programming today either. They told us that babies with Andy's problems are prone to respiratory infections, and have trouble with their breathing.

It's possible that in time I'll be able to see Andy programmed from nine in the morning until ten at night, while running a 102 fever. But not today.

The treatment worked, folks, but the patient died. Even Jack didn't give me an argument about canceling today's programming.

Sunday, November 10, 1974

No programming today. Fever dropping, but slowly. I don't want to read myself writing that much more. The frustration I feel at not being able to get going again is increasing every day. If Andy's temperature drops to 100, I'll reschedule tomorrow's programmers.

Monday, November 11, 1974

Andy was very sick last night and on into this morning. He got no sleep at all, coughing badly, still with a high fever.

Todd seems to have the same thing. It's like a tiny revelation. Andy has something normal. It's something I have to try to remember the next time he catches a cold or a virus or something. He's a kid. He catches things just like any other kid does.

By late afternoon, the fever was nearly gone. I have my fingers crossed and I haven't called off tomorrow's programming.

Tuesday, November 12, 1974

Andy had a seizure.

I can write that pretty calmly now, but I didn't feel calm when I was watching him have it. I felt helpless and just as sick as I did the last time. And I took him to see Uncle Murray despite all my good intentions about handling these things myself, because I felt no better able to cope with the situation this time than the last time.

So it's confession time. I was wrong to go to Uncle Murray. He doesn't really approve of this type of programming. I ended up sitting through twenty minutes of "I told you so" after which I had a royal battle with poor Uncle Murray. Which was really stupid because I love him and I know he loves us, but it's no good people giving you their opinions when you really don't want to hear anything but support for your own decisions.

And of course, since the seizure was over by that time, I also felt like a jerk, sitting there. I didn't *need* Uncle Murray. I'd managed myself!

Jack didn't want me to take Andy to Uncle Murray. He was right. I think I even knew he was right when he was yelling at me. It just made me feel stubborn and unable to change my mind. I'd said I was going, so I had to go— that kind of thing that you look back on and feel silly over and wonder why you couldn't behave like an adult. And going meant canceling the morning programs. I felt terrible about that!

We started programming at one o'clock and went through until ten. It was a small consolation to me that we did that. And there won't be any cancellations tomorrow, no matter what. I don't know if Andy can handle it or not, but at this point I'd rather see him coughing and crying on the patterning table than coughing and crying, doing nothing, in his crib.

Wednesday, November 13, 1974

My dearest little boy! What an effort! We had a full program today, and I do mean a full program! It was our first time all the way through to the end and, of course, Andy cried a lot and he was drowsy and slow and there was no progress. There never has been any progress. But we completed the program! And it felt incredibly good, that simple fact.

We completed the program.

10

It was Sunday morning, precisely two weeks after the start of the programming. Four people who were no longer total strangers stood around the patterning table—a stockbroker from center city, a cashier from the Acme, an undergraduate student from Temple University, and one of Judy's good friends. These four would work the hour from ten to eleven, the second hour of the daily program. At least one of them would be terribly afraid. Andy's limbs were so stiff that to force them into the pattern was like trying to move the lever on a rusty hand brake.

That morning, as on all the mornings of these two weeks, there was no noticeable response from Andy.

Upstairs, in the back bedrooms, Scott and Todd were shuffling behind closed doors. In the master bedroom, Jack, just home from work, was pulling on pajamas. It was still a matter of discomfort to Judy to see him undress with a house full of people downstairs.

The past few days had been frantic. She'd gotten totally off her carefully devised household schedules. The upstairs bathroom was decidedly dingy and she'd been so tired that she left last night's laundry undone. Large, unwieldy piles of clothing stood in all three bedrooms. She couldn't find the notepad with her shopping lists. And Todd's left shoe had vanished.

"He fought everything during the nine o'clock program,"

she said to Jack, watching him out of the corner of her eye, thinking he looked ill, a bit pale, the flesh of his face drawn tight.

"He kicked that nice woman from the beauty parlor when it was time for the masking, screamed when they used the little flashlight down in the basement, and threw up when they were rolling him on the rug. He liked all the cuddling and tickling, though," she said thoughtfully.

"It's so hard to move his arms and legs and head," she said hesitantly. "I think a lot of them are afraid. It seems like you have to break a bone, forcing him into the pattern."

Jack looked up. "He has to learn this before he can go on to cross-pattern and normal crawling."

She knew that. She was just tired. It amazed her how exhausting it was to see unending hands on her baby. To know she couldn't rest on the couch, couldn't nurse a headache in private, couldn't be alone in her own living room. Couldn't leave the house either, if it came to that. Not if Jack was asleep. Not even to take a little walk to refresh herself.

Then there was the Family Hour. CNR's treat. That hour allotted, minus programmers, for the family dinner each night. She'd tried to make it special. She was fully aware of the importance of this time together. But it had quickly become apparent that the atmosphere in the house had made even eating dinner together something of a trial.

Watching the clock. Trying to find appetite. Discovering, instead, a constant lump in her throat.

There was never an end to worrying. Large worries and small. Thinking about all the bills piling in. About the absence, one morning, of clean socks.

Monday, November 18, 1974

Andy was a little less cranky today. Still no sign of progress. The programmers stand and move his arms and legs and head, and when they stop, he lays there. There's been no apparent movement initiated by Andy himself. He doesn't seem to understand what the programmers are doing

Tuesday, November 19, 1974
No progress.

Wednesday, November 20, 1974
Andy didn't sleep well last night, but he hardly cried at all during the entire day's programming.

God, he's such a beautiful little boy. Why did this terrible thing have to happen to him? How did it happen? I can't stand the thought that a perfectly normal child was damaged like this through the negligence of a man I trusted while I was lying in a hospital bed too sick to stop it happening.

Thursday, November 21, 1974
A day like all the others. Nothing happening.

Friday, November 22, 1974
Nothing.

Saturday, November 23, 1974
Andy didn't feel well today. He completed his program coughing and crying. I wouldn't have stopped the program early anyway, but Jack seemed to think I might. He stood glowering over me for most of the day, which meant he missed his sleep, which means he's terribly tired tonight.

He's also turning into a stranger.

Sunday, November 24, 1974
Hour after hour. Same exercises, different hands, same response—none whatsoever. Have to be careful. Feel myself falling into depression.

Monday, November 25, 1974

_____

Tuesday, November 26, 1974

_____

Wednesday, November 27, 1974

Must be my imagination some of the programmers are starting to look disappointed. Must have expected a miracle. Just like Andy's Mommy.

Thursday, November 28, 1974

I woke up with a terrible headache this morning and feeling lower than dirt. Maybe because it's Thanksgiving. I had a long heart-to-heart talk with myself last night, telling myself all about my blessings, knowing that even this programming is a blessing of sorts because Andy's increasing awareness is an improvement I _can_ see, even if it's the only accomplishment.

But I can't make myself stop asking myself why? Why _my_ baby? Why why why! Jack says it's futile and stupid to go on beating a dead horse, that we'll probably never know the answer. He says just live for the day, and hope for the best for tomorrow.

You know what I want? Desperately? To see my baby crawl! Jack says be patient. How patient can I be? I may be really stupid to even say I hoped, but it would have been an awfully nice Thanksgiving present.

Friday, November 29, 1974

Andy was actually pleasant today throughout the programming. He seemed, if it's not a totally absurd thing to imagine, to be thinking about the programming. He was more aware of what was going on. This wasn't my observation alone. Several of the programmers commented on

106

it. It was as if he'd suddenly tuned in for a while, then tuned out, then decided to tune back in again.

I want to believe this is the first step to bigger things. That he had to first become fully aware of what the programmers are doing before he could begin to take an active part in the programming. But there's no sense in trying to make guesses about any of this. We just have to wait and see.

At least now I'm really looking forward to tomorrow's programming.

Saturday, November 30, 1974

It's one o'clock in the morning and I'm trying very hard to be the cool-headed mother I'm expected to be, and the capable woman I always thought myself to be, which is why I'm sitting here, on the bed, acting grown-up, writing dumb scribbles in this stupid little book instead of locking myself in the bathroom and having a really satisfying scream.

Jack called to say he has to work a double shift and since we so desperately need the money, and since we're so worried about possible layoffs anyway, it wasn't a question of whether he would or wouldn't work, it was just a phone call to tell me he wouldn't be home until late afternoon instead of at nine in the morning. And then he'll have to leave again for work a few hours later, which will mean practically no sleep at all for him, and no moral support at all for me.

His call woke me from my miserable dozing. I haven't been able to sleep for the past few nights and tonight I was so exhausted I think I blacked out the minute I hit the pillow. So I'd managed a little sleep, dreaming I was being chased, waking a bit, then dreaming again—an endless dream where I was running down a hospital corridor with people in all the doorways throwing con-

107

vulsive fits. I knew it was only a dream but that didn't make it easier, and the sound of the phone nearly drove *me* into a fit.

Andy had a seizure before Jack left at eleven. It wasn't that bad, I stayed calm and matter-of-fact, maybe because Jack was here with me. Andy fell asleep around midnight, then woke coughing and crying, then fell asleep again, then the phone woke him, naturally, and he's been coughing and choking and crying ever since.

I finally put Todd in with Scott. It was the one "good mother" thing I could do. Nothing else I've tried seems to have accomplished anything. Andy's coughing sounds almost constant right now, I'm trying not to keep running in to him. I rolled him around on the floor for a while until his breathing seemed clearer, then put him on his tummy, in his crib, and covered him up, and came back in here and in a little while if it's necessary I'll go roll him again—I get so frightened!

I'll try to write more later . . .

Just finished rolling Andy on the rug, then carrying him around upside down for another half hour. It was the only way I could think of to keep him breathing freely, he's coughing that badly. So tired. Can't think. Never been this tired. My head feels like a solid block and the headache's blinding. I should call Uncle Murray's emergency number, but couldn't stand another lecture. Can't call Jack at work and what could Jack do if I did call him?

It's quieter. Andy's quieter. Maybe rolling him and holding him like that did do some good. Maybe I don't need to feel so worthless.

Can't sleep. Don't know if that's bad or good. Can't stop thinking, either, feeling sorry for myself, so disgustingly self-pitying. Never seem to feel any better.

Don't expect to feel *good,* just *better.* Never seem to get myself together anymore. Don't care how I look. Don't care how the house looks. Don't care about anything. It's always something with Andy, something bad to erase the small bits of good. He's always sick, there's no point glossing it over, even when he's trying his hardest he's coughing, having trouble breathing, up sick at night and me with him, rolling him on the floor. How can a little baby be expected to do all that when he's never well enough to do anything?

You wouldn't expect it of an adult!

No matter what I try won't help. No choices left. He'll make it or he won't, and if he doesn't . . .

I know I'll be sorry for writing all this negative slop! I'll go back and read it over a year from now and wonder how I could feel such mean things about my own baby. How I could sit here, seeing life as it would have been without Andy. Seeing Jack and Scott and Todd and me, normal and happy together

. . . I actually dozed off and it was a mistake—the baby's worse, I woke to hear him gagging and choking. Been carrying him around again, it's three o'clock, I'm ready to drop—Scott got up to ask me should he do anything, yelled at him to go back to bed, don't know what's the matter with me, need something besides a kid I'd only have to give directions to, stand over, *supervise* for God's sake! Need somebody to help me, take this responsibility off me for a little while.

Sunday morning finally dawned. It could be they were right, whoever it was who'd said morning always comes, eventually. Judy greeted the dawn through swollen lids, waking slowly and numbly from a short, heavy sleep.

She didn't know why she felt it was wrong to have been asleep.

109

After a while, she heard sounds from downstairs. She must have dozed again. She turned her head stiffly and saw, to her horror, that it was nine-fifteen. Then memory returned, in bits and pieces. She'd called Phyllis at three in the morning, crying and half-dead on her feet, Andy back under her arm, twisting in seizure.

And Phyllis came. Dear Phyllis. In a lifetime, she'd never forget she'd been able to count on Phyllis.

The voices from downstairs were the first set of volunteers. How ridiculous—Andy had probably died in the night while she slept the sleep of the dead herself. Why would anyone program a dead infant?

She struggled up from the bed and crept across the hall into Andy's bedroom. The crib was empty. Todd's bed was made. In the back room, Scott's bed was made up too, and the room empty.

Phyllis had roused the family, fed them, sent them on their way, made the beds, cared for Andy. Put Judy to bed. Greeted the first-hour programmers.

Judy's eyes filled with the helpless tears of exhaustion.

But she really did have to stop the programming. She got as far as the head of the stairs, then stumbled instead toward her bedroom, changed her mind, crept into the bathroom, shook out two Fiorinal and swallowed them down, then allowed herself to feel her way back to bed.

Phyllis wouldn't do anything wrong for Andy. If Andy couldn't be programmed, Phyllis would stop the programming. Phyllis was a mother and today she'd mother Andy.

For today. Just that. A few minutes. A few hours' clemency.

And if Andy could manage, Phyllis would supervise the programming.

Judy dropped down on the bed and slept soundly.

Andy completed most of the day—child of contradictions. It was no surprise to his mother. The surprise came from Jack— she wondered later exactly what Phyllis told him. Home from his sixteen-hour shift, Jack stopped the programming at six

110

o'clock and called the evening's volunteers to cancel the rest.

And then called Phyllis back. Phyllis, who'd just gotten home to her own family. And then called Pediatric Hospital to alert them that Andy was coming in. His breathing problems were worsening. With Phyllis to babysit the two older boys, he bundled Judy and Andy into their coats and out the front door.

December came and went and was not a month for fond remembrances. Andy was admitted to Pediatric Hospital and put in a mist tent, on nothing but juice and water. Thorpe was notified immediately.

Andy was in Pediatric for a week while they watched and waited to evaluate a seizure. After, they allowed Judy to bring him home, with some new equipment to keep him company.

They'd wanted her to let him sleep in an oxygen tent, set up around his crib. She refused. She'd use the breathing equipment at night, if she had to.

Wednesday, December 11, 1974

> Must think I'm completely out of my mind and no mother at all. Wanted me to let Andy sleep in an oxygen tent, in the bedroom he shares with Todd!

They taught her percussion. From that moment on, aspirating Andy became one of her nightmares. There was such a wealth of nightmares, a growing collection . . .

She told Thorpe about the new equipment. Also about the nurse who came to supervise and to give her some needed rest, and add to her anxiety by proving one more expense not covered by Jack's health insurance.

The programming started again three days after Andy's return from Pediatric. They'd tested him for cystic fibrosis. Little matters for gratitude and family congratulations: He did not have the disease.

She reported that fact, too, to Thorpe and wondered, uncharitably, if he was disappointed.

She had to use the new equipment four times that day—the

day Andy went back on programming. If the baby was tired, his mother was exhausted by day's end, and this utter weariness, like her savage headaches, was swiftly becoming a natural part of her.

December 10th, Andy's first birthday, brought little gifts from over half the programmers. Judy was amazed they'd remembered. That they'd known the date to begin with. She was grateful that so many of them cared, that they'd taken the time to buy gifts, that they'd wanted to do something a little special—truly, she *was* grateful.

She just didn't want to have to say how grateful.

One week after his birthday, Andy developed an eye infection that grew steadily worse for the next two days and required still more medication.

Doctor's visit and medicine reported immediately to Alexander Thorpe, via telephone.

December—chill and ugly. Christmas came and Christmas went and they were Jewish, it was true, but it was rotten, anyway, having such a grim Christmas. It wasn't a lack of gifts for the children. More gifts filled the house than in any normal year—courtesy of the programmers. But the program itself surged right ahead without regard to holidays and the holiday spirit lay somewhere dead in a household waiting for the real gifts of normalcy.

The days were dark gray. The money was vanishing. Jack's mouth was growing grim and his eyes were turning secretive and frightening. The trip to Pediatric, the stay, the nervous terror, had affected both Judy and Jack. For Jack it was another small dose of desperate reality. For Judy it was trauma, the equipment she had to use . . . to go down into the baby's nose and throat. . . .

She made it her business not to dwell on it. Just to do it. Not even Jack was forced to do it. It was her own private purgatory.

Andy had seizure after seizure that month. Once, he stopped breathing. And the feeling of Andy's awareness Judy and some of the programmers had sensed, back during Thanksgiving week, had vanished in the weeks since. There was no apparent progress in the programming.

She stood alone in the bathroom one cold morning, staring at herself in the small mirror over the sink.

"They don't like me," she told her image out loud, but softly. "They," after all, were right downstairs in the dining room, programming.

"They think I should walk around smiling. Or never smiling, depending on exactly who you listen to complaining. They think I should treat each one of them with a special warmth, like a hostess at a party, that I should remember their husbands' professions and their kids' ages and names and their own special interests. They think that because I can't always tell them apart, I don't really appreciate the tremendous sacrifice they make, coming here one hour a week to program my baby."

The young mother whose own child was sick. The young married woman who couldn't seem to conceive. The grandfather whose children and grandchildren had moved far away. The teenage girls who spent all their pocket money on gifts for Andy.

They were part of her life now, and their hurts and achievements and immediate concerns were becoming part of her emotional framework, but she hadn't the strength or the time to stand around being compassionate. To take a minute from the sixty minutes to ask the caring question that would lead, as questions always do, to a long discussion.

Late that night she found herself standing over Andy's crib, thinking of all the little everyday things they could have done if she'd used a diaphragm instead of having a tubal ligation. The zoo with Scott and Todd in the fall. A ball game in the spring. An hour plus five or ten or fifteen minutes for dinner, at five or six or seven at night. In a normally set up household, with no back doorbells ringing every hour on the hour.

A bathroom unused by any but the family.

The privacy to sit in it and read a book.

And they could have kept the puppy they'd bought for Todd.

113

This last wandering thought brought her fully awake, hanging over the crib in the dimness of the room, with the hall light behind her. It was, to date, her silliest and most maudlin thought, and she actually grinned over it. They could have kept Candy, Todd's German shepherd. They'd had it such a short time, bought during her pregnancy with Andy. And they'd given it away to a nurse at Pediatric, for the dog seemed disturbed by Andy's odd sounds and movements.

She sighed, glanced over at Todd, curled facing the wall, then leaned forward and gently patted Andy's sleeping head and went to her own bedroom.

Days came and went and she thought about things like the lost puppy and sank deeper and deeper into a mixture of self-mockery and misery. Into despair floated faces from Midtown Hospital and she tried to rally, to be worthy of what they'd tried to impart, but couldn't get up the energy.

She needed a definition. There was no place for anything that was happening to her. There was no room in her life for living, no private place to step to the side to regard herself objectively.

At the beginning of January, they went back to CNR for the first evaluation of the programming. She went with a sad heart, knowing there was no grand miracle, no progress. But John Unruh smiled, and added a few new things to the program.

She didn't understand why anything should be added to it: It increased her feeling that matters of grave importance were passing right over her head. It made her dismally certain she was too tired to see the obvious, right in front of her face. Because she couldn't see any sign of progress, could she? A reason to add anything to the program? Andy wasn't moving his own limbs at all, let alone crawling. She found she couldn't picture her son down on the floor hotfooting it from wall to wall in an ecstasy of excitement. Andy wasn't responding at all to anything, yet Unruh smiled his approval and added things to the program.

114

Andy managed to swallow a small part of a soft-boiled egg that night and she sat, regarding him, one eye on her watch, one ear cocked as always for the downstairs doorbell.

Andy must be coming along. They'd added steps to the program. Or maybe, came the predictable, cynical thought, he was simply doing so badly they'd added on more things to try to get him to react to *anything*.

Get on with her life? Her life was a still life. There was no real, recognizable, thinking focus in the picture. Not for the family, her family, now thoroughly dehumanized to fit neatly around all the "things" that made up the picture.

Still life—patterning table.

Still life—breath mask.

Still life—medicines filling a cabinet.

Still life—bills collecting.

Still life of the empty shell of a soft-boiled egg on a meagerly supplied dinner table in a house without laughter.

11

Monday, January 6, 1975

We started Andy's new program today—hardly a *new* program, more an extended one. He seemed tired as he usually does, but it doesn't really matter, he makes no effort to respond to the exercises—so how much can it affect anything if he's tired?

Sometimes I think it wouldn't even matter if they programmed him while he was fast asleep.

The programmers were happy to have a few new things to try, fluttering around, making noises at the baby, and I stood and watched them indulgently, feeling myself watching, if you know what I mean, wondering why nothing feels immediate or real, wondering why I was standing outside myself that way, watching myself—watching.

I haven't been able to get up any energy. My headaches are becoming an inseparable part of my day. The Fiorinal I used to take so sparingly seems to need renewing constantly. The headaches are there when I open my eyes—I must sleep with them. Disgusting headaches, up the back of my neck, down over my forehead to sit behind my eyes, squeezing tight.

The problem is, I feel vulnerable. I worry endlessly about my health. I think, if I get sick, what happens to everything? I worry about the volunteers—if they stopped coming we'd have to just give up on the programming. I worry about money—I can't afford to even *think* about worrying about money.

One day at a time, Jack says.

One step at a time, Thorpe says.

One stage at a time, Unruh says.

Nuts to what everybody says. Not one of these philosophers is the mother of a brain-damaged child.

Wednesday, January 8, 1975

We had a small party tonight, at ten o'clock, when Andy was in bed, for Scott's eleventh birthday. The presents were small—a sweater from Jack and me that Jack picked out, and a belt Jack bought to be from Todd and Andy. There were tons of cards, about which Scott couldn't have cared less, but I cared, I wanted to see exactly who forgot his birthday.

I was never small-minded in my life. What's wrong with me?

I'm very tired tonight. I could write a song about being tired if I had enough strength. I wouldn't have the energy right now to take a trip if somebody gave me one free. I wouldn't have the interest to enter a contest if I was told for sure my entry had to win. It's all I can do to get up every morning and go through my now-normal routine.

Happy Birthday, Scott! Things have to be better for everybody next year.

Thursday, January 9, 1975

Andy was up sick all last night—a predictable climax to Scott's birthday. Scott stayed in his room, closed his door, and never opened it once to see what all the noise was for—Andy coughing and choking. I knew I'd be using the breathing equipment all day today, and I wasn't wrong.

Todd crept out of the bedroom sometime during the night and I found him curled up beside Scott this morning. For some reason, that upset me terribly. I realized how completely I'm losing touch with my older children. And what can I do to change that? Can I ask Andy to hurry up? Can I tell Andy it's not fair for me to spend every ounce of my energy and every second of my time with just him? Can I ask Andy if he's figured out yet that the wild-eyed redhead with the swollen feet is called "Mommy"?

I wonder what the world looks like to him—all those faces looking down. Rows and rows of changing faces. Staring. Hands prodding and shoving. Voices always chattering. No silence. No privacy.

Don't want to write anymore. Feel like crying.

Friday, January 10, 1975

Becoming deeply depressed. Absolutely no response from Andy in programming. Bad headache this morning, took Fiorinal on rising, again at mid-morning, afternoon, tonight. Feel sick to my stomach, probably from so much Fiorinal, can't be coming down with something, don't have time to die nicely.

117

"I need a little emotional pick-me-up here, John. Give me some help!"

"I can't help you. You have to help yourself!"

Her hand grew sweaty, clenched as it was around the phone.

"It's always such a treat talking to you, John!"

"I'm not a shrink, Judy," Unruh's voice was practical. "I'm a physical therapist."

"Give me a guarantee, John. For anything. Tell me he'll live through all this and not be a flake when he's finished. Or that he'll reach age twelve, mentally. Or fifteen. Or give me a really great boost, John, and tell me he'll be normal.

"Tell me, John, tell me anything at all. I'll believe you. I'll make myself believe you, just for today. Help me out today."

"I can't."

"Just like that?"

The line hummed.

"It's normal for you to feel frustrated, Judy. I think you know that without me saying it to you."

Of course she knew it. She'd known better than to expect empty promises when she'd called. She didn't even want empty promises.

She had to get her act together. She had to find again whatever courage she'd learned at Midtown. She couldn't go crying and moaning to every stranger. That wouldn't help her, and it certainly wouldn't help Andy.

Thursday, January 23, 1975

> It gets harder and harder. I was never very good at giving myself pep talks. If there was just a tiny indication, the smallest bit of hope . . .

The last programmers had gone. Judy had retired to the bedroom some minutes earlier. Jack stood in the dining room, by the patterning table, holding his youngest son.

It was utterly silent in the house.

The living room floor was a great expanse. The child looked tiny and defenseless there. Jack placed him gently on his stomach, stared blindly at the far wall, then gripped one leg in both strong hands.

He pushed the leg up to the baby's chest in a partial crawling position. Then, he waited. There was no response. There never had been any response to any of it.

After a bit, he pushed a little harder. His own mind imagined pain. He didn't know what Andy felt, or if Andy felt anything, and the seconds ticked by, became a minute, more than a minute.

The child seemed finally to squirm. Jack stared at the small back, the silken hair, gritted his teeth, and held on. More minutes inched past. Minutes spent in a shuddering anxiety.

He pushed a little harder.

The child protested sharply—angry, guttural sounds. The muscles of his small leg seemed to go into spasm, but it might have been Jack's imagination . . .

Tick tick tick . . .

There was a haze before Jack's eyes. "Please . . ." Beads of sweat ran down his left eye.

Tick tick tick . . .

"Please," he whispered. "Come—on . . ."

The child made a choking sound, squirmed again, harder, began to whimper. Jack's hands felt numb.

"I love you," he moaned. "I love you so much, please, please push off, come—on—and—try—for—me!" The icy sweat was making him feel sick now.

Tick tick tick tick of the clock.

"Andy," he whispered his son's name.

The leg straightened with force and the child pushed off.

Jack gaped at him. He released the leg and sat back on his heels and stared at his son, who was crying now in earnest, then lifted him and cuddled him and kissed the small head, staggering to his feet, lurching for the stairs.

"Judy!"

Friday, January 24, 1975

Andy did great today! It was his first really good day—a full day. He wasn't cranky and he was alert—I'm almost afraid to say that, but it's true, he was aware again, like that other day, so long ago.

I'll always believe it's because of Jack, because Jack had the courage to force him to react last night!

It was the first success. Not grand miracle-type success but success to build on. I can hope now that there's really something there, something to work with. If he could react to the pressure Jack put on his leg, he can react to the rest of this patterning business. Maybe, until now, he just didn't realize *he* was expected to do anything during the exercising. It's always been a bunch of people moving his limbs for him. Maybe it simply didn't occur to him, it didn't connect up—this idea that these other people are moving his arms and legs to teach *him* to move them by himself.

Saturday, January 25, 1975

I think Andy's starting to accept the fact of the programming. Today was a carbon copy of yesterday. He seemed to be cooperating and once, I thought I saw him try to move his own leg. The programmers weren't sure, but since it didn't happen again, I won't put too much hope on it. And I'm sure my expectations are still too high, despite all the sensible things I keep telling myself.

Jack is naturally pleased as punch! I hadn't realized how tight and grim he was starting to look. I just hope we'll have a more substantial success soon. There's a limit to how long the good feeling of one small movement can last.

As for me—I'm falling behind with the housework. I don't know why I should be having such a stupid problem. I just have to make up my mind to get myself together and be more rigid about working to this schedule.

Wouldn't it be great if I inherited a million dollars and at least had the money worries out of the way?

On second thought, I wouldn't believe I really inherited a million dollars even if they sent it in cash in a big box.

Sunday, January 26, 1975

Andy's really zooming along, so far as awareness is concerned. He's much less cranky and seems to be learning to concentrate on what's being done to him. He almost held a toy this morning, which may not seem like much for other kids his age, but believe me, it would have been a real leap forward for Andy!

I kept telling myself for the rest of the day that it was a real attempt, that his little hand really did try to close on the toy, that it wasn't just something that looked that good because I was wishing for it so badly. The programmers told me you couldn't really call it *holding* the toy, so I probably shouldn't even have entered it in this diary.

Do I sound negative again? Step step step. I think I'd better have another one of my famous heart-to-heart talks with myself before bed. Not in this diary. In private.

Monday, January 27, 1975

Andy moved his legs in the beginning of a crawling movement today! That's right. Go back and read it again! Andy moved his legs—both legs—in the start of the movement and I could *feel* the rightness of it, I could feel *him* feel the rightness of it, like a light bulb lighting up in your head when you get a bright idea.

It's not crawling. Not yet. It's the beginning of crawling. The first movement, the first step. I know that Andy was fully aware of what he did today. That what he did was what was expected. I know he felt that was a real, true thing, and that he was proud of himself for the first time in his life!

121

I've been so depressed but my God! I feel good today! Finally, I can begin to believe that this *was* the right decision for Andy.

Tuesday, January 28, 1975

Andy seems to have completely forgotten what he accomplished yesterday.

There was no rationalizing away what she felt that night when Andy was in bed. She was on a seesaw of emotion these days and the total unresponsiveness of her baby throughout the day's programming stripped her of every residual feeling of warmth from the day before and plunged her even deeper into melancholy.

Wednesday, January 29, 1975

I'm too depressed to write much. I must sound like a schizophrenic.

Andy was up all night, sick, crying, actually trembling in my arms. He seems utterly exhausted. Could it possibly be that the exertion he went through to move his legs in some way weakened him? That he really did feel the thrill of moving ahead, and that it was too much of an emotional drain for such a sick little baby, and that all it's done is make him *really* sick all over again?

I can't bear it. If that's the case, how will he ever accomplish anything?

Thursday, January 30, 1975

No progress. No movement.

Friday, January 31, 1975

Nothing.

Saturday, February 1, 1975

Andy's been very good in programming for the past

few days. It's a goodness without response, if you can picture that. He's looked like he was determined to tolerate all this indignity.

But I realized something, watching him today. In some way, he's demanding more and more attention from everybody. I think if he could squeeze a grin from a chair, he'd manage it just for the pleasure of having something else focused on him constantly. He patterned this morning with a smile, though he was terribly cranky for the rest of the day.

Patience. I'll learn that gift, through all this, if I don't learn anything else!

Sunday, February 2, 1975

Andy was very cranky today. Absolutely no progress.

Monday, February 3, 1975

Andy tried to put his fingers in his mouth this morning—no small feat. What amazed me was that he nearly made it, and seemed aware of that, and tried it again, and again and again all day!

It's the first time anything's interested him enough for him to stick to it. No high hopes. Tomorrow's another day.

Can you believe this? I'm sitting here, praying my kid will progress enough to stick his fingers in his mouth!

He had another bad night, hardly any sleep at all, which may be fine for superbaby but definitely isn't the greatest thing for superbaby's bone-tired Mom.

Tuesday, February 4, 1975

Andy very irritable today. Kept trying to get those fingers into his mouth. Seemed frustrated when he couldn't.

No progress.

123

Wednesday, February 5, 1975

Still can't get the old fingers into the mouth. Tried very hard but was very tired and toward evening threw, what I imagine, was his equivalent of a temper tantrum.

After, his little face, all wet and red, seemed sad.

I think I'm going crazy.

Thursday, February 6, 1975

Andy was bright and cheerful today. He had a good sleep last night, and it really doesn't make much sense that I lay there awake through all those peaceful hours, strung out tight, listening and praying not to hear anything.

I couldn't have a normal husband who works normal hours and could share these things with me!

Friday, February 7, 1975

Andy waved bye-bye this morning—at least that's what it looked like, then immediately stuck his fingers in his mouth. That's right. All the fingers of his right hand in his mouth. This pleased him so much that he kept doing it all day long, playing the ham, grinning and giggling, which the programmers lapped right up and which, for no reason at all, finally started to irritate me.

I think the world may have lost a great infant comedian.

So we have a double accomplishment: Fingers in mouth. Bye-bye.

Saturday, February 8, 1975

I think I'm suddenly the mother of a stuck-up child. Andy couldn't be more pleased with himself—the little turkey. He never stops waving bye-bye and sticking his fingers in his mouth. He's very proud of himself. I think he's developing a clown personality.

He seemed a little more tired than he's been. I hope he'll sleep well tonight and wake up fresh and raring to go in the morning.

Sunday, February 9, 1975

Andy had a good day today, alert and pleasant. He had his picture taken today—the husband of one of the programmers is a photographer. I even had him out for our first walk since summer. He gets absolutely no time to be just a baby. Even the walk wouldn't have taken place except that he ate his lunch so quickly we had fifteen minutes before his first afternoon program.

She needed to see him crawl. She needed it desperately. There was an easing of the deep pain in her heart when he waved bye-bye, when he found his mouth with his hand, but these were small things that needed bolstering with solid progress.

In all the more important areas, they were apparently going nowhere. Three months and nowhere.

Sunday, February 16, 1975

Andy was unbelievably awful today! He fought the program, fought every single masking, seemed to hold himself more rigidly than usual, even kicked one of the eleven o'clockers in the chin.

Gave me my only laugh of the day. Can't stand the woman! She misses most of her appointed times, and never calls to give me the chance to replace her.

Laughter turned to tears. Think I'm having terminal blues. Disgusted with myself.

Monday, February 17, 1975

A litle better today. Not me. Andy.

Tuesday, February 18, 1975

Okay.

The house seemed overly full. It was the end of the hour. There were the four seven o'clock programmers, and the four waiting to start the next hour. Two neighbors who'd stopped by to see if they could lend a hand. Judy, Jack. Scott was somewhere in the house and Todd was running back and forth from the kitchen constantly, watching the programming and asking endless questions of everybody.

"Oh.. Oh, look. Look!"

Andy was on the patterning table, on his stomach. The exercise called for three of the volunteers, and was aimed at impressing on the healthy cells of the brain the movements required in crawling.

One programmer turned Andy's head. Another stood on the side of the table toward which the head was turned, and flexed Andy's arm and leg. The third, on the opposite side, extended both limbs. Then the baby's head was turned to the opposite side and the positions of his arms and legs reversed with it.

They'd been doing this same exercise for the past three months.

It was the programmer on the left side of the patterning table who cried out. Her call brought people running from each room of the house. There was a silence then, so vast and total, that Judy could hear three different breathing rhythms at her back. Her knuckles were white against the doorframe. Her own breath had virtually stopped.

The programmers' hands had gone easy, light. The baby's arms and legs and head moved in the familiar patterning position as they all watched. It took a long second, a remarkable, aching second, to realize that Andy was moving, inching forward up the table, in the crawling pattern.

Himself!

A bursting cheer reverberated throughout every level of the house. Judy swayed, the room blurred, and beside her Jack's hand groped, found her hand, gripped tight.

Andrew Polikoff, aged fourteen and a half months, had broken the first bonds of his terrible affliction to move forward on his own!

Monday, February 24, 1975

Andy's crawling with authority! Don't mean to make it sound less than remarkable. It's just that I can't express what I felt when I saw the first movements, and everything after that tends to be anticlimactic.

The programmers act like they've been given a shot in the arm. Everything has a greater probability of success now, after this first real success, with the crawling!

What exactly do I feel? I can't explain this, but I feel tense. Like I keep expecting something terrible to happen, to take away the good feelings of these past few days.

Wonder if I need iron supplements. Or pep pills. Or a little red sports car and a trip to the Bahamas. Or if anything at all would *feel* normal.

This diary was supposed to be for Andy. It strikes me I haven't been totally glowing and positive. I may have to tear out some pages.

Tuesday, February 25, 1975

Andy was up sick all night. Reaction from crawling? Kid's a test case, reactions from everything—exercise, air, water . . .

Wednesday, February 26, 1975

Crawling beautifully. Up sick again all night.

Thursday, February 27, 1975

—————

There was a long string of apathetic days where she lost track of time, events, everything but the programming. The momentary thrill of achievement was lost with desperate swiftness, new thrills were needed and seldom quick to make an appearance.

Monday, March 10, 1975

Andy turned half over this morning, then looked so surprised I burst out laughing—everybody did—and then I realized it's been longer than I can remember since I laughed like that because all the muscles in my chest hurt after.

Then, this afternoon, thinking God only knows what thoughts, what did the little ham do but a total flip-over. All the way over, all by himself. Once he'd accomplished it there was no stopping him from doing it over and over and over. A regular little whirling dervish.

Andy thinks he's the greatest. So does everybody else. His Daddy's probably sending away for college applications. Even his Mommy's impressed.

Some of the programmers seem to be growing territorial—that's the only way I can describe the possessiveness they show toward Andy himself and each achievement. They vie for position, if that makes sense. They get hurt if they think they're being short-changed in their own participation in these accomplishments.

Andy doesn't seem to feel well tonight, which is exactly the routine he's been following whenever there's a great exertion.

Tuesday, March 11, 1975

Andy's still able to turn himself over today. And over. And over. Don't know why I expected him to forget how to do it overnight. Guess I've gotten to the point where I actually expect the six steps backwards.

Today, Andrew Polikoff discovered chocolate kisses!

Monday, March 17, 1975

Weekend went normally. Andy's still crawling. Still turning over.

No horrors.

Tuesday, March 18, 1975

Same.

Monday, March 24, 1975

Andy put food up to his mouth at lunch. Nearly made it all the way up and in. Keep you posted.

Judy and Jack brought Andy back to CNR during the last

week in March. The program was upgraded. Cross-pattern was added. The goal—creeping.

Friday, March 28, 1975

I think I've finally been, at least temporarily, jolted out of feeling so absurdly sorry for myself. Because that's exactly how I've been feeling. There's no nicer way to put it. Always asking yourself why you're in a particular situation is feeling sorry for yourself, and there's really no glossing over it.

But Andy tried to creep today. To creep! And for some reason, that excited me so much more than when he actually started crawling. He pushed up and started to creep!

It only lasted a second before he collapsed, and he didn't try it again. But it was there, for that single second, the ability to progress from one step to the next, and I saw it and it did something to the lump I've been carrying around in my chest.

Now I'll probably lie in bed all night afraid to sleep, expecting breathing problems to reward this effort. Payment for attempting progress.

It can't happen! No steps backwards this time. Just this once, let it be an unqualified success!

Saturday, March 29, 1975

Andy sick—no progress.

Sunday, March 30, 1975

No progress. Back to crawling lethargically. No further attempt to creep. Very bad night.

Wednesday, April 2, 1975

Andy cries whenever I come near him. Just what I need. A real shot in the arm—rejection!

Friday, April 4, 1975

Andy sick, having trouble breathing. Surprise—right? Lots of rolling on the floor last night.

129

Monday, April 7, 1975
Andy was sick all weekend but we programmed as usual. No progress.

Friday, April 11, 1975
Andy has a cold. Played with a ball today. Sneezing, nose runny, but no fever.

Friday, April 18, 1975
Todd has chicken pox.

Friday, April 25, 1975
Andy having trouble breathing again. Had to be rolled all night. Find myself using the breathing equipment endlessly. Heavy heavy congestion. Todd whining and scratching. Don't mean to make him sound like a flea-bitten dog. Scott hanging around, looks like he pities me. Can't imagine why. Great relationship!

Tuesday, April 29, 1975
Andy has chicken pox.

12

It was a tunnel with landmarks that were swiftly outrun, leaving behind anti-climax. She never knew, after, where the entire year of programming, the entire year of 1975, had gone. The days, weeks, months—there was a blurred memory of winter turning to spring, spring to summer, with her only definite knowledge of the passing seasons being the up and down position of the house windows.

It was horribly hot in the house that summer. Hideously uncomfortable, pushing and pulling at Andy. Draining to hear him whimpering. Sweat stained her old housedresses and she knew she'd never after, for all the years of her life, be able to bear the sight of a button-up-the-front housedress.

Summer, waking dully to birds chirping outside the window. Andy tried again to creep in the middle of that hot summer. Tried once. Tried twice. Gave up trying and settled back to a past success—crawling.

Summer peaked and died unwillingly in the flame of crisp autumn.

Andy tried to creep again as the air cooled and the leaves went golden. Tried once. Tried twice. Tried a third time and made it!

Autumn. Her favorite season. More innervating than ever before due to this sight of her child, up off his belly. The worries remained, of course; the money worries. Sheltering behind moments of pride, hiding in dusty corners of her mind. Terrible, hysterical money worries.

Thanksgiving arrived—the second Thanksgiving of the programming—and seven different programmers brought Thanksgiving dinner to the Polikoffs.

It was odd. Afterward, she tried to rationalize. You loved some, hated some, were neutral toward the rest—a natural state of human affairs whether the people were neighbors, business associates, or programmers. You viewed gifts as welcome or as charity. It depended on so much more than just the gift.

Seven full Thanksgiving dinners.

"Happy Thanksgiving, Judy!"

Turkey and stuffing and mashed potatoes. Cakes and pies. Vegetables. Enough for a party, a feast, a veritable orgy. The refrigerator went through seven reorganizations, food piled, plates tilting and sliding.

By eleven o'clock her chest felt like bursting. That seriously alarmed her. She hugged one of her steadiest volunteers, an old friend, and found herself swallowing tears. She was unnaturally silent throughout the rest of the day, swallowing continually.

Late that afternoon, she opened the refrigerator cautiously. She stared inside, bit her lip, closed the door carefully. Walked through the dining room past the current set of programmers and nodded, smiling brightly. Climbed the steps to the upstairs, humming, then locked herself in the bathroom. She sat on the toilet seat and began to giggle hysterically while tears of gratitude and helpless mortification fled down her cheeks and she thought, I can't bear this, this will kill Jack. And she wished, wished with all her heart, that they hadn't brought seven full Thanksgiving dinners. It demeaned her to be in such desperate need. It would break Jack's heart!

That night, in the hour allocated for their dinner, she sat in her place and watched Jack and Scott and Todd. There was so much unaccustomed food on the table she could barely *see* Todd.

Scott looked glassy-eyed and ill. Todd—his was a baby face and you couldn't decipher the blandness of his gaze. Jack took turkey and stuffing and vegetables and ate, silent, not meeting Judy's eyes. She herself, to her own enormous surprise, ate nothing.

Andy had a soft-boiled egg and some mashed potatoes. Through it all, watching the faces of her family, Judy heard it over and over again in her head—"Happy Thanksgiving!"

Of course, it passed. The season of holidays. It passed as things always do. Chanukah and Christmas came and went, the house again buried in the programmers' gifts. One of the eleven o'clockers, a constant canceller, a professional excuse-finder, gave Judy a vial of expensive perfume. One of her steady three o'clockers, a dear friend, with her since the beginning, always on time, never absent for any reason whatsoever, gave her a box of paperback books, all brand new—love stories and mysteries with a haunted house or two.

She placed the perfume on a back shelf. The paperbacks went on the bookstand in the bedroom.

There were scores of presents for the children. Home-baked

132

sweets. Boxes of elaborate candies. Candy canes and stocking stuffers, all accepted with a discomfort due to the impossibility of being able to reciprocate.

But the holidays passed, and after a while she even managed to forget them.

It was a long dark tunnel. There were some surprises along the way and these came suddenly and were quickly spent. It was a tunnel you were stuck in, having come too far to turn back, yet it showed no signs of ending. No daylight. No place to sidestep, look around. Just a scary, single-file walk into mystery.

January, 1976, was bitter cold. Andy's second year of programming. One year down. One whole year—gone. To go—?
Maybe God knew. Judy didn't.

Wednesday, January 21, 1976

Andy's Bingo was last night. I know, I know—what Bingo? If this is supposed to be a diary, why didn't I take a minute a week ago or two weeks ago or a month ago to mention a Bingo for Andy?

I wouldn't even be mentioning it now if omitting it didn't seem heartless and totally ungrateful. The Bingo was arranged through Brith Sholom, two lodges working together, but it ended up being a total community effort. Not only did the members of the lodges do an incredible amount of planning and setting up for it, but people from the neighborhood, hearing about it, pitched right in and made it into a regular "event." And the night of the Bingo, *everybody* turned up.

To help us.

There. You get the first inkling of why this is my first and last mention of the Bingo. Me, the girl who loves "events." If it was for somebody else, I would have been at the front of the line, pitching in, having myself a great old time. Like all these people had themselves a great old

133

time. Because it's fun, doing things like this, *for other people*. Funny how you never stop to think what they feel—those *other people*.

There's no way on earth that anyone untouched by something like this could possibly understand how I hate even having to *write* these words: To Help Us!

There was a raffle. Beautiful food baskets were raffled off—to help us.

Other things. A bunch of girls from the neighborhood went around to all the houses collecting canned goods to make up into big packages, also to be raffled off.

There was a cake sale. There were so many things going on, all those people coming, giving their money . . .

To help us. Because we can't help ourselves!

I've tried not to dwell on it here, on these pages, but it must be clear by now, the Bingo was held because we had to have something, *anything,* to put toward Andy's medical expenses. Because there's nothing left. Nothing! It's the middle-class nightmare you never really believe could happen to you, losing not only every penny you ever had but even the chance of making up the loss, even that, and not enough coming in to make a dent in an unbelievable, skyrocketing debt.

When the Bingo was advertised around, the "care packages" started coming in. Food boxes, brought every day by a different volunteer. Phyllis, or somebody, had to have set it up, but I'm so ashamed I can't even make myself ask who it was. And I accept the food boxes—that's my shame—because that's the major component of our breakfast, lunch, and dinner. And I have to think of the children!

Sitting there, at the Bingo, was the single most terrible night I've had since we found out about Andy's brain damage. Phyllis begged me not to come, but I had to come, I couldn't hide while all those people were doing this for us.

I talked to John before I left. When all this is over, I'll never forget John. He doesn't only take care of the programs for Andy, he listens to me whenever things get too much and I need to be tongue-lashed back to sanity.

"I'll have to thank them, John," I said, as if he didn't know that, as if he couldn't guess. "And I can't. I've already said so many thank you's in these past months, I'm thank you'd out."

He didn't say anything for a minute. I was afraid he wouldn't say anything at all. It's a very hard thing to have to admit, to somebody else. To myself. That I don't want to have to be this grateful to everybody. That I don't want to have to depend on anybody but Jack and myself!

When John finally answered me, he surprised me, as he always does.

"You stand up, Judy," he said, "and you thank them all for being faithful friends. Then you tell them how thankful *they* can be to have Andy Polikoff in their lives!"

Do you know how much I would have liked to do just that? I thought about it all the way to the Bingo. It would have given me self-respect, showing them it wasn't all a one-way gift—their gift to the Polikoffs. That maybe one or ten or a hundred of them became better, in some personal way, for doing this momentous thing for Andy.

In the end, it didn't matter what I planned or didn't plan to say. All those eyes on me, so kind, waiting. I choked up, then I started to cry, and I could see their concern, I could *feel* their pity—my God!—and I just sat down and didn't say anything.

These are the most hurtful words in the language if you have to say them often enough. Thank you thank you thank you thank you . . .

The money will help. They made over $3,000. It will pay some bills, buy some time—not enough, though. Not nearly enough.

*　　*　　*

135

Even at the start, when the challenge was high, even then when it was all new, when she and Jack had hoped for the miracle of instant success, when their optimism was at its peak, to undertake the rigors of the programming and its disorganizing effect on the family's life was too much to ask. Too much, if they'd let themselves view it rationally. If they'd made themselves sit and consider it as cold fact, devoid of the human element at its core—Andy. If their sense of survival had overruled their hearts they might never have undertaken the programming. Day after day. Week after week. Without the distant focus of an ending year.

Promises?

No promises.

It was more than anyone should have had to decide to bear, and they carried on with it because—because there was nothing else, no reasonable choice. And Andy *was* progressing. Slowly. Coming along. It was necessary to remember that, to hold each victory dear, to prolong the joy.

Months after starting, fatigued and in unspeakable debt, living for every tiny smattering of success, even pride began to flake away—all the small things, the humanizing forces drifting into a limbo world where they were easy to forget.

It was two months into the second year, a bitterly cold night. Judy had paced and paced, downstairs and up, through endless hours, until the sky finally lightened.

There were small scuffling sounds from the kitchen. She stopped pacing to listen. Jack was still at work, so it had to be Scott or Todd, poking and prying into cupboards for something to nibble on.

She crossed to the master bedroom.

The room was dim. She strained to see the clock. It read eight-forty-five, which didn't make sense, and she stood and stared at it for some time. It seemed impossible that the night had finally passed, after waiting so long, praying and sweating and despairing, walking with the baby, rolling him on the rug to clear his lungs, stopping at the window, watching for dawn.

A terrible night, the latest in a long chain. Nightmare hours for Andy, who was sick, always sick, with the breathing problems she'd been warned of. Regressing after every success, not strong enough to just keep going, even more congested than usual this night. She'd walked with him, and walked and walked, back and shoulders burning with weariness and strain, and she'd felt a bitterness she couldn't control, her mind shivering, her heart threatening to burst. Until, suddenly, here it was morning, with somebody rummaging in the kitchen and the first programmers due to arrive at nine. And the laundry she'd been too tired to do last night was sitting in the basement, in the middle of the basement floor—had she actually left it there, like that?

She hurried to the kitchen, where Todd stood staring vaguely into the empty refrigerator. He turned when he heard her. Glancing at his baby brother, his young mouth curled. She ignored this. It was only natural to feel antagonism toward a creature who'd kicked you out of your own mother's heart.

Jack was due home around nine. All the talk of layoffs at Century Steel, months before, had died down. Jack would come home, exhausted and peevish, his stomach almost surely tight, his head aching, and she hadn't started thinking about his breakfast or, for that matter, provided any breakfast for Scott, who'd apparently already left.

She started cooking an egg for Todd—the last of a dozen brought four days ago by one of the volunteers. The egg looked pitifully small, alone there in the pan, while Todd loomed suddenly, starvingly large. She shifted Andy to her hip and turned up the stove light.

The back doorbell sounded as the egg congealed. Judy scowled and lowered the light and raced down the steps. Sure enough, the laundry basket sat smack in the middle of the floor, the family private business, underwear and smelly socks with holes in toes and soles and old soft things with tiny stains and tears. She kicked it impatiently aside.

Programmer A smiled a welcome, stared at the greasy fork

Judy was clutching, and looked momentarily disconcerted. Todd shouted something Judy couldn't quite catch, and Andy punched her in the stomach.

Up in the living room, the four newcomers took charge of Andy.

"Mom!" shouted Todd.

"Smells really good, Judy," said Programmer B.

Judy stared at her blankly. Smells good? The baby?

"Mom!"

She fled to the kitchen, Programmer B behind her. The egg was burning. She shoveled what remained on a chipped plate and dropped the whole before Todd, who eyed her with a curious expression on his freckled face, then began eating morosely.

"Judy!" Programmer B's attention had been abruptly diverted. "Andy's soaking."

"Here," said Programmer C, smiling, "I'll change him."

"It's not the programmer's job to change diapers," said B, severely.

A semi-audible argument ensued between them.

"And it's after nine," Programmer B rounded out her complaint. "Changing diapers and starting late . . ."

"We'll catch up," Programmer C interjected easily.

In the kitchen, by the stove, Judy's eyes misted. A spectrum of personalities. A wealth of dispositions. Programmer C was a darling, who never looked into closets or peered into lidded pots or used the upstairs bathroom. If all the programmers could have been like C . . . Judy wouldn't even have minded being scolded by Programmer C, but then C never scolded. C knew when to look away or cough or comment on the weather.

They wouldn't catch up. They'd be behind all day.

"You know we're always on time, Judy," B wouldn't let it go, that was *her* personality. "Why do you find it so difficult lately to have Andy ready? If we're late, all the programs will be late for the rest of the day. Don't you understand that?"

Judy, utterly exhausted, stared at her condescending face and delved for some suitable retort, not too prim, not too tart, and

138

found nothing. Besides, over B's shoulder she caught a glimpse of Programmer D, disappearing around the bannister.

"Me for the little girl's room, Judy," she twittered, halfway up the stairs before Judy could point out, for the thousandth time, the convenience of the basement bathroom. She stared listlessly after D's disappearing legs, thinking of the sodden towels still hanging over the edge of the tub, refusing to dry in the damp weather. Jack's shower towels from last night and Scott's face towel from this morning. She hadn't stopped to gather them together. A picture filled her weary mind of the bedroom doors standing open: the unmade beds, the pervasive clutter.

She looked over at Andy, lying on the patterning table, and finished diapering him with programmer C alongside, as Andy giggled and kicked her.

Todd was pushing his last bit of egg around. Jack was a missing person. A horn blared at the curb—the car pool to take Todd off to nursery school, and as he got to his feet Judy saw, for the first time, that he was wearing the same clothing she'd dressed him in yesterday.

She swallowed and pulled him around then hesitated, mind skittering, and Andy started to whine, then the car horn blared again and Todd stared, deadly stare of the four-and-a-halfer, and she thought, so what, he doesn't sweat, and there's no time to change him anyway.

At nine-twenty she began supervising the start of the nine o'clock program. She was desperately weary. She hadn't felt well for longer than she remembered. Her weight kept falling, her clothing hung. Only her feet claimed a life of their own— hot and swollen. And the headaches—the headaches had finally achieved the status of "normal." They were with her always.

The house was growing more crowded. The second set of volunteers had arrived, two of a supposed four, meaning there would be two vacancies. Neither absentee had called in advance so she could make other arrangements. These last-minute hassles were happening more and more lately.

"That's a lovely ashtray, Judy," one of the new arrivals said as Judy passed through the living room on her way to recruit a trusty neighbor.

"Odd, isn't it?" The woman's tone of voice had altered, pitched lower, aimed at the other volunteer alone, but unfortunately also reaching Judy.

"Just having the Bingo for them," she continued, as Judy paused in the door. "I hear she calls around to perfect strangers, begging money for medications for the kid, says they can't afford milk for the other little boy—what's she doing buying expensive new ashtrays with our money?"

Betty Kelly, who lived three houses up the block, opened her door to Judy's bright red face and stared at her curiously, then agreed to come and help with the ten o'clock program. Betty had never missed her own scheduled hour and was filling in quite willingly these days for several recent dropouts.

It was bitterly cold on the front walk. The wind stirred Judy's damp hair, lifting whole strands around her face. Her skin felt taut. Every drop of blood seemed to have rapidly left her head.

Ashtrays. Candlestick holders. Pretty little things. Small, forgotten possessions. Gifts from other days—packed away in boxes. She'd rummaged through one such box and found the ashtray. She'd put it out, to be able to look at it, to extend the pleasure of her memories, to try to raise her spirits.

A hotness scalded her cheeks and she brushed numbly at her face and re-entered the house. One of the volunteers still waited patiently on her couch. The other, the whisperer, was rummaging through the refrigerator while the four nine o'clock volunteers, in the dining room, finished up their segment of the program.

"Something cold if we're going to have to sit and wait, Judy?"

Judy glared at the woman. "I have no soft drinks in the house. No extra juice and no milk." Her tone was sharper than she'd intended; she'd had a terrible night and Jack—just where was Jack anyway? Scott was too young to give solid support. Todd was only a baby, sent off to school in yesterday's clothes,

140

with one sad, donated egg to warm his stomach.

The programmer looked surprised, then grimly displeased, her lips folding in a thin line. Judy felt dull panic, the same panic she'd been feeling for months now, product of all the growing excuses and absences, panic that this woman too, objectionable though she might be, could elect not to return and thereby deprive Andy of yet another set of helping hands.

Betty arrived. Judy heard her cheerful, pleasant voice. And Andy, up all night, companioned by whatever dark ghosts and goblins joined him, determined at that precise moment to compound his mother's problems by falling into a deep sleep in Programmer C's arms.

Judy returned slowly to the kitchen to fetch the bucket from under the sink. She filled it, carried it to the dining room, and there stood Jack—it was a miracle. She'd actually stopped wondering where Jack was and here he stood, looking at their peacefully sleeping son, hands in his jacket pockets, his mouth soft. She could vaguely remember him looking at her much like that just after making love.

There was a surge of self-pity she staunchly ignored.

Jack had come home. She wondered when. She avoided his eyes, even as he avoided hers.

She put the bucket down on the floor, and Jack reached out and gathered in the sleeping child, then grasped him by the ankles and plunged the baby's face into the icy water.

There was an immediate uproar. Screams of fright and shock.

Near faint from Volunteer D, blasphemy from B, grim disapproval from A. Programmer C stood silently nearby, her eyes filled with tears.

Jack was pariah.

She? She was only—poor Judy.

Tuesday, January 27, 1976
Had a truly awful day!

141

13

It was a damp, bleak Friday morning. The entire week had been drizzly. There was a persistent smell of snow in the air, a promise which never materialized.

Despite the open curtains, the living room was dim. In the dining room, the overhead light was on, and the programming continued as usual.

From her bedroom Judy heard the front door open. Then, there was silence. No voices greeted the new arrival. She glanced at the clock. It was ten of twelve, which meant it was almost surely Scott, who had special permission to return home at lunch to help her in whatever way was necessary.

She sat, too lethargic to move, staring at her toes, swelling through the cloth sides of her old slippers. She'd been sitting in bed for most of the eleven o'clock program. She felt achy and desperately weary. Grunting, she finally pulled up off the bed and made her way slowly down the stairs to the living room.

Scott stood in the middle of the room, making no attempt to remove his jacket, the sleeves of which covered his arms only to just below the elbows. He watched his mother make her halting progress down the stairs, looking like Grandmom, worse than Grandmom, exhausted and bleached out and with the fun vanished from her eyes and full mouth.

It made him angry. He had just turned twelve but that was old enough to feel a terrible hurt, caught between childhood and adolescence and burdened with the cares and anxieties of distant adulthood. He was desperately, furiously angry at Andy.

His mother smiled at him vaguely and placed a lifeless hand on his shoulder. He was tall, thin, handsome, his eyes nearly on a level with her own. He looked at her, nervous to be stared at with such blank, unswerving candor, then he saw the love in her tired eyes, a flashing of it, and it made him prickly and it also gave him the foolish courage to ask what he'd faithfully promised himself never to ask her.

"Mom?"

She waited and he shuffled, determined but afraid.

"Who do you love best, Mom?"

He forced all his muscles loose with the asking, wriggling his toes around inside his shoes, but it didn't work—his palms were wet inside his tightly locked fists and his stomach threatened to turn over.

"Who do you love best? Todd? Or Andy? Or me?"

With a touch of reproof, as if he'd stabbed her in the back when she wasn't looking, when she was already down and being trampled, she looked helplessly at him, then toward the window. And still he waited. He couldn't pull his eyes away from her ravaged face.

Finally, she focused on his features, and he saw a glint in her pupils, a swift narrowing, and knew quite suddenly and with more acuteness than a boy his age should have possessed that she'd thought up a good one. To make him happy. *Her* truth she wouldn't lie, she'd soothe him with her vision of reality.

"I love you best," she said. Scott heard it through a buzzing in his ears and dared to hope his feeling was wrong, that the words would stay right, that he'd heard his own yearned-for truth. "Because you're my first. Because we went through all that business about your dad together. Because you've always been there for me, and I could lean on you and depend on you and love you. It didn't matter that you were just a baby. I had you there with me then, and that comforted me, and having you with me now gives me the courage to go on." Desperate wariness crossed her face. "You're very wise, Scott. You're older than your years. You've made me brave, always."

Because because because. If the answer had been the one he was looking for there would have been no need for "because."

Her eyes had softened out of focus, and Scott wondered apprehensively if she was about to burst into tears. Then, she

143

steadied herself, the glint was back in her eyes, and he knew he was about to get the knife in the ribs.

"And I love Todd best," she continued with gentle emphasis on Todd's name.

"Because I had Todd with Daddy and he's special in his own way, our middle child, and because I wanted a brother for you so much."

This last she threw out as an afterthought, hopefully. He watched it curve toward him. She expected him to believe that? That you had a kid for reasons like that—him having a brother? He'd never even wanted a puppy. His throat tightened, but he remained silent. After all, she was tired. He was old enough, and more than sharp enough, to understand she was tired.

"And I love Andy best," her voice droned on. She was speaking faster now, as if aware she might have carried it too far.

Scott went deaf. He'd learned to shut out everything with Andy's name attached. Consequently, in the past year or so, he'd missed an incredible amount.

"Because . . ."

He stared at his mother, fascinated, for she seemed to be considering the why of loving Andy. He thought of leaving, going back to school, but she'd probably only stand here, finishing her speech, and the programmers would hear her voice and come and find her talking only to herself.

". . . because he's Andy."

It didn't seem like a very good reason to Scott but then, he was only twelve. A small smile lingered on her mouth, then it went tense. If only the new shift of volunteers would arrive, a passage of people to intervene, break this up.

The back doorbell sounded. His mother stirred herself, wrenching her eyes from the sight of his face.

"I made you a sandwich," she glanced toward the back of the house. "Fried egg."

Then she was gone, to make meaningless sounds of gratitude at the arrivals in the basement. For all his life, before Andy, there'd been no need for servile gratitude. His mother had always been proud.

As he heard the creaking of the deteriorating basement steps, a fantasy, tiny and vicious, passed through his mind. He could clearly imagine the basement steps collapsing, taking them all down—the programmers, and with them, Andy.

The sandwich lay congealed, one cold egg between two slices of stale white bread. It rested on a green plate. There was no longer such a thing as a matched set of anything, a hot meal for lunch, a feeling of warm well-being in his stomach. He could clearly recall thick meat sandwiches from his childhood. Peanut butter and jelly on fresh bread. Chicken salad and sweet pickles. They made everything worse, these memories.

He lifted the plate, one of four donated by somebody at Christmas, and balanced it in the palm of his hand as he watched the four new programmers emerge from the basement doorway to join the four just finishing. All eight of them stood around, poking and cooing and making clown faces at Andy.

Andy, now two, smiled enigmatically at everyone.

Scott glanced toward the basement doorway. His mother stood there now, leaning against the doorframe, squinting against one of her interminable headaches, elbows hugging a body growing thinner and thinner, her housedress old and washed out—something she would never have been caught dead in. Her hair seemed dried out, the color dull, not the red he once knew. Her face, without makeup, looked bleached, its features melding.

A sudden, unsolicited, unprecedented horror filled his mind.

She's gonna die, he thought.

He panicked.

An odd haze formed around his head. It seemed part of the dull hammering in his ears; his breathing grew short. He wondered if it might be the start of a seizure and the thought was funny, monstrously funny, the funniest thing he'd thought in days, months, years—that he, Scott, oldest and most "normal," might have a seizure right here in the kitchen, in front of company. He who was never a problem to his parents, who was thoughtful enough to never even catch colds, would lay jerking and flopping like Andy did, holding his fried egg sandwich and making grunting sounds like a stuck pig!

They wouldn't notice. They were all staring at Andy.

A deep and terrible rage shook him. He could feel his back strain, could feel his arm muscles jerking. Rage, making him breathless, dimming his sight. He heaved the plate, with his sad lunch, straight over the dining room table at the wall.

There was a sudden, total silence. Nine pairs of startled eyes jerked around to impale him in the kitchen doorway. Yellow yolk knotted the wall, white dropped, the plate, plastic, along with the bread, cardboard, bounced on the worn carpet. Nine pairs of eyes looked confused, stared at this mess, his mother among them, then eyed him again and looked politely revolted.

He heard himself breathing harshly through his mouth. The haze covered everything. He fled the house.

Friday, January 30, 1976

Andy tried to pull up today. Didn't make it. Scott ran away.

14

"Why did Scott run away to Pittsburgh to Uncle Ned?" Todd asked.

Judy pushed up from the couch to stare wearily at her second son. It was after eleven, and the last volunteers had gone.

It invariably woke Todd when she brought Andy up at ten, but tonight he hadn't even been to bed. He was still dressed. He looked revoltingly wide awake. And he'd asked this same question, in varying forms, over and over again.

146

"Where was Scott? Did he run away?"

That was on the Sunday night Ned brought Scott back home.

"Why was Scott in Pittsburgh with Uncle Ned? Did Scott run away from home?"

That was on the Monday morning after.

"If Scott can run away to Uncle Ned, next time, can I go?"

That was Tuesday. Now he'd waited for Jack to go to work, to bring it up again. It was supposed to be Jack who answered father-son questions.

"Ask Scott," Judy discovered, quite suddenly, the next best thing to Jack. Her emotional dependence on her oldest son was in no way diminished by his attempt to escape the atmosphere in the house. Scott's running away had terrified her. She hadn't thought she could still feel such an intensity of fright. But it hadn't changed her lifelong, nearly unconscious convictions about him.

Scott was deep, his thinking intricate, his emotions hidden for the most part—he had always been a private child. She'd long suspected Scott would dare a course of action outside the normal scope of a twelve-year-old. But she hadn't thought he'd run. She'd trusted him to be there, silent, background support.

Like Jack.

Todd, impervious to curtness and too young to be touched by the sight of obvious incipient exhaustion, refused to make himself scarce.

"I did ask Scott," he assured her. "He said a dirty word."

He waited confidently, then, for her reaction, but she merely sat all the way up straight and pushed at her limp hair.

"Wanna know what he said?" Todd asked, hopefully.

"No," she quelled him with one look. "I don't. You can tell Scott I sent you to ask him. After all," she said reasonably, "since he's the one who went to see Uncle Ned, he should give you his reasons."

It occurred to her, though, that this was trusting her oldest son to use wisdom. It would gain nothing, it might even injure Todd, if Scott decided to be vicious.

147

Todd, however, had his own ideas.

"He went to get away from Andy."

She looked at him with an aching coldness in her heart.

"That's not the kind of thing I expect to hear from you, Todd," she said finally. It was an effort to keep her tone gentle and calm.

"Why?" her middle child stared at her, bewildered. "That's really why, isn't it? I want to get away from Andy too. Can I?"

Her first impulse was to laugh. His little face was so serious, the question so naive and at the same time so very reasonable. Her darling child, planned for, wanted! Then pushed aside, of necessity, at the tender age of two, to make room in the house for . . .

Do you know what they call them in England?

She dropped back on the couch cushions and closed her eyes against a pounding headache.

"Always take a suitcase when you run away," she advised. "And check with me before you leave. I'll want to make sure everything's neat and you have bus money."

With which she took a swift peek through half-closed lids. Todd was gone.

Scott listened to the soft sounds from the next bedroom, determined not to bother investigating. He felt heartsick and mind-weary, and he really didn't care what Todd was up to.

Finally, unable to curb his curiosity, he got up and opened his door in time to see the younger boy slipping down the stairs. He hesitated, nearly went back to bed after all, cursed fluently under his breath, and followed him.

In the living room, his mother was deeply asleep. The inside door wasn't quite closed. The outside wasn't latched. Todd was on the porch, struggling to get his second arm into the sleeve of his jacket. He gazed with only mild surprise at Scott, accepting as normal enough this family gathering on a cold patio at midnight.

"I know," Scott said, acidly. "You've got a really great reason for being out here. Why don't you tell me what it is? It's late. It's also freezing, if you're too stupid to notice."

"I was thinking I'd run away like you," Todd confided, "but Mommy said take a suitcase and I can't find one." He looked hopefully up into his brother's brooding eyes, debated whether to ask for help in locating this elusive luggage, decided not. Scott took him by the arm and shoved him, unceremoniously, back into the house.

Judy slept like the dead. She didn't hear Scott locking up, taking Todd to the basement to throw in a load of wash, following the smaller boy back up to the bedrooms above.

"Scott?"

Todd had put on his pajamas as Scott said, and even contemplated his own bed. But sleep held no attractions, it hadn't for much of his life, because Andy shared his room and that gave him nightmares. Tonight would be one of the extra-bads, he knew it would, because Andy was making those awful breathing sounds again, and he knew he'd lie awake waiting for the sounds to stop.

He dimly understood it would somehow be worse if the sounds *did* stop.

It was twelve-thirty, but Scott was standing by the bedroom window, staring out at the night. He turned his head to eye Todd coldly.

"I'm busy. It's late. It's even later than it was half an hour ago when I said it was late, and to go to bed. I told you, you keep buggin' me like this, first I'm gonna knock you all over the room, then I'm gonna tell Mom to farm you out to Grandmom down in Florida."

Todd judiciously ignored such threats, part and parcel as they were of his relationship with his brother. Despite the long years that separated them, they'd always been close in this manner of meaningless insults and total loyalty to one another.

"You're not busy," he therefore remarked. "You're just standing there, looking out the window. You can't even see

149

anything out the window. It's too dark."

"I'm busy," Scott said with ice in his voice, "looking out the window at nothing. Go to bed."

Todd took this for encouragement and advanced into the room, closing the door first, softly. His older brother sighed and folded his arms across his chest and glared, without noticeable affection.

"You're a pain, you know that? What do you think you want?"

"You still didn't say why you ran away," Todd reminded him.

Scott's mouth went grim.

"And I told Mommy you said that dirty word," Todd warned, "so don't say it again."

Scott stared at him.

"And Mommy said since you ran away, you should say why."

There was a silence during which it seemed Scott was considering this.

"Well?" Todd prodded.

Scott didn't reply.

"You ran away to get away from Andy, wasn't that it?" Todd asked, a bit anxious. "That's what I told Mommy."

A look of incredulity crept acoss the older boy's face. "You said that to Mom?" his voice rose.

"Isn't it right?" Todd prodded.

Of course it was right. Right on the money, and something he hadn't thought Todd would pick up. After all, Todd was only four-and-a-half. But then, Todd had been forced to grow up fast.

It was an act of survival, running away. It was for the purpose of taking a deep, unhampered breath. He hadn't been frightened out on the road—he'd known he could get to Uncle Ned. All the fears of his life were right here, in this house. The fear his father might not love him as much as Todd. That was a killer thought—Scott adored Jack. The fear that his mother was

150

drawing away, turning inward, losing her laughter, growing ill—the fear of death.

The fear of Andy. Truly, he was terrified of Andy.

He couldn't say anything of this to Todd. He was responsible for Todd. That was a fact. Ever since the programming had started, no one else had had the time to supervise Todd.

"I shouldn't have run away," Scott said. "It's punk to run away from things. You have to face them out!"

Todd settled comfortably on the bed and gazed soulfully up at his older brother. This answer seemed to strike a responsive cord. He was silent for a second or two, then set his lips, and gazed sideways at Scott.

"Mommy doesn't love Daddy anymore."

Scott, taken completely off-guard, stared at him for a long moment. He thought about fleeing, then remembered what he'd just said, and faced Todd squarely.

"She loves Dad. Don't be a stupid baby!"

"If you're so sure, why are you calling me names?" Todd asked politely.

Scott's mind was a total blank.

"Is Daddy gonna go away?" This with a nonchalant and worldly air, spoiled somewhat by the catch in his voice.

"You're totally ridiculous, you know that?"

"Is he?"

Scott laughed bitterly. "And leave Andy?"

It was out before he could stop it, before he even knew he was about to say it, and he was sorry for that because he saw the peculiar blanching around Todd's young mouth. He dropped down on the bed beside him.

"I didn't mean that, Todd. I'm just tired. I have to go down and put the wash in the dryer and wake up Mom and tell her to go to bed. I've got my own problems, and you're buggin' me."

They sat there, neither moving, in silence.

"Sometimes," Todd finally said, with dread, "I hate Andy." He didn't look at Scott when he said it, eyes pinned blindly to a spot on the far wall.

151

"I hate him to death, almost," he confessed in a rush, then shivered and closed his mouth tight. "Is God gonna punish me?"

Scott was quiet for a long minute. He gave this question due consideration.

"I think it's okay," he said finally. "I think it's normal to be jealous of all the time that gets spent on Andy."

Todd looked doubtfully into his eyes, wanting to believe this. There was another small silence.

"Do Mommy and Daddy still love each other?" he asked, his voice very small and quivering.

Scott felt vastly tired. This was a damaging question. It should be left alone, not voiced, not even thought about. He felt as weary as his mother looked. As weary as he knew his father felt. He wondered if they'd both felt like this—sad and old—for all the time since Andy's birth. The thought was insupportable. He wondered if he himself would feel this worn and depressed for the rest of his life. It wasn't fair. They were old. He had his whole lifetime left to live.

Todd was sitting there, eyes huge and strained, waiting for words of wisdom from his older brother.

"They still love each other," Scott said. He stated it with determination and, to his surprise, found himself believing it.

But Todd was shaking his head, steeped in gloom.

"Listen to me," Scott spat, anger coming, as it often did, as the only way to breathe through an atmosphere of overwhelming unhappiness. "All you have to do is look at Dad when he's looking at Mom. When she doesn't know he's looking."

"Then it's just Mommy that doesn't love him," Todd said flatly.

"Mom loves Dad," Scott sighed, for though he'd been young and self-absorbed at the time, not much older than Todd was now, his memories were clear of the battles between Judy and her first husband, of the emotions he'd stored up without knowing it. He had a gut feel for his mother's thoughts, her

152

hopelessness and anger during the last months of that marriage. Of her final emotional state concerning a man she once had loved and loved no longer.

His father.

It had been different with Jack—from the first, and always.

"Mom's just tired. She spends all those hours with Andy and the volunteers. She feels like she's been at it forever, being nicer than anybody should have to always be, just so the volunteers won't get mad and leave her and screw up the programming. She worries a lot. She doesn't always know it's even *for* something. She'd probably feel better if somebody said everything's gonna end up straight, but nobody's gonna stick out their neck to tell her that because nobody knows if it'll ever be right for Andy. Andy could end up being slow forever."

"He's a lot better," Todd retorted, with a dry edge to his voice beneath an overly brisk assumption of brotherly concern. "He can do whatever the programmers want him to do."

"Andy's starting to be able to do some simple, basic little baby things, but he's two years old and that's too old to be just starting to do those things," Scott explained. "Because he still can't do a lot of the things kids younger than him can do. So that means he's getting closer to *looking* normal. And I don't think Mom or Dad want him to just look normal. They didn't go through the programming so they could sit him in a chair in a restaurant and fool people into thinking he's normal if he's not really normal.

"They want him to get all the way normal, Todd, like everybody else. I don't think Mom could stand the idea that he wouldn't be able to have anything he wants when he's grown up, or that he wouldn't be able to do all the things other people take for granted, like going to college and getting married and like that . . ."

But Todd had gone pale.

"What's the matter?" Scott asked.

There was a glazed, shaken look in the child's eyes and strain

153

lines around his nose and mouth. His freckles stood out livid on his nose, the way they always did when his skin went too white.

Scott dropped a careless arm around him.

"It's okay," he said awkwardly. "It'll all turn out."

But Todd was staring at him and where the pallor had been only moments before there was now a rising flush of rage.

"You mean," Todd said, trying to extract sense from what was essentially gibberish to one his age, "that it's gonna stay like this? That it's never gonna be any different? That all these *people,* all this *stuff,* won't ever end? That it's gonna be forever?"

Scott looked at him dully. It was one o'clock in the morning. He wanted nothing more than to crawl under the covers and sleep for a year. The running away to Uncle Ned hadn't helped. He was proud of himself for doing it—he'd hitchhiked all the way to Pittsburgh without the least bit of difficulty. But it hadn't helped, because he'd felt deliciously free for just a bit, then guilty, and then, of course, he'd had to come home anyway.

He was suddenly completely out of temper with Todd. He'd tried his best to be patient with him. Todd had no right to feel so misused. He was cared for. He belonged. He'd never had to suffer, not really. He just wanted more than what he had— which made him a spoiled brat.

"Listen, you think you're gonna sit around whining over everything?" Scott pressed. "You wanna cry over how unfair it all is? Nobody went and burned out a part of *your* brain, did they?"

Todd, gaping helplessly, tried to rise but Scott caught his shoulder in a heavy-handed grip that kept him firmly where he was.

"I don't remember seeing Mom running you around, doing errands or anything. I don't remember Dad even making you keep your room clean. Just what exactly is it you *have* been

154

doing all this time to make you feel so depressed and misunderstood?"

This attack had the predictable effect of erasing Todd's desire to whine and rousing his fury instead. It was totally unfair of Scott. He'd suffered the same agonies Scott had suffered. He'd been unwilling witness time and again to their mother's search for funds. Hiding in the hallway, where she couldn't see him, listening while she talked on the phone. He'd heard her when she'd called the market one morning, pleading for free food, for free milk for her children. It horrified him to understand that he himself was one of these children. And when the groceries had indeed been sent, he'd watched her face to see if this gift brought joy back to it. It didn't. Her face was white and drawn. After the phone call. After the charity. He was very young and didn't know the word "charity" but he knew what it had done to her.

He retaliated against Scott's attack in the only way he knew.

"We're poor!" he snapped, collaring that fact and brandishing it wildly. "Because of Andy!" His mouth curled around the name.

"For God's sake!" Scott muttered. "You think we were rich *before* Andy?"

"At least we were happy!"

Scott stared at him, then burst out laughing.

It grew silent in the room as the brothers watched one another warily.

"It's all *Andy*," Todd said finally. He sounded deeply exhausted. It was, Scott realized, the overriding characteristic in this house. Total, helpless exhaustion.

"All of it," Todd whispered. "All the time. Mommy never stops looking at him, like he'll disappear or something. And Daddy stands around and looks *stupid!*" His small face crumpled. "Stupid, the way he stares at Andy."

Scott was back at the window, looking out.

"It hurts me," Todd whimpered.

155

But his older brother didn't turn or speak. He waited a bit, for it was unbearable to have said this terrible thing to nothing but a silence, yet there was nothing else from Scott.

He turned and left the room.

Jack Polikoff drove slowly toward home. He felt dangerously muddled, an odd sort of feeling, not simple weariness or even the bone-aching tiredness of physical breakdown. It was his insides that felt tired. As if he could actually *feel* them. As if he could monitor every organ and blood vessel. As if his liver had been ignited. As if his intestines had been looped into a huge, square knot.

The layoff was the last straw.

The house would be empty of programmers until nine o'clock. If he went right home, he'd be there by seven, which would scare Judy to death—or not. He considered this possibility in a lethargic, semi-detached manner, then decided against it. He'd get home early but it wouldn't scare Judy, Judy wouldn't even notice his return, because his comings and goings weren't part of *her* schedule.

If he waited until nine, the house would be crawling with people. If he was lucky, the first shift would be arriving. Four women, bent on harassing Judy in any of a hundred tiny, unutterably cruel ways. It would give him a chance to hang up his coat and go to the bathroom. If he continued lucky, he wouldn't find that terrible woman with her weak bladder locked in the family toilet.

If he came home after nine and wasn't lucky, there'd be women standing around in his living room to intercept him. There always were women in his living room. Of late, some of them had even started bringing their own small children for Judy to babysit. For free. While they programmed Andy. And how did you tell them to stop? How did you dare tell them anything?

If there were women standing around in his living room

156

when he got home, they'd make polite noises at him, ask him inane questions, and he'd feel obliged to answer and flash his phony smile, his inner eye watching Judy all the while. Wondering what she thought. Wondering what she felt. Wondering when she'd come back to him.

Scott would have left for school. He never saw much of Scott. The car pool would have carried Todd off to nursery. A blurred little face through glass—that was Todd.

Jack's head began to ache and he scowled and clenched his teeth and tried to come to a decision. When to go home. When it would be safest. Safest, to have a second of privacy with Judy.

A blur of images filled his mind—the ruin of the family. No, not that, not the ruin, the deterioration of an atmosphere. Scott had run away because life had become unbearable. At age twelve—it had to be some kind of peacetime record. He, father of the house, hadn't been available to hear the source of the trouble and that single fact lacerated his already damaged ego.

Todd? Todd always watched Scott. Therefore, Todd knew that Scott had run away. And with his obviously sharp intellect, he must have figured out why. Todd adored Scott and might seriously consider emulating him. That thought had haunted Jack's nights since Ned brought Scott home.

It felt as if hot needles were piercing his throat. He wanted desperately to go home, now, while it was still early. To crawl into bed and gather Judy to his heart and perhaps, perhaps, cry a little. He'd never cried in all his years of manhood but then, he'd never been so tired before, so totally spent.

But he dared not. She was the mother of a brain-damaged child. He couldn't stand to have to tell her why he was home early, he couldn't stand the panic he'd arouse in her. Her mouth would tremble with sympathy in that second before she'd recall she was iron, cold, unique, and alone. He turned the car viciously toward West River Drive and did not go home.

*　　*　　*

157

ROBERT CARR, M.D.
Elm Square Clinic
Elm Street at Dale Road
Philadelphia, Pa.

February 9, 1976

Re: Andrew Polikoff

To Whom It May Concern:

Andy has been our patient since September 4, 1974, at which time a thorough neurological evaluation was carried out. Following evaluation, he was admitted to Midtown Hospital, in Philadelphia, for contrast studies. He was discharged on October 6, 1974, with diagnoses of:

> Chronic Encephalopathy
> Brain and Cortical Atrophy
> Severe Psychomotor Retardation

He was then placed on an intensive program of rehabilitation therapy, under the aegis of the Centre for Neurological Rehabilitation, and has made remarkable progress under this program.

Mr. Polikoff is now temporarily unemployed by Century Steel. Any assistance you can provide this family in meeting their extensive expenses would be greatly appreciated.

Robert Carr, M.D.

15

Monday, March 1, 1976

Andy had his first swimming lesson at the Jewish Y today. CNR thought it would be a good thing to try, and the swimming instructor at the Y seemed very confident he could help Andy.

Had it all approved by Thorpe—naturally.

To be perfectly honest, I didn't expect much. I mean—swimming? Andy was scared to death, and why not? But the lesson seemed to go okay, Andy seemed interested in this new world, and the instructor smiled at the end so at least it wasn't a washout.

Jack will paint the pool in return for Andy's lessons. It's becoming unique these days to find a chance to give service in return for service instead of constantly accepting acts of charity. I don't know how Jack feels about that or if Jack feels anything at all other than bleak and rotten because he can't find steady work.

When he told me about the layoff, I took it too well. I stood there and felt myself taking it too well. It didn't penetrate. I must be growing a numb spot all over my emotions. I must be turning into a tired robot. When the numbness becomes hard calluses over my heart and soul, maybe I'll feel lucky.

P.S. Andy's doing pretty well in programming.

It snowed. Not much, a mere sprinkling, but Judy held Andy up to the window to look, and talked a lot about snow, regaling him with tales of herself and her only brother, Ned, as children. She ended this monologue in tears, but Andy didn't notice.

Jack was out walking. She envisioned him in different outfits, walking in virtually any weather. Waterproof overcoat and

159

boots in a tidal wave. Weighted pants and shoes in a tornado. Heated underwear and shirt and jeans and shoes with little blades across the sole and heel to walk on an ice floe. Pop-out cleats to walk up an avalanche.

The bills kept right on coming, while Jack walked.

She'd called a neighborhood synagogue the week before, and they'd donated thirty dollars. She kept lists of amounts and sent everything to Alexander Thorpe. She had no idea how deeply she'd come to rely on Thorpe's constant support. How much she'd unconsciously shifted such needs away from Jack.

She really didn't have the time to wonder about the realities of their finances or the reactions of other people toward their escalating need. That was a sure route to depression, and she also hadn't time to court distress. She reacted to every new situation by gut instinct, with a minimum of planning or retrospection.

Monday, March 8, 1976

If things can possibly happen to produce an air of depression in the house, they will. Andy seems to be coming down with what, in anybody else, would be just a cold. In his case it will almost certainly cause breathing problems. He was badly congested all night, crying, wouldn't come to me when I tried to comfort him. Doing very badly in programming for the past day or two. Won't even make an effort. No further attempt to pull up. Is apparently regressing in this sense. Even the creeping, which was nearing perfection, seems to have been forgotten, hopefully only for this short period.

Canceled swimming lesson.

Tuesday, March 9, 1976

Andy wouldn't let me hold him today. Seems afraid of me or mad at me or something. Can you believe this? He actually cried every single time he saw me today. Made me feel like I'd better skulk past him. Saw the smirks on one or two programmers' faces, the ones I can't stand anyway, so maybe it's only in my mind.

It's not only in my mind. I won't start thinking that. There are always those people who delight in other people's discomforts.

And Andy only made it worse by giggling and snuggling with absolutely everybody else.

Jack hanging around constantly. Didn't take a single walk today. Kept looking at me, sideways, when he figured I wouldn't catch him looking. Must think I did something gross to turn Andy from me.

I decided it was my turn to take a little walk for a change. Did. Nobody missed me.

Wednesday, March 10, 1976
No programming. Andy sick.

Thursday, March 11, 1976
Andy very sick. Congestion. Fever.

Friday, March 12, 1976
Still very sick, making me so scared, wonder if it's possible for him to lose all he's achieved and go right back to the beginning. Seems I'm always having horrible thoughts like this, always either scared or depressed.

Saturday, March 13, 1976
Andy's better today. Just like that. Not gradually better but completely better. Maybe he's just being cute, trying to drive me crazy. Short trip!

Sunday, March 14, 1976
Full day of programming.

Judy called CNR on Monday afternoon to talk to John Unruh or, more accurately, to shout at John Unruh because she

161

was growing convinced he wouldn't hear a word she said if she spoke softly. Nobody else did.

"I tell you, he doesn't respond to me. I'm his mother, John, and there's absolutely no normal response to me. We've been on this program for nearly a year-and-a-half, and this is the total result of all that effort? That he still hasn't figured out I'm his mother? What do I do for the rest of his life? What's my role, John? Just another pretty face? One in a million?"

She was shouting, but it was okay: The programmers were gone for lunch, there was only Scott peering at her from the kitchen doorway, and Jack was invisible somewhere in the house with Andy. She didn't care if Jack heard her or not.

"That's enough, Judy!"

"What?" She stared, affronted, at the phone.

"I don't mind if you yell yourself hoarse if it ends up making you feel better, but you're not thinking constructively. It's okay to have a really terrible day, Judy. It's normal to have lots of terrible days. You're allowed to have terrible, stinking, putrid days and weeks and months. Didn't anybody tell you?"

She stood glaring at the wall.

"I thought *I* told you," Unruh added, thoughtfully.

"That's it?" she retorted. "I'm *allowed* to feel sorry for myself? That's the best you can come up with after all this time? I call you at the end of my rope and you make a nice neat noose for me to stick my head in while you stand and watch? You want to kick the chair out now and watch me dangle for a while? I'm allowed!"

"You're allowed to feel anything you feel. It's not unnatural to wish you'd never started the programming. It's not evil or abnormal to think how much better and easier life would have been if there'd been no Andy. It's *normal*, Judy. Are you listening to a word I'm saying? You don't have to pretend you don't feel like that. It's normal to feel you've been singled out for a disaster area. You have."

She swallowed.

"Now, what did you call about?"

162

When she slammed down the receiver without answering, her blood was hot and she felt like tearing up the house. The crawling, desperate, self-pitying lethargy had fled.

That was why she had called him.

He never tried to soothe her or pat her on the head. He didn't treat her like glass. He didn't smooth her down, like Jack did.

He made her mad. He made her want to fight and live!

Tuesday, March 16, 1976

Andy's doing fine today. I still can't believe all he had was a cold. I guess at this point it's hard to believe that anything Andy gets will be that simple.

Also—Andy's creeping again. The movement's perfect! That made me feel calmer. I even had a heart-to-heart with myself.

And I've made myself a promise! To find an area of calm inside myself. No matter how strung out I feel, I won't let go, I won't break down. I've come too far, brought Andy too far, to lose it all now by growing disgustingly weak. I will not have anybody telling me, Ahh ahh Judy! That above all else. I will not be pitied.

And one depressed adult to a household is the limit. Right now, "Depressed Adult" status belongs to Jack, exclusively.

The last half of March was gray and chill. The house was shabby, distinctly shabby. The carpet, despite the removal of shoes in the basement, was worn thin, the color inconsistent, the nap totally gone from the areas that got the greatest traffic. The programmers were a given, a natural part of existence, like her lungs and liver and swollen feet.

And the falling away of volunteers was continuing, the rate increasing. It was getting harder and harder to fill the vacancies. Judy was taking part in the programs herself, hour after hour, day after day. It was utterly exhausting. There were more and more sessions with only one or two programmers, and then

163

Jack would work the hour as well, while they both prayed the next set would be better attended.

Jack, his face too white, started going out on the street and stopping people.

"You. Joe. Wait a minute!"

The mailman turned, hesitating. Jack's face was grim, his size overpowering. To the mailman, small-boned and middle-aged, he had the appearance of definite trouble.

Judy ran down the front path and dragged her spouse back into the privacy of their household.

"You can't do that, Jack. Joe would help if he could—he *has* helped. You know he programs on his day off. You can't expect people to jeopardize their jobs for Andy." She found she was holding onto his tense forearm, restraining him bodily.

"We'll get through the set okay. You and me and Martha."

She turned and smiled warmly at the one woman who'd come and Martha, with them from the start, received this heartfelt glow and flushed. She also changed her mind about telling Judy and Jack she wouldn't be back after this particular hour.

Jack was fidgeting. Judy had never seen him fidget. There was a set look around his mouth and his eyes were smarting. He shoved her placating hand away and turned and went back on the street. She didn't follow him this time. She was too frightened.

"We'd better see what we can accomplish ourselves, Martha."

The young man Jack brought back held a sample case to his chest, shield against possible insanity. The sight of the two women, Andy, the patterning table served to ease his mind a bit about Jack. He'd said he'd come and see what the problem was and here he was. Then, he looked into Judy's tired blue eyes, sighed, dropped his case on the rug, grabbed a leg, and listened to the instructions Judy gave him.

Late that night, Judy thought about the young man and lay giggling nervously as she recalled his expression. He would have been a Category Two, she was sure of it. From the start, she'd found her programmers falling into one of two categories.

Into Category One fell the deeply sympathetic, gushing early callers, the very first names, in some cases, on the Hope Line list, the ones who made sure to call their friends the minute they signed up, to spread the word of their own generosity. These were the programmers who came for two or three months, then recalled favorite beauty parlor appointments, or made conflicting personal dates and discovered pressing obligations that removed them time and again from their scheduled hours. They were the group that didn't bother to reschedule, and that left Judy perpetually shorthanded.

Category One.

Those who liked to talk about it.

Then there was Category Two: the tentatives. Some had taken weeks to call at all, perhaps hoping that by that time all the spots would be filled. The embarrassed ones. The sometimes painfully honest ones. The revolted ones, who stuck it through despite personal inconvenience, despite the fact that they hated coming at all. The ones who saw a duty and couldn't make it go away. Who didn't tell their friends because they were afraid they might be called "do-gooders." Who hated the whole process from first to last, but who pulled their weight because they viewed life as a membership kind of thing, complete with dues owing. Thank you, God, for all my blessings. Here's a payment on my dues. Keep me blessed, God, that's all I'm asking.

Faithful friends were in a category by themselves. Never in her life would she forget them. Never would she do them the disservice of dissecting their motives. They were loyal through it all. Her own intrepid army.

Her cousin Phyllis was always near. Her dear friend Marcia. Both had come, in the middle of the night, to give her some rest, in these long months of breathing problems with Andy. More neighbors than she'd known she had. Store owners: The credit they'd extended over a long period of time was in totals beyond comprehension.

The family: Uncle Murray and her brother, Ned. Little gifts in the mail, checks that seemed to appear at the very worst times, carrying them over impossible barriers.

No category for the faithful friends. Just love, and easy gratitude.

And another elite group: the women of Midtown Hospital. Hardly a day passed without at least one call, quick check-ins to say hello, to say take care, to say keep your chin up off the floor and get your life going, girl! Chiding calls and laughing calls and gently bracing calls. She felt cushioned and lulled by each of these calls and, as time passed, with her new resolve, Jack finally came back into focus.

She felt a dread, aching, endless sorrow for Jack. She would have liked to hold him if they hadn't grown so far apart.

He was taking any job he could get. Substitute watchman. Babysitter. Painter. Short-haul truck driver for one of their friends. He'd gone away from her since he'd lost his job at Century Steel. Far away.

It didn't seem to matter that the plant had closed. That the fault wasn't his. They needed money desperately and he wasn't bringing sufficient money in.

Jack was ashamed. She could feel his shame. It made one more barrier between them.

Andy kicked her one day when she reached down to lift him, then shrieked with alarm when she grit her teeth and swung him up anyway. She felt a sudden, deep hatred for this youngest child, and put him back down, very, very carefully.

Friday, March 19, 1976

Losing Jack. Know it. Losing the boys. Scott never talks to me anymore, and Todd won't even look at me. Losing volunteers right and left. Must be my personality. Losing Judy. Could be I can't stand myself either. Andy? Andy was never mine to lose.

166

Good thing I'm keeping my chin up, isn't it?

But that changed. That deepening sense of loss. It changed because of Andy.

The little push toy was Todd's and Judy had brought it downstairs for Andy. The abortive efforts to pull up had been resulting, finally, in some tottering successes. One day, in late March, Andy started cruising, and from then on there was no stopping him. The brightly painted push toy, with its stout handle, became a permanent part of the living room decor, leaning tantalizingly against the end table.

She'd never forget. Never. The look on his face the first time he let go of Jack's hands and gripped the knob on the top of the push toy. And teetered. And steadied himself. And took one faltering step, secure in the feel of the stout handle.

And balanced. Light dawning on his small face. And walked. Andy and the push toy. Alone, together.

16

By late March, the shortage of volunteers was approaching critical. Judy got in touch with a reporter who'd covered the very start of Andy's programming. His trip to the house, and the resultant article and picture of Andy walking with his push toy, brought in, over the next six days, more than two hundred new names through the Hope Line.

Some Category Ones. Some Category Twos. Only time would tell. Disaster was, for the moment, averted.

There was a small spate of follow-up coverage. She'd thought Andy was old news if news at all, but one of the three major television networks called about doing a possible documentary. The thought made her dizzy. Hot lights, people over-running the house, dragging coils of heavy wire, entangling the programmers—surely, that was what would happen if they filmed a documentary.

She needn't have worried. Thorpe's office forbade any more exposure than had already been necessary. The word "trial" actually passed Thorpe's thin lips—a word she hadn't heard or allowed herself to think since the start of the programming.

Wednesday, March 31, 1976

They've intensified the brushes we use to stimulate Andy's skin and tongue. This isn't in response to any new problem, the problem's existed all along. We just lost track, more or less, of our rate of success in this particular area because we've grown so high on the major break-throughs we've been fortunate enough to experience.

Andy started to walk and that was a huge success. It drove other aspects of the overall programming just a little bit off dead-center. So we were brought up short by a little surprise the other day. Here's what happened.

We had a snowstorm—nothing major—a few nights ago, and the following day, at lunchtime, Jack went out to shovel the path and sidewalk. I took Andy to the storm door to watch him. It was still snowing a little and the wind was vicious.

When Jack was nearly through, the phone rang, and I went to answer, bringing Andy into the kitchen. When I hung up, a minute or two later, Andy was gone. He wasn't in the dining room or the living room. Where he *was,* was standing outside, having somehow pushed open the storm door. Standing on the front walk, in only a thin shirt and pants, watching Jack, whose back was turned, shoveling.

The point I'm leading up to is this. It was a bitterly cold day, gusting wind, and Andy wasn't even shivering.

So we're intensifying the brushing. For gross tactile stimulation. To span this particular gap, to complete a circuit broken by the brain damage. To stimulate Andy's senses. To make him somehow aware that he could freeze to death, standing out in the snow and wind, and that it's supposed to be uncomfortable freezing to death, not just a pleasant little interlude.

You really do have to grow a callus over your heart if you hope to live through this programming.

ROBERT CARR, M.D.
Elm Square Clinic
Elm Street at Dale Road
Philadelphia, Pa.

April 5, 1976

U.S. Government
Internal Revenue Service
600 Arch Street
Philadelphia, Pa.

Gentlemen:

This is to certify that our patient, Andrew Polikoff, has been under our care since the fall of 1974. During that time, we have done extensive testing to determine the degree of brain damage he incurred. We have placed him on a rigid program of rehabilitation which continues to this day. The testing continues as well.

Necessarily, these procedures were quite expensive. The diagnostic procedures were the most sophisticated screening procedures at the time, and since then, Andy has been maintained on medication to stabilize his condition so that his rehabilitative therapy, which was, in itself, costly, could be effective.

If you have need of our charge records for the last quarter of 1974, or the full year, 1975, please contact us and we will make them available to you immediately.

Yours truly,

Robert Carr, M.D.

Spring finally came. Judy and Jack took out a second mortgage on the house to try to push back a part of their immediate medical debt. Also, to put food on the table. To buy shoes for three sons.

By spring, Judy felt they'd hit up every friend they'd ever had. It was probably fact. She'd forgotten what it was like to have something called a bank account. But spring came anyway, unmindful of such transient human affairs, and she could open the windows and breathe fresh air, damp soil, new growth, then worry about drafts and the probability of Andy's catching pneumonia.

There were so many bills she finally stopped tabulating them. As usual, she sent them straight to Thorpe.

But there was also the positive side to things. She got a part-time job as a fast-order cook. And Andy knew her. He finally knew she was "Mommy." Andy learned she was somebody special before she permitted herself to leave the house.

"I want you to buy a distinctive perfume," Unruh said at their last program upgrading. "Something potent. If you can find one that really stinks, buy up a case of it!"

She'd eyed him narrowly, though she really should have known he wasn't kidding.

"For this phase of the programming you won't be able to help with the exercises. Stay away from Andy until the last five minutes of each set. For that five minutes, take him into an empty room and hold him and caress him and talk to him softly. Keep talking to him. Make him look at you. Kiss him a lot.

"And make sure the perfume's very noticeable.

"We'll see if the assault on his sense of smell, along with the extra cuddling and privacy, separates you from all the other ladies in his life."

Tuesday, May 11, 1976

Made a new sign for the basement. NO ONE MAY WEAR *Vamp* WHILE PROGRAMMING!

Don't know why anybody would want to wear Vamp, ever. Smells like . . . Well, skip that. We'll see what Andy thinks of it.

The bedroom was cool and dim. Outside the window, there was birdsong. Judy had been wearing the perfume for the past three weeks. Now Andy sat on her lap, facing her, playing with her hair, gripping it in both hands and pulling, then gazing up into her face.

It was very quiet, but for the birds. Speech was still beyond her child. He made only guttural sounds, accompanied by insistent pointing toward what he desired. A cookie. Juice. A loved soft toy.

Andy looked up into his mother's face and his little nose twitched. He giggled, pointed at her, shifted, and cuddled into her arms.

17

"I want to *know*," Scott said, grimly.

He positioned himself in his parents' bedroom doorway, arms folded across his chest, and showed no signs of moving.

"I want to know how much longer we're gonna have all these people living in our house!"

Neither she nor Jack commented on his belligerence. It would have been ridiculous. And it was a fair enough question. If anything, they were both surprised he hadn't demanded an answer sooner. Judy herself would have welcomed an answer, but she couldn't very well say such a thing to her twelve-and-a-half-year-old. She could hardly put herself in such an absurd position. How could she say, "Look, son, I don't know how much longer, I don't know if we'll ever finish, I don't know if what we're trying to do is even possible to accomplish. They won't tell me, so how can I tell you?" She just couldn't say that to her son, could she?

But she and Jack went downstairs with Scott and Scott went out on the street to find Todd, because both Jack and Judy had agreed this should be a family conference. It took longer for Scott to find Todd than Judy had expected. It was nine-forty when they finally came home. Todd wasn't even five yet and should surely not have been wandering the streets at night.

Time to tighten the reins. Time to resolve to notice all these peripheral family things.

From the dining room came the bustling sounds of the day's wrap-up. Jack appeared seconds later, carrying Andy up to bed. Judy watched him go up the stairs, then turned to Scott and Todd.

"Sit down. You'll wait for Daddy."

They sat, looking oddly out of context in the living room. The living room was a waiting room for strangers, not an intimate meeting place for the family. She sat too and listened to the soft sounds of Jack putting Andy to bed. He was quick, suspiciously quick. She thought he must have stuffed Andy fully clothed into his crib, but when she went in later to kiss him goodnight, he was neatly pajama'd, neatly covered—she wished she could bed him down with such swift, neat efficiency.

She sat and regarded her two older sons as Jack sank into his favorite armchair. Scott looked angry, as he had in their bedroom doorway—angry, distant, and cold. Todd looked totally disinterested. She didn't believe in such disinterest. She didn't want to believe in it.

"Scott wanted this family conference," Jack announced to the room at large, but particularly to Todd.

Todd looked startled and moved a bit away from Scott.

"Mommy and I hadn't really considered having a family talk," Jack said carefully, "but Scott seems to feel it's time we got all this business out in the open. About Andy."

Todd was staring at the carpet between his sneakered feet. Judy saw his young mouth twitch.

"Why?" he finally asked, lifting his head, eyes innocent—far too innocent.

Scott's face was frozen. He stared belligerently at his father and avoided looking at his mother completely.

"If you mean why does Scott think it's time," Judy roused herself and sat forward, "he probably thinks it's time because we've been in programming now for over a year-and-a-half, and it seems like it's never ending. And if it seems like that to me, at my age, it must seem to both of you that it's always been this way. That there was never anything different."

Todd looked at her with a cool derision that made her flush.

"Is this whole talk gonna be about Andy?" Todd asked.

Jack sat forward.

"This talk is about the family," he chided.

Scott smiled. It wasn't a particularly pleasant smile.

But Todd seemed interested in the concept of a discussion

173

centering on something other than his younger brother.

"Can we talk about school?" he quipped. "Nobody ever lets me talk about school."

Judy shifted.

"Or about baseball," Todd went on to suggest. His tone was eager but there was a glint in his eye that made Judy feel uneasy. Todd was too young to be baiting his parents.

"Maybe," Todd said, inspired, his child's face suddenly less childish, "we won't be poor anymore if Andy ever gets normal."

"We're not finished with Andy's programming," Jack put in smoothly. "It's time to talk about it because it obviously bothers you and Scott very much, yet neither of you has come and talked about it to Mommy or to me. And keeping it inside doesn't help. It made Scott run away . . ."

Scott's stare became malevolent and Jack met it with a cool detachment that aggravated the situation that much more.

". . . and I don't doubt for a minute," Jack said to Todd, "that it's made you confused and sad and inclined to hide behind a fresh attitude."

Todd looped his fingers together and yawned in his father's face.

In the ensuing second of silence that greeted this gross insubordination, a swift sideways glance passed between the brothers. Jack's eyes met Judy's an instant later in their first totally shared understanding since Andy's birth. Scott and Todd were a unit. They were reacting as one.

"We've come a long way with the programming," Jack said quietly, watching both boys carefully. "But we're not done, we still have to go a little farther to make it all worth something. We don't know exactly how much more it needs, but we can guess the worst is past. Andy's catching up to where he would have been naturally if he hadn't had all these problems."

"Then why doesn't that mean he's better?" Todd asked. The sneering impertinence wasn't even masked. There was another small glance at Scott, as if for approval, but Scott was unresponsive now, staring bitterly at the far wall.

"Exactly what do you mean by 'better', Todd?" his mother asked gently.

"I mean," Todd raised his voice aggressively, "normal. Not a retard."

A dreadful pall fell over the room. Jack sat forward. "That's not a good word, Todd," he said.

Judy's eyes had filled with weak tears. She saw her middle child through a swimming haze. He was a baby, just a baby. How could a baby with freckles look so hateful?

"It's true, isn't it?" Todd challenged, his eyes too wide, looking hard at Jack, trying desperately to be mean, to overcome the liability of being so young.

"No, Todd, it isn't."

Todd looked at him in scornful silence, then his eyes dropped.

"Andy's not retarded," Jack insisted. "He's brain-damaged, and that means . . ."

"It means his brain's dead," Todd spat out. "Scott said so!"

Scott stiffened, turned his head, and glared at his sibling. For the first time, Jack saw a faint flush rise to bathe Scott's face as he became aware of a certain precariousness to his own position.

"Is that what I said?" Scott asked viciously. "That his brain's dead? Is that what I *said?*"

Todd squirmed. It made him look what he really was—a baby, in a rage.

"You said part of his brain's burned out. I remember, Scott!" His voice trembled and a faint flinching thing happened to his shoulders as he tried to face down his big brother.

"Is that all I said? Just like that?" Scott was hotly furious now, desperately aware of the silence of his mother and father and of what they must imagine had been the thrust and tone of this brotherly conversation.

Todd stared at him, then moved back against the arm of the couch and chewed at his lower lip, trying to remember exactly.

"You said he'd have to learn to use the good parts instead, and that's what the people come for," Todd finally imparted.

Scott glanced at his parents, then relaxed a little. But Todd, feeling unjustly diminished, turned on him with a child's anger.

"So if he learned to use the good parts, why isn't he better? Why's he still a retard?"

"You know who the real retard is?" Scott asked grimly.

"Scott!" Judy's voice was strangled. On the couch, Todd cringed, the blood swooping into his freckled face. His eyes had widened enormously. He looked horrified. Stabbed to the heart.

"Scott?" he whispered, unintentionally echoing his mother.

"How many times," Scott asked, "did we talk about all this? How many times did you ask the same stupid questions, over and over and over? How many times did you hear me say it takes time, lots and lots and lots of time? You hear me say that, Todd? You remember me saying that? Didn't you believe me when I said that?"

Todd's eyes, to Judy's surprise, suddenly overflowed with tears, and his mouth trembled with anguish.

"I believe what you say, Scott." There was reverence in his voice for this role model, his brother.

"Then what's your problem?" Scott asked. "What's with all this 'retard' business?"

"I just want to know when he'll be better enough!" Todd's small chin went up.

"Better enough for what?"

"Better enough to have all the people stop coming to the house. Better enough to act like everybody else. Normal," he added, shooting a malevolent glance at his mother.

"Normal" had become one of Judy's least favorite words. Jack knew this. Scott knew this. So, apparently, did Todd. Jack interceded swiftly.

"Andy's much better than he was. It's even possible he won't need the volunteers much longer. We have an appointment at CNR soon, and we'll hear what they have to say then about Andy's progress, and about how much farther he has to go in programming.

"But the important thing you have to understand, both of you, is *why* Mommy and I spent all this time on Andy's programming."

Judy was shifting fitfully in her chair, still hooked on that deadly word, "normal."

"Normal," she interrupted, "means different things for different people."

Scott's gaze narrowed at this revelation. Todd squirmed and rubbed his face. Jack, seeing the glint in Judy's eyes, was determined not to let this discussion switch to monologues on semantics.

"We're not sitting here late at night to discuss words like 'normal', are we? We can do that any Sunday afternoon when all this is over, if you think it's important enough."

Judy shot him a rapid glance, then looked at Scott. Scott had turned off. She saw this. It was the oddest sensation, as if he had stood and left the room or inserted ear plugs.

Jack saw too.

"This isn't a lecture, Scott," Jack said.

Scott's awareness returned. He glared into Jack's face. It was a cold, adult glare. He smiled slightly at his father, a secret, disturbing smile which Jack returned with a long, cold remoteness of his own. It made Judy frightened in a vague, nameless way. She sat forward abruptly to drag them back from wherever they'd gone—Scott and Jack.

"It's important for us to talk this out," Judy forced herself to continue. "What we want you to understand, what you *have* to understand, is that we've done all this for your brother to try to make him a person, yes, for himself, but not only for that, for the rest of the family as well. To make him *live* because we couldn't just sit back and hope he'd learn to live all by himself!"

Scott looked polite, Todd morose and perhaps disbelieving. She wondered if Todd was too young to understand what she was saying, but he glanced up then and she saw the malevolent gleam in his wide-set eyes.

"You mean," said her middle child, "you don't want Andy

177

to stay a lump for when you and Daddy aren't here anymore? You thought Scott and me shouldn't have a vegetable to take care of when you and Daddy are dead?"

"Todd," she said weakly, then began to laugh. Helpless tears filled her eyes and she dropped her head against the back of her chair, shaking with the laughter. Her husband came to his feet and her oldest son turned and said something to his hapless sibling and still the tears came, coursing down her cheeks. Jack was kneeling now in front of her and she was aware of the boys being sent from, or simply exiting, the living room.

Jack's strong arms went around her. She sat limply, then managed to raise one hand to his hair. The laughter had stopped. Even the tears were stilled.

The silence in the house was total.

Jack got work at the brewery, but it didn't last long. He was the newest man on. When the layoffs came, he was the first let go.

It would have been a novelty, finding a job where layoffs weren't a part of the status quo.

Judy added babysitting to her hours at the diner, knowing full well how Jack felt about her working, knowing what it did to his ego. But they'd long since passed a point where she could afford to stay home and stroke his ego and be unemployed with him.

He went back to taking any odd job he could get. Never in his adult life had he been content to sit still. Now, with his financial responsibilities snowballing, his frustration was liberally laced with guilt.

Judy knew. She couldn't help him.

The holidays came again. This time one old friend brought Thanksgiving dinner and stayed to share it with them.

"Listen, Marcia!" Judy commanded, sitting Andy on her lap as Jack and Scott and Todd finished up their platters.

She bent her head and kissed Andy's ear. "Tell Marcia what you want now," she suggested, hugging Andy tight.

178

"Uhh," he said, pointing at the plate of holiday cookies.

"What's that?" she asked.

"Uhh," he repeated, annoyed. "Uhhhhh!"

Judy set him on his feet.

"I guess Andy doesn't want any cookies," she said sorrowfully to her friend.

Andy yanked at her hand and shrieked indignantly.

"Yes, love," Judy said, looking down at him gently. "But how do I know what you want? What do you want, Andy?"

One small index finger stabbed the air, gesturing wildly toward the plate. The small mouth set belligerently.

"Judy . . ." But Marcia fell silent at the look Judy gave her.

Judy reached over calmly and took a cookie, a huge gingerbread man, all iced in white. She nibbled at the leg delicately, rubbed her stomach, said, "Mmmm, that's so good!"

Andy disappeared into the living room. Seconds later, sounds of ill temper reached the group around the dinner table. Jack sat easy, watching his wife. Scott tapped at the table top. Todd looked vaguely disgusted. Marcia took a cookie, felt unwell, replaced it.

"Judy," she tried again.

Judy smiled at her slightly. "He can say it, Marcia. He's just lazy. He can't say it very clearly, but he *can* say it. We're going to ask at CNR about speech therapy. I think he's ready. And when he really wants something, he's capable of naming it."

Marcia never had proof of it that night. Andy finished up his tantrum and fell asleep on the living room floor. But later, when Judy lifted him and kissed his head, and he woke, he stared into her face and shivered and gripped her hair and clung tight.

"M-ma?"

"What is it, lovey?" she asked.

"Wan coo-ey."

They looked into each other's eyes.

Judy smiled and hugged him, then kissed his cheek.

"Then let's go get one," she said, turning toward the kitchen, still holding him. "How can I know, until you tell me?"

He rubbed against her with delight.

Winter came and went and she was terribly cold in her old worn coat, going to work, coming back. But there was one plus to being grown up. Unlike Scott and Todd, she didn't outgrow the coat.

Tuesday, March 1, 1977

There are so many blank pages in this book. It's ridiculous to call it a diary. It's been so long since I wrote, such a long and trying time since I've had the energy or the desire though things have happened, of course, things I wish now I'd put down. All the successes in the programming. Andy crawls. And creeps. And walks. And for quite some time now, we've been forcing him to *say* what he wants. As a result, his vocabulary is increasing rapidly, though his speech isn't clear. He'll need speech therapy at some time in the near future. Up to now, he hasn't seemed ready. He's just starting to find joy in expressing himself to anybody who will stop and listen.

I have a specific reason for opening up this diary and making this entry. It's to note down a change in atmosphere. A "feeling." There's a change due for the Polikoffs. I don't know what that change is, only that it's near.

It may be Andy, finishing the programming. It's almost got to happen, so that's no revelation. And I'm a little afraid for them to say he's finally finished the programming.

Or the change may be something totally different, positive or negative—something out of left field. A new "test" for Jack and me. Something else to deal with.

But whatever it is, it's coming. With the delicate tread of an ox. Not my imagination. Real.

NAME: Andy Polikoff
BIRTHDATE: December 10, 1973
AGE: 3 years 3 months
TESTED: March 4, 1977

TESTS USED: Stanford-Binet

REASON FOR REFERRAL:
A psychological evaluation was suggested to determine Andy's intellectual development, his current level, his potential learning abilities and possible future educational needs.

TEST RESULTS:
Andy achieved a Stanford-Binet IQ of 94, which was within the low Average range. However, due to his difficulty in short-term attention, concentration, and memory skills, as well as in fine-motor, perceptual-motor coordination, and verbal expressive abilities, Andy was considered at high risk for need of special education.

18

They were sitting once again with Dr. Carr, at CNR. Jack, a working man again, had taken the morning off. It was the culmination of every update of the programming, coming here to silence and relative peace to hear a summing up of the findings. All such things had become a matter of routine.

"We—I—am very pleased."

This was not routine. Indeed, it bordered on the effusive. Judy stared at Carr, her nerves twitching.

"You know far better than I what you and Andy and your entire family have been through for the past two-and-a-half years. The initial starting up. All the new things added periodically to the program. What a tremendous effort it all took."

He sat and regarded them both—Judy and Jack—in silence for a second, then leaned forward.

"You've witnessed your son's every smallest achievement in a way that parents of normal children rarely do. Every accomplishment was noted and kept fresh and special in your minds, and these pictures will be with you forever."

Patterns. She had internalized each and every rhythm, each and every trauma. She would remember the routines, the waiting, the backsliding, the small triumphs, the big ones, as long as she lived. He was right. Of course he was right.

"We're finished."

A vast blankness filled her mind at hearing the very words she'd dreamed of over and over, sometimes with fear, for the past two-and-a-half years.

"We will, of course, continue to look after Andy. We need to see him regularly and to keep up his vitamins and some medications. But as for the programming—all those volunteers of yours—go home and give them their marching orders.

"You're free."

She was amazed that he could make such a statement. Free. She wondered if he really imagined they could ever again feel free.

"The programming has, in our opinion, taken Andy as far as it can. There would be no point in continuing it."

They took Andy home. Without a new set of exercises. And Jack went off to work, back at the brewery for the past three weeks. Judy herself had nowhere to go, having quit her own part-timing when Jack could no longer supervise the programmers.

So there she was, with Andy. She stood him up on the living room rug and sat herself down on the couch and proceeded to stare at him vaguely. He, in turn, grinned back hugely, then toddled over to put clumsy arms around her legs while she gazed at his head, then patted him.

"How about a nap?" she finally ventured.

He became interested in his shirt buttons, pulling at them appreciatively.

Judy gathered him to her heart in a crushing hug, then stood and took his hand and led him up to bed. She felt unfocused, without purpose. Two soft toys were already in the crib. She added another. Andy settled in and looked at her expectantly and she bent and kissed his head, then stroked the superfine hair and kissed him again.

The house was too empty. She wandered back downstairs and sat on the couch and studied the walls of her living room. The walls seemed overly close together, leaning in on her, she was quite sure, moving closer and closer to where she sat. The room, she felt, was growing smaller as she watched it.

She felt a small surge of hysteria and made herself sit very still, listening to the quiet. No women's voices, talking over her child's body. No hiccoughing wails from the patterning table. Andy was singing softly to himself in bed, but it was nevertheless uncharacteristically quiet. In time, the older boys would come home from school and all the ordinary things of life would commence, but for this moment there was a vacuum around her, a numb lack of acceptance.

It was spring. Again. Andy was three-and-a-half. Todd was nearly six. Scott was thirteen-plus. She herself was thirty-four, a hundred and four, a thousand and four. Jack was thirty-eight. She had no idea at all how old Jack felt.

The house was too quiet, too warmly spring, she was a young woman still and the normal things of life could begin for her again. Carr said. No more volunteers, no more roaming the streets searching for help, no more phone calls to beg the essentials of life, smiling and pretending she wasn't dying. She was free to be herself.

There was just one small problem remaining. She didn't

183

know how to admit this to Jack. Not even to herself. That she couldn't quite seem to remember: how to be Judy, or who Judy was.

She was too tired to learn about herself again. She leaned her head back on the couch cushion and closed her eyes as tears streamed down her cheeks.

Jack was indeed older. She finally understood that fully. There were lines in his face where there hadn't been, and his hair had a peppering of gray. But more than anything else, he wasn't easy to be with.

She'd watched him hungrily for what seemed like hours, ever since dinner. It was still strange, knowing Jack worked days, knowing Jack would be home beside her every night. She'd sat and listened to everything he said, no longer wanting to be remote, no longer wanting to stand alone and untouchable.

"There's nothing to worry about anymore." Jack made this blanket statement. She would, at one time, have argued about it or derided or ignored him.

Now, she sat and stared at her husband and absorbed the words, expression, tone of voice.

"We got him this far, we got the good news that we're a success, now it's time to loosen up and just live a little. You don't look for things to store up for future nightmares, Judy. You don't start thinking, 'How normal *is* he?' You don't keep wondering where we'll find his limits."

All that was exactly what she was thinking. It amazed her that Jack should know.

They were in the living room, just the two of them, the boys upstairs amusing themselves.

"We got him this far," Jack repeated thoughtfully. "And nobody can see tomorrow. We just have to wait, like with everything else, even normal things. There aren't any guarantees."

A whole new set of challenges? The programming was to stop, but there was one condition. Andy was to have a sched-

184

ule, a well set up day, and that meant nursery school, a whole roomful of kids with one teacher and Andy.

Endless possibilities.

"Try to take it easy, babe," Jack said gently, studying her tense face. "It's okay. You earned taking it a little easy."

She smiled at him tremulously and he stared at her for a second, then sighed. She watched him stand and cross to the window. She went to him then, crossing the room, and put her arms around his waist, cuddling against him.

He stared at her, astonished. Looking up, she saw the widening of his eyes and his very shock wounded her mortally. He made no immediate move to return her embrace, perhaps frozen as she herself had been so often through those months and years. After a minute, feeling foolish, she released him and wandered away upstairs.

Tired and confused, he watched her leave him.

III
THE FAMILY

19

ROBERT CARR, M.D.
Elm Square Clinic
Elm Street at Dale Road
Philadelphia, Pa.

May 17, 1977

Jewish YM and YWHA
Broad and Pine Streets
Philadelphia, Pa.

Re: Andrew Polikoff

To Whom It May Concern:

This is to advise you of the considerable medical expenditure
required of the Polikoff family for the maintenance of Andy's
health. The word "considerable" is actually modest in
describing the cost, both for professional services and extensive testing, in addition to the cost of his current medications.

Any documentation you may require in your consideration
of this family for one of your full scholarships will be gladly
provided. Do not hesitate to call on me.

Sincerely,

Robert Carr, M.D.

                              *   *   *.

The JYC—the Jewish Y's and Centers—took Andy on full
scholarship, first for summer camp, then nursery school. The
nursery school was tops, and had the added attraction of being
housed in the Center's beautiful grounds, less than a mile away.
It was a perfect, immediate solution for the problem of restruc-
turing Andy's day.

Three weeks passed between the awarding of the scholarship
and Andy's first camp day. Those weeks gave Judy unwelcome
time for all the quaking fears, the insecurities she couldn't help
feel. Andy had never been away from her. Andy might simply
refuse to go. He'd hate being away all day, pushed into a
strange new grouping of his peers. Surrounded by children for
the first time in his life. He'd be terrified.

She'd be terrified.

And the ease of his acceptance on full scholarship made her
wary. There had to be some obstacle in the offing. Her day-to-
day life had become a crawling through endless obstacles. And
when the obstacle to all this perfection did, finally, appear she
was almost relieved to stop waiting for it.

She was summoned to the office of the JYC on Andy's third
day of camp.

"We can't keep kids Andy's age if they're not completely
toilet-trained, Judy." Susan Greenbaum, the membership director, was sympathetic but definite.

Judy, sitting opposite her desk, already knew the words, all
the set phrases that had to be coming, all the ugly little digs, all
the things she'd heard echo in her heart for years, all the revolt-
ing attitudes she'd imagined or experienced for the sum of
Andy's life.

All the questions, statements, excuses.

Questions like, "Have you ever considered a *special* school
for Andy?"

Statements like, "We have only so many scholarships available, and hundreds of applicants waiting, and on further consideration we really do think that our scholarship would do more
good elsewhere."

                              190

Excuses like, "We just didn't fully understand the scope of the problem, that he's *still different,* we're just not set up to handle differences in the children."

She thought she'd schooled herself not to let anything crush her, to let nothing penetrate her fierce Midtown Hospital armor, yet she knew she'd die if any of those words were spoken in this utterly normal room.

"What with all the other kids," Susan was saying, "the counselors can't possibly worry about keeping him dry. He's such a big boy, too, for his age, that when he does wet, he wets absolutely everything! A diaper just doesn't work with kids as well-developed and active as Andy."

She really couldn't sit out the strain. Susan, a true diplomat, could probably dance around and around the point, softening the blow until she went insane.

"And?"

Susan looked perplexed. "And?" she repeated doubtfully, then her eyes widened. She pushed back her hair, tucking it determinedly behind her ears. "And," she said, "we'd really appreciate you giving some serious thought to solving this little problem. Andy's a great little kid, the counselors already love working with him, he's so enthusiastic about everything and he relates beautifully to adults, maybe because he's always had so many adults around him. And he's nice. You wouldn't believe how many angelic looking little kids can be so unnice," she smiled ruefully, then straightened and eyed Judy kindly.

"Look, Judy, anybody who could make it through what you and Jack made it through for two-and-a-half years just can't convince me they'd have any trouble finishing Andy's toilet training. He's practically trained now, he's not one bit worse than lots of little boys, we've had plenty of mothers in here and they didn't like it one bit," she grinned broadly, "just like you, but they did something about it because they knew I was right, and so can you.

"Andy gets so absorbed in whatever's going on that—well— he just forgets to go to the bathroom when he should, and then it's too late, and he has an accident. He has to learn it's important not to forget, especially since he starts nursery school soon."

Judy removed her miracle child from summer camp and took him home, and told him what had to be accomplished to win his return. The outrage on his face surprised her. Andy, snatched from his first freedom, so terrifying, so exciting, Andy, brought home in utter ignominy, understood perfectly what his mother was imparting and, to his own and his mother's intense gratification, was daytime dry for the next three days running.

Nights . . . The night wetting was nobody's business.

He was returned to camp in triumph. There was no more daytime wetting.

Summer was a soft succession of days that formed easy strings of things called weeks, and Judy felt lethargic but not unhappy. Carol stayed in touch. Carol always had. She'd programmed, of course, and taken up scores of empty slots when the going got rough, so when Carol called or dropped by, Judy drove herself to perk up because her moods seemed to worry Carol.

Phyllis came too. She wished they'd both stay home. Her friends were growing impatient, all the old friends, not just Carol and Phyllis—all the old friends wanted to welcome her back to the fold, and all these friends were exactly the same as they'd been, but she herself was not. All the small and feisty interests of her previous life were no longer remotely interesting to her. She didn't have the need or the desire to be with people. It was, in fact, a definite chore to have to be with people.

And she wisely gave herself time before trying to find work. The bills were still enormous, the back debt a horror, but she'd gauged her capacity to perform and had determined, quite rightly, that her tank had gone dry. No reserves. No obvious, easy way to refill it.

She spent hours that summer on introspection that hurt. All

her thoughts were dead-end, all her questions without answers. She'd worked so hard for so long without letup that she was deeply exhausted.

In September, Andy started nursery school, still under full scholarship at the JYC. Two days after his first class, Susan Greenbaum was back on the phone, asking Judy to come see her.

There'd been weeks and weeks of uninterrupted quiet. All of July. All of August. Hot, sybaritic, soul-steaming—the intensity of summer soothed her and relaxed some deep rigidity in her stomach. So it was that the office of the JYC seemed oddly threatening.

Andy had had a small seizure that morning, Susan informed her.

At four o'clock that afternoon, the living room was prepared for Andy's homecoming. She'd seeded the area with all his favorite toys, putting the cuddly ones on the couch, putting his blocks enticingly on the floor, sitting his puppet, Icky Roo, on the table close at hand, then settling Andy himself in the midst of all this opulence and herself flopping down beside him.

"What's up, baby?" she asked, studying him calmly.

He glanced at her, then at his cuddly Snoopy, touched nothing, stared at his legs, began kicking them.

"Want to keep it all to yourself?" Judy asked. "After all," she added, "you certainly have a right to your own privacy."

There was a tiny, flickering look of inquiry on his face at this new word—privacy.

"Privacy means keeping some things for secrets. But it's only fun to keep secrets and have privacy for happy things. When I feel really rotten about something, I don't want to have privacy. I want to talk to somebody who loves me, so they'll kiss and hug me. That way I'm not sad anymore."

Judy once? Judy gone. Not the Judy who'd avoided Jack for all the time of the programming.

Andy was staring unblinking at the far wall, too young and

193

self-absorbed to understand or even note this double standard.

She patted his cheek playfully.

"Do you like your teacher? I saw her today. I've known Jo for years and years and years. I always liked Jo. I think she's a very nice person. Do you like Jo?"

"Like Jo," he avowed, listlessly.

"Do you like your classroom? I walked down to see the pretty decorations and the mobiles hanging from the ceiling, but I didn't stop to talk to you because I didn't want to interrupt your fun. Your classroom looked so bright and nice. I was thinking I'd like to go to school in a classroom like that. Do you like your classroom?"

"Like it," Andy muttered, nervously biting his lower lip, then yanking it between his long fingers. Kick. Kick. Kick.

"Do you like the other kids?" Judy pressed on—"guessing game" said her tone. She tried to keep it like that, light and easy. "I remember when I started school—years and years and years ago, I didn't like some of the other kids at first, because I didn't know them, but later, when I knew them better, and when they knew me better, they were my friends. That made school a very very happy place to be every day."

"Not *all*," Andy said, mutinously.

"All? *All* the kids? Don't you like them all?"

"All *your* friends?" Andy asked, gazing at her with hard bright eyes.

Her mind grappled with this. "The kids when *I* went to school? No," she admitted cheerfully, "they weren't all my friends. I didn't want them all for my friends. Just the specially nice ones ended up my friends. Friends wouldn't be special if everybody was your friend."

Andy was silent.

"Is there somebody in your class who isn't your friend?"

Andy pulled and yanked and tortured his lip and she nearly reached out to restrain his hand, but stopped herself because this preoccupation at least gave him an outlet and left him sitting

194

relatively still. Without it he'd be banging around the living room. Refusing to hear a word she said.

After a bit, she picked up a squeeze toy of which he was inordinately fond and compressed it near his ear, making a hideous squawking sound with it. Then she tickled him hard in the tummy with the head of the toy. He forgot his lip, snatched it from her, squeezing it himself, then staring at it admiringly.

"Like Bobby," he finally said, when she'd despaired of him saying anything. He looked at her, squinting. "Like Amy. Nice." He rubbed the toy against his own cheek and extended it to her.

"Rub, Mommy."

Dutifully, she rubbed it against his arm, his chest, his belly button. He sat in peaceful receipt of these ministrations for a minute.

"Not Mickey," he said.

"Mickey?" his mother asked. "Why don't you like Mickey?"

Andy poked his forefinger into the soft belly of the toy, his eyes distant.

"Is Mickey mean to you? Does he hit you?"

"Hit everybody," Andy said morosely. "Kick Jo. Spit," he added with considerable relish, doing a creditable job of blowing a stream of saliva into her face.

"He's just a mean little boy, then," Judy said, relieved, surreptitiously rubbing at her cheek. "Pretend he isn't there."

Andy looked at her, surprised.

"*Is* there," he told her, disgusted by her stupidity. "Spill juice in my hair," he added disconsolately. "Jo wash it."

Judy received this confidence in silence.

"Say diaper," Andy added mysteriously.

His mother studied his averted face thoughtfully.

"Did Mickey come into the bathroom one day during camp when you still wore diapers?"

The child made a gesture resembling a shrug, then looked at her out of the corner of one eye. She sighed, tried to think up a

195

neat solution, turned to him hopefully.

"Don't you think you could show him you don't wear diapers anymore?"

But Andy was down on the floor, examining his building blocks, and didn't answer.

She sat back, thinking she'd have to talk to Jo. This was not what she'd expected when they'd told her of the seizure, that Andy would react in this fashion to a classmate. She hadn't known Andy was developing sore spots. Connections. Sensitivities. Subtle sensations for which he hadn't been programmed.

ROBERT CARR, M.D.
Elm Square Clinic
Elm Street at Dale Road
Philadelphia, Pa.

September 20, 1977

Jewish YM and YWHA
Riverside Branch
Philadelphia, Pa.

Re: Andy Polikoff

To Whom It May Concern:

The above-named patient has a history of convulsive seizures and is maintained on anti-convulsant medications for their control. Please administer Andy's medications to him as prescribed, and if there are any questions, do not hesitate to call me.

Yours truly,

Robert Carr, M.D.

20

Andy was nearing his fourth birthday, attending a normal private nursery from nine to four, like other four-year-old children with working mothers.

Judy had taken a new part-time restaurant job near the house, tiring, finally, of her self-imposed inactivity—a good sign overall. Now she had her own routine, like everyone else in the family, to carry her through the days until she met up with the real Judy. She didn't have the slightest idea where to go or what to do to discover this identity.

All the gentle, silly, spontaneous things that had once characterized her were missing from her personality. She envisioned a gaping hole there, a wind tunnel. All her easy relationships had vanished into a void. All the kindness she'd naturally felt toward the human species was a little contrived now. She smiled and laughed and said nice things but as an onlooker, watching her own performance, not wanting to hurt or offend anybody.

She didn't *like* any of the people she knew, not even the ones she loved. She was caustic enough and honest enough to suspect this was because she didn't like herself. She'd lost touch with whatever it was she and Jack shared that made them close before her test: Andy's birth.

Scott was bar mitzvahed in January in a small ceremony. That meant Scott was a man. The thought made her laugh. She'd sat on the bed and laughed and cried, with the tears falling into her lap, and Jack had looked gentle, then a little afraid, then a little annoyed because after all—what could Jack say?

Scott was a man because he'd turned thirteen. Scott, who'd reached adolescence when Andy was born. Who'd been a teenager when Andy was diagnosed. Who'd been a young adult when Andy was programmed. Who'd been middle-aged ever since. Scott was really a very old man, if you considered all this.

And Todd? Todd was six. A baby and not a baby. That was all she knew about Todd—that she didn't know Todd.

Tell me all you know about this individual, Mrs. Polikoff. This one—Todd? He's six.

He's six? That's it? The whole bit? Sorry, lady, my mistake, I thought you were his mother.

And Jack? Jack was feeling better, it was true, he'd lost that pinched, frightening look, but the trauma of the years was stamped in shadows on his face and there was a grim solidity still about the barrier she herself had raised. She couldn't seem to break it down. She couldn't seem to kick it out of place. She couldn't climb over it, dig under it, move around it—it was sturdy, well-built, a monument. Now, when she needed to be warmed and loved, when she needed reassurance of a normal life after limbo, now, when her needs were alive and deep, Jack had gone and appropriated the very shell she'd discarded herself after so many years alone.

She decided in autumn that her family was a mess, and in need of a new focus. They were a disaster area, crawling with open wounds around the old bloody arena of the house. What they needed was something innocuous and new, something funny, perhaps joyous, and unrelated to the past. If she couldn't heal the wounds of the family overnight, she could at least bring rollicking warmth into these rooms.

And Andy's birthday was coming, the perfect time— warmth and love and Andy's birthday and Candy.

She'd been thinking of Candy again. Todd's long-lost German shepherd. The immediate and obvious cause for this remembering was her neighbor's new litter of collie puppies. She kept her little plan secret until dinner.

"I've been thinking about a little surprise," she said at the table as the family began eating. "And I thought we'd all go around to Helen Jacob's house for a few minutes tonight so I can show you something."

She felt absurdly excited, clasping her hands tight in her lap and watching their faces expectantly.

Jack looked wary, which made her smile. Scott groaned for no apparent reason, but then Scott seemed to be at the age where he groaned over everything. Todd was silent, watching his mother from under a brooding brow. Andy exhibited a total lack of interest, playing happily with his food and getting more on his face and hands than in his mouth.

"Helen has something special to show us," Judy said brightly, though a bit damped by this wholesale lack of interest.

Andy glanced up, squashed carrot on his cheek.

"Her collie just had a litter of beautiful puppies."

The appalled silence that greeted this announcement was so profound it left her momentarily shaken. She looked doubtfully around the table, at her offspring, at her husband.

"S-so I thought," she stuttered, more than a little hurt, "I thought we could go see what the pups look like, and if they're really as cute as she says they are, maybe, just maybe, we could bring one home when it's old enough."

The silence deepened. Jack was frowning. Jack was thinking, she knew, about the added expense of a dog, but she'd already considered that. There weren't many extras she took in stride, let alone seriously contemplated, but Jack was working and so was she and the bills were being paid, if slowly. And a puppy wasn't exactly a fur coat. Or a trip to the Bahamas. Or a party for fifty people. Or a standing rib roast every few weeks, either.

"Puppy?" Andy finally tuned in.

"A dog?" Scott sounded disgusted.

It was Todd, though, who was staring at her intently. His eyes were glittering, so odd in their stare that she thought for a moment, before she knew better, that it was rapture she saw there. Then she knew she wouldn't recognize joy on the face of this child. She didn't know Todd well enough to understand the nuances of his expressions or the subtleties of his character. What she did know, suddenly, vividly, was that this gift must *not* be for Andy.

She smiled at Todd, on her left, and reached out to squeeze his hand.

"You'll be the one to pick out the puppy," she said softly.

Todd watched her, silent, not returning her smile, his hand limp under hers, not returning her clasp. Judy's discomfort grew. She moved her hand away and returned to her dinner, avoiding Jack's eyes now, avoiding them all. When she finally dared look up again, Jack was finishing his dinner; Scott was pushing his vegetables around his plate; Andy was mushing everything together with his spoon and muttering incomprehensibly. And Todd still sat staring, his eyes shadowy pools, his mouth drawn out in a thin line. All the natural expression of a guileless face was gone—replaced by a complex maturity. She gazed into his wide-set eyes and felt a vast, debilitating shock.

Todd was laughing at her.

Her appetite was quite gone. She stood and began clearing the table.

The puppies gamboled around their bored mother. There were four of them, four gawky bundles with outsize feet and snuffling noses. One had its head buried in the bend of its mother's hind leg; another tried in vain to suck. The remaining two did stunts on the heavy, crumpled newspapers covering the kitchen floor.

Todd stared at the litter, then turned and went home alone, and it was Andy, tumbling down, squealing with excitement, who was overrun by stampeding paws and licking tongues.

The clumsiest pup, the one that kept falling over its front feet onto its face, the one that grinned broadly with an amiable stupid look from head to tail, the most active pup chose them for best friends. It was Andy's biggest thrill in the following weeks to go visit this rapidly growing menace and hold it, kiss it, hug it. When the puppy was finally old enough to bring home, he followed it around, watching Judy feed it, train it— Todd's lack of enthusiasm was more than compensated for by Andy's total devotion.

Scott remained remote and amused. Jack, who loved animals almost as much as he loved children, forgot his early reservations and rolled wrestling around the floor, to the delight of his youngest child and of his wife, and to the cool contempt of his oldest son.

Only Todd was not around to be impressed or unimpressed. Todd absented himself from the start. So that the coming of the collie, which was meant as a family focus, in reality meant that they all saw even less of Todd.

And in the end, it was no contest. Jack was playmate, big toy, sometimes walker, and all-around good sport, but Andy was the constant adorer. The pup became Andy's dog.

Scott pulled a favored blue sweatshirt over his head while the collie sat watching on his bedspread. The house was quiet. When Scott turned, straightening the sleeves, he saw Todd eyeing him from the doorway. He hadn't heard Todd come home or sneak up on him.

There was an uncomfortable little silence.

"Mom wouldn't like it much, messing up your bed," Todd finally remarked, then vanished.

This was undeniably true, but it got Scott's back up anyway. "Todd!"

Todd ignored the summons. They were alone in the house. Andy's car pool would deliver him in the next fifteen or twenty minutes, with their mother arriving at almost the same second.

Scott thrust the demanding puppy off his bed and strode out into the hall to Todd's doorway. Todd, to his surprise, was neither changing his clothes nor punching the walls, but was sitting on the edge of his bed, morose, staring at nothing. The dog followed Scott to the threshold, then wisely stopped. Todd's bedroom was off limits and when Andy wasn't home, this was definitely Todd's bedroom.

"What do you want?" Todd asked peevishly.

There was nothing Scott wanted except, perhaps, to find out what was bugging Todd. But it was a difficult business asking these things, sticking your nose where it wasn't wanted. The collie licked his hand and he petted the narrow head absently,

201

and Todd's eyes narrowed to venal slits at this minimal display of affection between man and beast.

"You could at least try to like the dog," Scott was annoyed. "I mean, why shouldn't you? It's a nice enough dog. If you gave it half a chance, it would be all over you. Mom meant it to be yours," he added accusingly.

Todd laughed and jerked his head toward Andy's bed. "She bought it for him. Don't try and fool me. It's bad enough everybody else lies to me!" He looked with loathing at the dog.

Scott had been trying for months to evaluate his sibling. Todd was too old for his age, with an aggressive personality and an attitude to match. Scott knew full well where Todd had learned the attitude, not that he took full credit by any means. Todd's friends weren't exactly a bunch of hothouse orchids.

"You had a dog of your own," Scott reminded him with some vague thought of establishing a common ground. "Candy. Don't you remember?"

It was a remarkably stupid thing to say, which he realized seconds later. Todd's too-cool eyes regarded him with a sneering sort of triumph.

"Yeah. I had a dog of my own. I remember." He laughed harshly and it was like having somebody spit in your face. "He was pretty, too," Todd admitted, as if he were doing Scott a favor. "Prettier than that!" This with a head jerk at the grinning collie in his doorway.

"He was pretty," Scott unwisely argued the point out of a sense of fairness. "I don't know if he was prettier. I don't think he *could* have been prettier."

"Of course not," Todd said caustically.

Scott's jeans seemed to interest the restless dog, which proceeded to do dog things, snuffling loudly and with a snorting huffing enthusiasm that made Todd look nauseated.

"Candy." He seemed to gag on the name. "It was Mommy who named him Candy," he stared at Andy's collie, his mouth grim. "Because when she was little she had a shepherd named Candy. But it was my dog and I should have named it myself.

She didn't care how stupid it made the dog feel, having a name like Candy."

What was stupid, remarkably stupid, was for Todd to be getting so worked up like this. It was possibly even crazy—Scott considered that coldly. Coming unglued over a stupid long-gone dog. Going ape over a name like Candy. It made Scott watchful and very wary.

"It was a boy dog," Todd continued. "It should have had a name like Spike." This with, perhaps, some measure of justification.

Scott absorbed this in silence, then pushed the collie away from his leg. The pup, appropriately christened Rocky by none other than Andy, yelped in outrage, then danced into the hall and tumbled in riotous good cheer down the steps to the living room.

Todd was picking viciously at a loose thread on his jacket, not looking at Scott.

"You were just a baby when we got Candy. You were too little to name him yourself."

Todd ignored this. "They had him killed," he said, his voice shrill. "They had him killed so he wouldn't eat Andy!"

It had the effect of shaking Scott totally out of his normal thirteen-year-old composure. He stared, shocked, at his brother.

For a moment or two, he didn't know whether to laugh or not. Then he decided not, definitely.

It was Todd, watching *him,* who laughed nastily.

"That's right," he commended the older boy, "pretend they didn't."

He stood then, shrugged out of his jacket, and tossed it onto the bed his parents had recently bought when Andy kicked his way out of the crib permanently. Their mother hated it, he knew, when he tossed his clothes on Andy's bed, so the jacket would still be there when she got home from work. He wondered if she'd say something this time, or just let it slide the way she'd taken to doing lately.

203

"They didn't have Candy killed, Todd," Scott felt impelled to point out. "They just figured they'd better give him away, because of all the volunteers coming in and out. He was a German shepherd, Todd, and shepherds are watchdogs—they'll take out your tonsils if you look at them funny. He'd have gone nuts having to watch all those people around and him not allowed to chew on any legs."

Todd was neither amused nor convinced.

"It had nothing to do with the volunteers," he informed his older brother angrily. "They got rid of Candy before the volunteers. They took one look at Andy when Andy was born and came home and got rid of Candy, so Candy wouldn't take one look at Andy and chew *him* up!"

It was close enough to the truth to keep Scott silent. Scott, who'd been ten at the time, knew it for a fact—it was a precaution, not a reaction to an actual problem. He remembered quite clearly, he could even see himself squeezing out some tears, watching them leave the dog at Pediatric where one of the nurses had agreed to take it. He'd felt little personal loss, suspecting he was crying only because he ought to feel something and not because he cared very much about this puppy that wasn't even his. It was Todd's dog. Scott had never personally had the least desire for one.

So maybe it was inevitable for Todd to feel nothing for Andy's dog. Except that Todd did feel something: He loathed Andy's dog. And Todd should not have harbored grim memories. Todd shouldn't even have been able to evaluate the loss of the shepherd, or relate it in any way to Andy. He'd been a baby, for heaven's sake, when they got rid of Candy.

It made Todd a continuing surprise, which wasn't really pleasant, not when you had to live with him. Scott, having isolated himself inside his own grievances for the past two years, had the adult suspicion there'd be trouble with Todd.

It made him uncomfortable, but it interested him too. He went downstairs to wait for Andy's car pool.

21

It was the first renewal of the holidays in a normal setting—an aching, strangely nostalgic December, as though they'd been years away, and not with one another. There were no frantic hour breaks this year from an unrelenting round of programming. No strangers bearing gifts. No outside limits placed on the interaction of the family. No acts of charity either.

Their giving to each other was tentative. They'd forgotten this special knack of unselfconscious giving. The gifts themselves were small and inexpensive, which didn't matter, a nice little pile of gifts, really, and the very acts of purchasing, wrapping, exchanging were oddly difficult, emotionally embarrassing and fraught with fear.

January came and brought the midwinter doldrums, which Judy had expected in this drifting time, devoid of great distinguishable landmarks. They'd grown so used to the strict rhythms of the programming that normal life seemed undemanding by comparison. And unreal. There was no reality without trauma.

Andy was still in nursery school from nine to four, and Todd and Scott had their own expanding schedules. Jack worked a normal day and looked more relaxed if not happier, and Judy—she worked her own odd hours as cook, as babysitter, as anything else she could find to raise some extra money and still preserve the illusion of freedom from the type of rigid scheduling that ruled the programming hours.

But it all boiled down to a single truth, a single inescapable condition. It was imitation of life, existence inside a blinding shroud, because of one irksome reality: the possibility of a trial.

"We have to wait. More waiting," Judy told Jack. They were

in their bedroom and the house was quiet. "If I've learned anything I've learned that. Things have to happen in the right sequence, or everything falls apart. We've come so far. . . ."

But she really couldn't bear to contemplate the long road past. "I really think we have to see what happens when it's time for Andy to enter public school."

Jack looked at her. "Why?" he finally asked.

"*I* have to know," Judy whispered. "How they rank him against the other kids his age. How they compare him." She swallowed. "If they'll put him in a normal grouping, in a normal classroom, in a normal school."

"He's in school now," Jack said quietly.

"I'm talking about real school, not nursery. Because we really don't know, do we? If he'll start showing signs of learning disabilities?" Her voice was tight. She felt ill, contemplating it.

"Another year," Jack said.

Judy turned and looked at him. "Another year," she agreed. "At least that." She stared at her own hands, clasped in her lap, then lifted her head and straightened her back. "He's so beautiful, isn't he? We've worked and worked to make him well. And yet, all along, look what we've been building. Past proof in his records and in the opinions of his doctors. Carr's well respected, an eminent doctor. The proof of Carr's evaluations at Pediatric and at Midtown and at CNR, the *fact* of Andy's programming and the five hundred volunteers, the bills, the continuing debt . . ." she paused for breath.

"Patterns," she sighed. "We've been building a pattern for all these years to prove an abnormality.

"So I think we have to wait. To see him out in the real world. Out there, where real people compete. With other kids his age, in the first competitive setting we all have to experience."

Tears grayed her eyes and she trembled with tiredness. "Real school!"

22

"Mommy?"

She turned too quickly, a nervous reaction she hadn't yet mastered whenever she heard the voice of her youngest child.

Andy stood in the kitchen doorway, staring at her.

"Am I still brain-damaged, Mommy?"

The juices of the raw chicken leg she was clasping dripped unnoticed while her mind did a skitter. It had happened before, when Scott hit her up for a best-loved-son rating during programming. She'd managed an answer then. This time there was no happy inspiration.

"Who said you were brain-damaged?" she fought for time, making her tone easy and curious, despite Andy's fierce scowl.

"Bobby."

Bobby Walker, whose mother had helped with the programming.

"Why would Bobby say such a thing?"

"He said I couldn't play with him and Pat because I'm brain-damaged," Andy announced flatly, his words rushing together, becoming nearly incomprehensible as they always did when he was upset.

"Am I?" He glared at her.

She dropped the chicken leg onto a plate and washed her hands carefully, each finger, each fingernail, and he came to stand beside her, tugging at her pants leg.

"Am I?"

There was no diverting Andy. Andy, more than either of her older children, would dog her remorselessly, asking the same questions, over and over and over, with no visible sign of tiredness or boredom. Night could fall and seasons could change, but Andy would be there, waiting and prodding, until she gave him an answer.

She dried her hands and bent, putting an arm around his sturdy shoulders, marveling at how he'd grown, at how beautiful he was, with awareness in every line of his face. The intelligence to want to know.

In that second she made the irrevocable admission to herself that Jack, with his calm steadiness, could handle some things, things like this, better than she could.

"I'll tell you what. This is a very important thing you want to know. I think this is the time for your very first man-to-man talk with Daddy."

Andy looked suitably impressed and she felt a rueful tugging at her heart, an intolerable sense of letting go.

"Okay then?" she asked, and the anguish abruptly eased. She could not raise Andy by herself. She didn't want to raise Andy by herself. "We'll wait until Daddy gets home?"

"But am I?" Andy asked.

She merely grinned at him. "Man-to-man?" she asked again. "Like Scott and Todd?"

He sighed, very theatrical, carbon copy of his big brothers. "Okay."

But his tone informed her she was being less than reasonable. He needed an answer. He needed to *know*.

So it was that Jack came home, tired, desirous of peace, to find himself faced with this less than delicious treat from his adoring wife, who at least had the grace to smile in weak apology. He took their youngest son up to the master bedroom before dinner for a heart-to-heart man-to-man talk.

"Mommy tells me you had a fight with Bobby Walker today." He sat on the side of the bed and Andy came to stand before him, between his legs.

Andy shook his dark head.

"You didn't? Then Mommy must have misunderstood you."

"We didn't have no fight," Andy said slowly. "He just said I was brain-damaged. Am I?" There was a narrowing intensity to his stare, and Jack met it as frankly as possible.

"Did Bobby tell you what brain-damaged means?"

The child considered this, then lifted a corner of the blanket in both hands and began to stroke it. Finally, he shook his head.

"Do you know what brain-damaged means, son?" Jack asked.

Longer pause this time. Then another shake of the head.

Jack sighed, then was immediately sorry, for Andy looked up swiftly, far more quickly than he normally reacted, with worry twisting his young mouth. Jack put a hand on his son's shoulder and looked directly into his eyes.

"Brain-damaged is when something happens to part of your brain. Here," he tapped his own skull. "Inside your head. It's like if you banged your elbow and got a scrape, or bloodied up your knee when you're playing outside."

Andy was listening intently.

"It's a boo-boo on your brain," Jack added, feeling absurd, but Andy's shoulders relaxed and he looked vastly interested in such a phenomenon.

"Did Mommy paint it?" he asked.

Jack grinned slightly, then shook his head. "Mommy would have loved to clean it all up and draw a beautiful Mercurochrome picture on it, son," he said. "You know how great Mommy paints those pictures."

Andy nodded excitedly.

"But she couldn't do that because it's all dark and invisible in there," he tapped Andy's head this time, "and you wouldn't be able to see the picture no matter how bright and pretty Mommy painted it."

Andy looked perplexed.

"So Mommy and Daddy took you to the doctor to ask him what to do . . ."

"Dr. Carr," said Andy helpfully.

"Dr. Carr," Jack agreed.

"I like Dr. Carr," said Andy.

"And Dr. Carr told Mommy and Daddy how to take good care of that boo-boo so it would go away, even though we couldn't use Mercurochrome pictures or even Band-Aids."

"Then it did go away," Andy picked up too quickly. It left Jack off-target and nonplussed. Andy sensed his father's discomfort as sharply as he'd felt pain that long-ago night, no part of his conscious memory, on the living room floor with his leg in Jack's grip. His face stiffened and Jack heard the labored sound of his breath in the silence of the room.

"Things that hurt your brain are invisible, son," Jack faltered. "You remember, I just told you that's why Mommy couldn't paint the boo-boo inside your head? And when something's invisible you can't actually *look* to see if it goes away or not. But if it doesn't cause any problems, if you don't even know if it's there anymore . . ."

But it was lame, he'd lost the whole thrust of his speech, and he was rapidly losing Andy. Andy's eyes were taking on a distant, blank glare.

"Nobody worries about it, though," Jack said swiftly, too loudly, grinning cheerfully and feeling the stiffness of the grin crack his face. He tickled his son hard in the tummy. "After all, everybody's brain-damaged."

He held his breath after saying it.

Andy took in this startling pronouncement, pondered it, absorbed it, debated it, perhaps rejected it. The blanket began to take on accordion pleats—no small accomplishment for so thick a material—and Jack forced himself not to babble on, not to over-explain, to just wait for another question.

Andy finally raised his head to look into his father's face.

"Everybody? Not just me?"

Jack feigned great surprise. "Just you? Of course not! You thought it was just you? Is that what that silly Bobby thinks?"

Andy giggled.

"Everybody has some kind of boo-boo up there," Jack said. "Brain cells get hurt from lots of things in all kinds of people . . ."

210

But Andy had lost interest and Jack wisely dropped the matter. The major panic of being different from everyone else had been, for the moment, allayed for his child, and though he had the suspicion Andy wasn't fully convinced, at least the worst of the fear, the worst of the tension, had passed. He put his arms around his son, giving him the great, crushing hug he loved, and Rocky heard the resulting commotion from the bedroom and came hurtling in protectively through the half-closed door. That was how Judy found them when dinner was ready, horsing around on her carefully made up bed, Andy and Jack and the collie too, in an indeterminate pile of rolling, barking, squealing love.

The fourth weekend in July was the annual Friends' Picnic. That's how they referred to it, among themselves, for all the years they'd held it. Bill Kramer remarked every single July that it sounded like a Quaker outing, though none of them were Quakers, but the Friends' Picnic was its name. The Polikoffs went along that year for the first time since Andy's conception.

The day was soft, not overly hot, with a storybook fresh green breeze. The sun was lemon through scudding clouds straight out of children's dreams. Judy felt nearly happy, nostalgic and maudlin—at peace. The dark shade of an old oak protected her head, and her back was pressed to the gnarled bark. Her friends lay sprawled all around, gossiping, the gossip the same through all that time, like a soap opera you could miss for months without missing any single element of plot. The names might change but the situations were static, and that too had a quality of unreality.

It wasn't until mid-afternoon that she started to wish she was home, safe, instead of outside, in a place without walls, in full view of everyone, watching and being watched . . .

There was softball and badminton, and game after game of wild volleyball. There were immense, obscene piles of food—it was sinful to waste so much, not that she'd ever before had qualms about waste at the Friends' Picnic. Judy, who wasn't

211

that Judy, and who couldn't find a new Judy to fill in for her, experienced all the old, taken-for-granted things distorted and discolored by different values gleaned through hard, hard years.

Everyone brought something, not just the regular picnic fare; among the surfeit of potato salad and chips and pretzels were the rarities that appeared year after year. Lobster salad. That was from Jean. A fresh fruit aspic that somehow survived the rigors of travel every year. A veal, chicken, and nut casserole from Karen, which disappeared with instant gorging, and which every other woman present would have given her own best recipe to learn to prepare. A cold apple/apricot/peach dessert baked under a cinnamon/brown sugar crumb topping that sat alongside the more traditional chocolate cake and cookies in every shape, flavor . . .

The last softball game of the day was underway. Judy sat with her paper plate on her lap and leaned her head against the tree trunk and closed her eyes, swallowing a nervous sickness, the very same sense of unwellness of the programming years.

In the meadow the game continued overlong—this due to Andy's turn at bat, which never seemed to end at all. Judy opened her eyes cautiously, then sat up straight, putting her plate carefully on the ground. As the ball looped toward Andy her throat went into spasm. Everyone was watching now, waiting, patient, cheering him on, urging him to hit it, to hit it, hit it, that's right, swing, just swing, hit it, and what she'd eaten for lunch congealed in her throat. She couldn't breathe, couldn't swallow, couldn't think, couldn't look away, or just get up and flee.

Sudden cheers bordering on hysteria brought her lurching to her feet as bat met ball—smack! Andy was lifted on Herb Stein's shoulders with all the rest of the men and boys crowding around in a cheering pack. A little parade around the field. She saw her youngest child's flushed face, it was ghastly, she didn't know why it was ghastly, she felt as if she might faint.

But there was more. There was a ceremony and a winner's

ribbon, laid out in a pretty little box on tissue paper the color of a fire engine truck, the ribbon itself cut from bright blue cloth edged with sparkly gold, shaped into a huge star. All preplanned, before the picnic, to stay until August if necessary, to find merit in Andy, to give Andy an award.

Judy was totally silent as they started the long ride home. Andy, on the other hand, was overexcited, nearly gibbering—a bad sign. There'd be interminable bedwetting—there always was wetting at night, especially when he was this excited. She pushed the thought from her numb mind. The ribbon ceremony had frightened and exhausted her. All their smiling faces, their opulent praise, their honest loving had rocked her world out of focus and snatched normalcy from her, launching her straight back into the nightmare anguish of Andy's diagnosis, of the decision to enter the programming, of the fact of the programming itself.

Rewarding a subnormal display. Expecting nothing better than a subnormal display.

Andy, in the middle of the back seat, babbled on madly about his prize. Scott sat silent behind Judy, Todd behind Jack. She felt danger at her back and knew it came from Todd.

Country roads wound inexorably in the fading light as the air cooled and the fragrance of some unknown night flower permeated the car. Judy stretched to relieve the tension. Her legs felt cramped and nearly rigid, and she rubbed her back against the back of the seat and tried to come up with something cheery to say to lighten the atmosphere.

Scott should have helped. She considered this bitterly. She didn't understand Scott, lounging there for all the world like nothing was the matter with Todd. When it was so obvious something was very wrong with Todd.

She had to think of something to say to make Andy be quiet. "Shut up!"

It was so much an extension of her own last thought that she

213

jerked around astonished when she heard Todd's commanding voice. Andy continued to babble, totally oblivious to his brothers on either side.

"I said shut up!" Todd repeated, a near shout this time, turning on his younger brother and pinching him viciously on the upper arm.

Andy yowled. Scott turned to stare at Todd. Judy half rose in her seat, facing back. Jack didn't turn or look, but merely spoke conversationally over the sounds of Andy's slowly decreasing wails.

"What's up, Todd?"

"Up?" Todd asked, then laughed theatrically. It was the family confrontation scene, heavy with danger and sarcasm. "Up?" he repeated more loudly. "What would be 'up'?"

The silence that predictably followed such a question was thick and uneasy. It forced Todd to carry the ball himself.

"I mean, I'm lucky, right?"

Judy opened her mouth indignantly, saw Jack's expression from the corner of her eye, shut her mouth and waited. Jack's voice was calm and stolid.

"I certainly think so."

Todd laughed again, but he'd lost the fine tuning, this was a child's rebellion, nothing more, and as such, almost pitiful.

"Just cut it out and sit back and be quiet," Scott admonished him.

Todd turned to glare at the older boy grimly. Scott's dark head rested lightly against the back of the seat, his eyes were half-closed.

"Sure," Todd sneered at his idol, "be quiet. What do you care, anyway? You're the original big deal now, aren't you, Scott? Hot-shot captain of the baseball team, superstar of everything. What do you have to complain about?"

He fell silent then, nursing his many grievances.

"And what exactly do you have to complain about, son?" Jack asked.

Todd's face flushed alarmingly. "Awards," he said succinctly.

Andy was still stroking his ribbon, still apparently oblivious to his own role in this scene. Judy, glancing back at him apprehensively, saw the tightness of his legs, held together rigidly from ankle to knee, and knew he was not oblivious to anything.

"You think you *deserve* that thing?" Todd shrieked at the younger boy, jabbing an offensive finger at the cherished ribbon. Andy moved with astonishing speed, clutching his prize to his stomach in a protective gesture as if Todd might tear it from him forcibly.

Judy sat trapped in the front seat, beaten down by a hollow thudding of her heart.

"You know why they really gave it to you, don't you?" she heard Todd continue, and without conscious thought, she lunged over and delivered a resounding slap in the mouth to her middle child to silence him.

Suddenly, there was a remarkable absence of sound in the car, then Jack shattered it as he drove over a creaking wooden bridge. Judy faced front, shaking, trying to steady her hands, keeping her eyes fixed to the road ahead, shutting out everything.

The sound of harsh breathing reached her from the back of the car. It might have been Todd. It might have been Andy. It was not Scott, who stayed as he was, slouched lazily in his corner, watching this family scenario through lowered lids, speculating.

When Jack entered their bedroom, Judy straightened, all pretense of reading a magazine abandoned. Across the hall, Todd went silently to bed.

"Well?" Judy prodded.

Jack shrugged. He'd had a talk with Todd. The talk resulted, as he suspected, in nothing. It left Todd with the impression he'd been unfairly berated, which perhaps was true, depending on how you looked at it. And it had already produced in Jack a feeling of inadequacy.

"Well, what?" he asked shortly, dropping down on his own side of the bed, then leaning over his shoes.

She scowled at his back. "Well, what?" she aped him. "What did you say to him? What did *he* say to *you* to excuse his behavior?"

Jack shrugged again. "He's understandably upset at Andy getting praise for something he knows very well he himself did better than Andy. They're not all that far apart in age, and he seems to see Andy as an equal who shouldn't be constantly treated with kid gloves and an extra dose of everything."

"I don't believe Todd sees Andy as his equal," Judy said flatly.

Jack didn't argue. He didn't see it that way either.

Judy sat there for a long minute, then rose and walked to the window.

"So now," she said, "along with everything else, we have to go through a good 'hate' with Todd. Todd's decided to compete with Andy, even though, everything else being equal, Andy would still be too young to compete with him. And he's made up his mind he'll hate Andy for whatever Andy might get that's special, from people who don't know how to be nice about Andy without also being stupid. That's the gist of it?"

That was the gist of it, but Jack felt it prudent to tread softly. "He doesn't hate Andy."

Judy laughed with utter disbelief and faced her husband squarely. "Sure he does," she corrected him, "and you know it as well as I do. And why on earth wouldn't he hate Andy, he must have resented Andy from the start, he must have lived a lonely nightmare we knew nothing about because he wasn't a screamer, he didn't carry on for attention, he just held it all in, building it all up so that now he can act really cracked!"

She went to the door, glanced over at Todd and Andy's bedroom, shut the door and returned, lowering her voice.

"And then, that stupid, *degrading* ribbon!"

Jack looked at her, then took his pajama pants from the drawer and began undressing.

"They meant well," he finally said. "They wanted to make Andy really belong. They wanted to do something special to show they love him."

But it was a limp remark and somehow offensive and she didn't bother to answer.

Jack, who really would have preferred not to belabor this point, nevertheless knew that Judy would agonize over it. And because he remembered all too clearly the silent years between them, he had no intention of just abandoning her now to her own guilt and remorse.

"There was nothing else we could do when we were programming, Judy, so don't start thinking we could have been one iota better than we were, because we couldn't! It took everything—*everything*—to be exactly what we were!"

She glared at him, hard and suspicious. "Sometimes I think if I hear that old line once more from you or anybody else I'll have a screaming fit. How do we know we couldn't have done better? We were warned of all the potential problems beforehand, weren't we? Why didn't we watch for them more closely? How did Scott and Todd get to be invisible? What happened to the family?"

Jack grinned suddenly, disconcerting her.

"What happened was that we're all still here, together," he reminded her. "You want to talk miracles? Don't you remember some of your friends from Midtown and the horror stories they told you about their own families?"

Stories she'd finally shared with him, just to start talking again in the weeks and months of relative peace following the end of programming, trying to draw close again, to rid the house of a sense of old secrets.

"We're all together and nobody's in jail and nobody's even mental," Jack said. "We did the best we could in an impossible situation and we pulled through, as a unit. We made something out of Andy, and if we don't know yet how much we accomplished, we do at least know we made the right choice in going with the programming. Because if we hadn't done any of that, if we hadn't gone through that experience," she saw a shadow cross his face, "if we'd sat back and just waited, what do you think we'd all be like now, having spent those years watching and praying and dying a little, leaving Andy to become something all by himself? Then again, maybe not becoming anything at all by himself. And starting to wonder now, pretty late, where to go to *do* something to help him."

She absorbed all this in hungry silence, knowing it to be true, but needing to hear it from Jack anyway. She watched him while he talked, her husband, this man who'd turned out to be so different than she'd expected, so much deeper, with so many sides to his nature. He was still standing there, naked to the waist, and she thought it would be nice, so nice, to run her hands over his bare chest. To feel the smooth skin, the hard muscle of his shoulders. To feel his strong hands on her breasts. Her nipples hardened just thinking it.

She stared at her husband, fully, sensually, for the first time in longer than she could remember, at his eyes, his mouth, remembering the feel of his hungry mouth, and a tickling ache spread between her legs, astonishing her.

But Jack was looking at her as he always looked at her now. Like a friend. Like her brother looked at her. Who wanted to share a bed with a live-in, roommate brother? She didn't know how to tell him this. How to tell him anything.

"We'll get Todd fixed up," Jack was saying, smiling slightly, putting more confidence into the words than he secretly felt. "We'll make him see we love him for himself."

Judy, hotly frustrated over this naiveté on Jack's part, retreated to her side of the bed. Jack began searching for a pajama top. She watched the line of his back, studied the shape of his head. She began to feel very sorry for herself.

"I'm the one Todd should hate," she said plaintively. "Not Andy."

Jack turned and stared at her, then laughed. "You really can be a little idiot!" he said kindly.

They lay not touching that night, as on all the other nights, the act of love still in hiding. And her mind refused sleep with her body so treacherously aware of Jack's hard length, so close . . . She didn't know why she couldn't just turn, reach out a hand, touch him, whisper . . .

"Jack?" Her hand brushed his shoulder.

He turned instantly toward her.

On a blanket of dark silence, she felt sudden terror, ridiculous fear that he'd reject her if she made the first move. She didn't think she could live if he rejected her. She took her hand away.

"I don't know what to do, Jack. About Todd."

He lay still for so long that her heart nearly burst. She'd heard the desperation in her own voice but was sure he would not correctly interpret it. Then, Jack seemed to relax on his pillow. Perhaps she imagined that he was disappointed, hideously disappointed, because when he spoke his voice was calm and impersonal.

"There's nothing to do, Judy. Todd's growing up. He's not showing a side to his personality that's great to see, but he's bitter, and so what? That's natural enough, isn't it, and anyway, lots of kids are bitter about one thing or another. What he needs is a change in his life. Not just the disappearance of the volunteers and less obvious attention to Andy, but more of everything for himself. The right kinds of everything for himself. From both of us."

"You think I neglect him?" Judy asked, the heat of her aborted passion filtering swiftly down to weepy depression. She felt the smarting tears in her eyes and hoped they weren't evident in the tone of her voice.

"No, Judy," Jack said hoarsely. "You never ignore or neglect the kids. But Todd didn't get a chance at the kind of single-

219

focus mothering Scott got when he was little. Scott was an only child, and of course, there weren't all those extra problems. And maybe Todd just happens to be the kind of kid who needs more than a normal amount of attention anyway. You'll figure it all out when you set your mind to it. Instinct," he added lightly.

That made her smile in the dark, though her eyes were still cloudy with unshed tears. Jack talking about instinct! It was possible he finally believed in it, now, after all this business over Andy.

She was bitterly depressed. She felt crawly. Beside her, her husband turned on his side, his back to her softness, clenching his teeth and staring grimly into the dark. He'd only imagined the longing in her touch. He imagined so much.

Together, apart, they slept.

She called John Unruh and told him about the picnic and its aftermath.

"They won't let Andy be normal."

"He's not normal."

"*You* say that to me? You can *see* he's normal. He's beautiful and he's normal and he'll do it, everything he wants to do, he . . ."

"He's brain-damaged, he'll always be brain-damaged, Judy, but it won't ruin his happiness if the people around him accept him for what he is rather than mourning what he's not. You can't go through life pretending . . ."

"You wait one minute, John . . ."

"I've said this before, Judy. You have three beautiful boys. They're all different, all three of them, in their abilities and their personalities and in what they enjoy doing and in what they don't enjoy. One of Andy's differences is that he's brain-damaged. Other differences can be expected to stem from that basic fact.

"The world, your personal world, Judy, knows Andy's

220

brain-damaged. You may be the only human being inside that world who can't accept that fact."

"Are you out of your mind?" Judy gasped. "Do you honestly think . . .?"

"What I think is that it's time you took a hard look at yourself, and at what you've been able to accept, and at what you haven't. You're the mother of a brain-damaged child, Judy!"

"Please . . ."

"For the rest of your life."

23

August was a blistering month, muggy and stifling. A month when tempers flared. When people weren't at their best. When diners out punched other diners for smoking at adjoining tables. When motorists on the expressway shot other motorists for honking or swearing.

Desultory days of unyielding heat. The sound of laughter was unsettling, and laughter in crowds was a threat.

Scott, coming slowly up the block one afternoon after baseball practice, the sweat thick across his chest and back, under his arms, down his neck, saw Todd and his buddies near the house. Andy was there too, hanging around Todd as always, being a pest. On the edge of every action, wheedling his way in from the minute he got home from JYC camp.

None of them saw Scott coming.

Todd and Billy Streeter had their heads together amid a gaggle of admirers—Todd was popular on the street. Scott saw him glance toward Andy, say something to Billy, move off by himself a bit and Andy, of course, follow. Then he saw Todd turn and stick out a fast foot, neatly tripping Andy into the gutter.

The grotesque scene nauseated Scott. Thirty feet off, swinging his bat gently, he kept his pace steady, listening to the howls of laughter from Todd's buddies and the screech of startled pain from Andy.

Scott closed the distance, and they saw him now, a menace through the very act of his regulated step and the pendulum swing of the bat. He stopped at the scene of the crime to gather Andy to his feet, eyed the bloody knees, and looked expressionlessly at Todd who stared offensively back. With a glance of utter contempt at Todd's suddenly silent friends, he pushed through their ranks, his arm around Andy, and felt the group dissipate behind his back.

The house was cool and dim. Scott hustled Andy up the steps to the bathroom. He could hear their mother on the phone, no longer working because Todd was home. There was no money for Todd to go to camp. There were no free scholarships, because Todd was normal.

Scott closed the bathroom door and locked it. Andy was staring fascinated at the seeping blood on both knees. He raised trustful eyes to his oldest brother's face and smiled tentatively through tears.

"I fell," he announced solemnly.

"I know. You're a regular little klutz, aren't you?" Scott chided as he washed the wounds gingerly, then searched the medicine chest for Mercurochrome.

"What'll you have?" he asked the child.

"B'loons," Andy crowed, delighted. He watched, breathless, as the older boy drew bunches of orange balloons on both knees, then leaned forward to blow on both to dry the Mercurochrome.

"Can I have Band-Aids?" he asked.

"How are you gonna see the balloons if they're covered with Band-Aids?" Scott asked.

"One balloons and one Band-Aid?" Andy suggested slyly.

Scott sighed and rummaged again, this time for the Band-Aid box, extracting a huge square that met totally with Andy's approval.

"It's lucky it's not my head again," Andy murmured comfortably, as Scott placed the patch delicately over the left knee.

Scott looked at him.

"Like before. When I got brain-damaged," Andy explained, "and Mommy couldn't see to draw b'loons or Band-Aid it."

Scott stared at him for a long moment, in silence.

"You're really a silly little kid, you know that?" he murmured with genuine affection, tousling the child's hair. Andy, taking this in the proper spirit, grinned lovingly up into his big brother's face and threw both arms around his neck.

The kitchen was dim. The summer night hadn't cooled a bit, and the house held the heavy heat of afternoon. Scott was still not in the best of moods.

"Come upstairs. I want to talk to you."

They'd had dinner, cleaned up, and Judy and Jack had taken Andy visiting somewhere on the block. The house was quiet. Scott had been waiting patiently for this opportunity.

Todd eyed him narrowly, then took a can of soda from the refrigerator and slammed the door shut. He leaned belligerently against the closed door and stared at his older brother.

"I'm in a hurry. Alan's waiting for me."

Scott told him pleasantly what Alan could do to amuse himself while he waited.

"You gonna come upstairs," Scott asked politely, "where it's private and won't matter if Mom and Dad come waltzing in, or do you want it right here, where they'll know if they come home what a little creep you're turning into?"

He watched Todd weigh this threat of imminent intrusion against the dangers inherent in facing the music upstairs. They'd never really fought—they were too far apart in age—

but Scott had meted out punishment through the programming years with enough frequency and determination for Todd to think twice before soliciting it again.

"Just say whatever you want to say," Todd finally decided. His shoulders had squared and his head tilted back in a swaggering posture.

Scott regarded this picture and made an instant evaluation. This was the streetwise loner, tough, cold, uncaring, a little dangerous. It was one of Todd's best and most convincing parts. It was how his friends perceived him, how he seemed to get through the rigors of life.

"I don't care," Todd continued brazenly, "what Mom or Dad hear." He licked his lips then, and glanced tentatively at Scott.

Scott wasn't impressed. Scott knew all about Todd's acts. He'd been monitoring them for years.

"You want this broadcast?" he asked softly. "Fine." He moved a step closer to his younger brother and saw Todd's muscles go rigid, but the grim set of the jaw didn't waver an inch. Neither did Todd's eyes.

Scott was very angry. He'd come to disparage most of Todd's behavior. The "martyred middle child" act had impressed him once, before he'd understood it was just that—an act. Before he'd started catching Todd out of character more times than in, before he'd seen Todd's eyes narrow with hate, before he'd learned to evaluate. And this—the "bad" act—had never moved Scott an inch. He pointed a finger at Todd's face.

"You're turning into a little punk," he said, then dropped the hand to grip Todd's shirt front. "Playing the clown for all your good buddies. You're a real big shot, aren't you, Todd? Bloodying up a little kid who just happens to be your kid brother. All that fun, just for a chance to get a laugh from your moron friends. Tell me, do you still think it was worth it?"

It occurred to Scott, suddenly, too late, that this was grist for the mill, stepping into Todd's street act, picking up the lines from Todd's own script. But Todd was trembling under the

224

force of his brother's grip, so possibly, just possibly, reality was forcing its way in.

"If I ever see you do a punk thing like that to Andy again, I want you to understand exactly what I'm gonna do to *you*," Scott said gently. "I'm gonna take you and turn you inside out and dump you right on your tail, for the special amusement of your friends. I want you to remember that, Todd, because it's a fact. It's real!"

His voice was super-soft.

"I'll take you apart and lay out all the pieces and make sure every one of your friends sees exactly what I'm doing. You think they'll get as big a laugh out of me bleeding you as they did today out of you bleeding Andy?"

They both heard the screen door open, Judy's voice, Jack's answering. They stood transfixed, two brothers, staring blindly at each other, seeing different things, remembering other summers.

There was a fixed look on Todd's face. Scott let go of him, feeling suddenly like a bully, then remembering Andy's bloody knees and no longer caring that he was older and bigger. He stared at Todd for a long second, then turned and left the kitchen.

24

Autumn arrived in a sneaking way. Judy thought she was aware, then it sprung all its colors in a glory not expected, too soon, too fast. Too quickly gone as well, a bright flash, swift streamers of time as life went on and the years seemed to shorten.

It was the Friday before Halloween when Andy brought

home the invitation from Adam.

"Mommy! Mommy!"

It wasn't pain or rage in his voice, but ecstasy.

"A party, Mommy!"

She stood watching him disentangle himself from the other children in the car pool, a grimy party invitation clutched in his hand, a look of almost gloating hysteria on his features as he jumped and skittered along the sidewalk.

She tried to take the paper from his rigid grip, finally bent down to read it over his shoulder, and froze.

It was later, much later. She and Jack had gone through a wild dance of joy all afternoon and through dinner with Andy. Scott sat and watched this display in silence and Todd somehow managed to convey an air of seeing and hearing nothing.

Finally, Judy and Jack were alone in their room. All three boys were asleep.

"What are we going to do?" she whispered to Jack.

"What do you mean, what are we going to do?"

"It's a birthday party and Halloween party all rolled into one, Jack," she hissed. "It's an overnight party!"

There was a small silence. Jack already knew it was an overnight party. Everyone in the house, probably on the block, already knew it was an overnight party.

"So what?" Jack asked.

"He can't sleep out!"

"Why not?"

"He wets at night, Jack," she spaced the words out carefully, trying not to lose her temper, not wanting to fight. "He soaks himself. He soaks the bed. Every night, twice a night, every single night of his life!"

Jack was silent. She pushed her hair back violently and ground her teeth.

"It couldn't have been a regular party, for an hour or two, at lunchtime! What are we going to tell him?"

"I thought I already made it clear. Let him go to the party."

"Go?" she croaked. *"Go?"*

"Go," Jack affirmed coldly. "As in, 'Sure, he'll come, thanks for asking him.'"

"Are you completely out of your mind?" She was genuinely horrified.

Jack merely looked at her, silent.

"He wets, Jack," she nearly danced with agitation by the side of the bed. "He wets. The bed. The sheets. The blanket. Every morning I'm surprised not to find a flood running down the steps into the living room!"

"Did you listen when they said he might stop if he had the motivation to stop?" Jack asked her, growing agitated himself. "He wets and we go in and change him, twice a night, we wash him and change him every single night of his life, and he gets extra attention that way."

She sighed wearily, dismissing it.

"They told us that at CNR, Judy. They told us it was at least a possibility, that things like this could be developmental, or medical—which it isn't in Andy's case, you know that, the urologist said so . . ."

"Or emotional," Judy finished the little speech for him. "I just love all the psychology business. I don't need a degree in psychology to know that he sleeps so hard, he sleeps so incredibly heavily, that he just doesn't *feel* it when he has to go to the bathroom."

"You *know* that's his problem!" Jack said acidly.

"I know when my own child's profoundly asleep!" she raged. "He doesn't even wake up when we change him. If he sleeps through the whole thing, how does he know we're paying all that extra attention to him?"

"You really believe he doesn't know we're standing over him?" Jack asked, astonished. "A kid who's been accustomed to hundreds of people standing over him every waking hour of his day? A kid who used to fall asleep on the patterning table with people talking to him and over him and moving his arms and head and legs? A kid who'd wake up without the slightest

227

disorientation the minute the nine to ten o'clock program ended and it was time for him to go up to bed?"

"They're not here anymore, Jack," her teeth were clenched so tight the words nearly got lost in there. "He's older now. He won't always react the same way he reacted during programming!"

"They're not here anymore," Jack agreed. "So everything's different now. And you really can't believe he might miss all the attention he was getting during the programming? Or that he's smart enough to figure out some new way to get additional attention? Not consciously, maybe, but unconsciously?"

Of course she could believe it. She simply didn't want to hear Jack believing it. Besides, in the short run, none of this mattered a bit. Not in terms of the party. Nothing was going to improve fast enough to make it possible for Andy to attend a slumber party. Somebody in his class liked him enough to invite him to such a special party, and she had to break his heart and tell him he couldn't go anyway. Small deaths.

Her whole soul rebelled at it.

"We could argue this forever," she told Jack wearily. "And it still wouldn't change the fact that we can't just pray he'll rise to the challenge. Not when we're sticking him in somebody else's bed, or wherever it is you put kids when they come for an overnight party. Even you have to admit I can't inflict that on some stranger, Jack."

"Let him go to the party, Judy. And if worst comes to worst, we'll apologize to his hostess and pay for repairs to her beroom."

It was absurd. It was irresponsible. It was letting go—a little bit. She knew she had to let go. And for a number of reasons she really couldn't unravel, she did decide to let Andy go to the party.

She decided to call Adam's mother that weekend, to thank her for the invitation and feel out the atmosphere. There'd been something familiar about the last name on the invitation, and she thought the boy's mother might have been one of her programmers. There was no answer when she called on Saturday or again on Sunday. Nor was there a response Monday morning or afternoon of the following week, or on Tuesday at lunch time. At that point Judy decided the name was definitely that of one of her programmers, and that the invitation had been extended out of kindness, not ignorance of Andy's situation.

For the remainder of the week, she convinced herself that it was highly unlikely Andy would even fall asleep after the party. He'd be too excited. And if he did, he certainly wouldn't sleep deeply, not when surrounded by a roomful of his classmates.

On Friday morning, she was still busy convincing herself. She packed a small bag for Andy as he watched, full of suggestions, stuffing additional toys inside every time she turned her back. His Teddy. His firetruck. Three extra pairs of socks. The children attending would be picked up at school by Adam's mother that afternoon and taken directly to his house, to be picked up by their own parents at noon on Saturday. By the time the car pool arrived, Andy was overexcited, but you never knew, she told herself, when another invitation would arrive and she wanted him to enjoy this day entirely.

The way Scott would. The way Todd would.

At two-thirty, the phone rang.

"Mrs. Polikoff?" The voice stirred her memory, though no face came to mind. "This is Mrs. Zitzman. Adam's mother."

Too late, Judy remembered the voice. Too late to reformulate her thoughts. Adam Zitzman's mother was one of the Category One programmers—absolutely never on time, never calling to cancel, never bothering to make explanations or seeming to feel guilt or embarrassment or anything other than complacency.

Judy's chest felt tight. A perfect match for her stomach. Nothing pleasant could come of this phone call. Of that she was certain.

"You probably don't remember me, so many names and faces in and out for all that time, but I was one of your programmers during the first year of Andy's rehabilitation."

First two months to be precise, then the cancellations started. A third month, with one visit out of a scheduled four. Dropout after that. No apologies, no formal withdrawal, just an empty space in the difficult-to-fill seven to eight o'clock spot on Wednesdays.

"When Adam told me the names of the four children he wanted to invite to his party, I really never thought to connect your little boy with the little boy he wanted. I mean, well, how could I? I didn't even know Andy was in regular school, and certainly not in the same class with Adam!"

Judy's breathing had gone shallow. It was possible she might stop breathing altogether.

"Even with an uncommon name like Andy—well, you see how I made my silly mistake, and then not checking immediately, but I've been so busy, in and out every day. And the days got away from me, I don't know where the time goes, and then this morning I was going over the acceptances and it occurred to me that this Andy just might possibly be your Andy, and of course Adam didn't know anybody's last name, they never do, do they, so after he left for school I called the JYC and asked for Jo and she said yes, it certainly was your little boy, and I thought I'd better call you. I wanted you to understand, because after all, you're a very practical woman, that's obvious from the burden you managed to carry so beautifully through Andy's rehabilitation, you're a practical woman and a mother, as I myself am, and you'll understand perfectly that there will be four other little boys here tonight, children for whom I'll be responsible, well, four counting my own little Adam and the three classmates he invited, *not* including Andy, of course, and only myself and my husband to supervise and not really my husband, either, because it's his night to go bowling . . ."

*　　*　　*

"What is it, Mom?"

Todd stood in the doorway, his books under his arm. It was later than she'd thought, very late, actually. She turned and stared at him blankly, still standing by the phone she'd hung up—how long ago? Had Scott too come in while she'd been standing there, frozen, and simply gone to his room?

"Mom?"

The car pool would be coming, bringing Andy home from nursery school. Home, with his little bag, soon . . .

"Mom?" There was an edge of panic in Todd's voice. "What's wrong?"

She couldn't believe she had just stood here, staring at nothing, for the whole hour between the call and Todd's homecoming. Nothing so banal as a birthday party was bad enough to hurt that way, to blank you right out. She stared at Todd, her own child, and the Friends' Picnic filled her mind—the picnic, the softball game, the ribbon, the hatred on the ride home, hitting Todd, her Todd. She bit her lower lip, then suddenly, helplessly began to cry great gulping sobs that filled the room, while tears poured down her cheeks.

"Mom," Todd whispered once more, swallowing hard.

"They don't want him," she heard herself wail, not meaning to say this to Todd, not really saying it to Todd at all, but to herself, to Thorpe, to Dr. Carr, to God. "Nobody wants him, they won't ever want him, we worked and worked to make him well enough to know that nobody will ever want him . . ."

Todd's face twisted terribly and he dropped his books on the floor and crossed the room at a dead run to throw his arms tight around her.

They went to a special dinner that night—a special dinner for Andy. He was even allowed to wear his Halloween costume, it was a special treat. They went next to a Walt Disney movie, through which both Scott and Todd sat with amazing grace.

231

Then they all took Andy out trick-or-treating, the whole family together, all this done, dinner onward, in a kind of nonstop frenzy as if they were all too deadly afraid he'd ask questions if they stopped and let him think or breathe.

By the time they got him tucked into his bed, he was too confused and agitated and exhausted to ask questions about anything. It really seemed, if you didn't have qualms about the expression behind his eyes and a certain tightness in his arms and legs, it really seemed as if he might have been induced to forget Adam's party.

Later, days later, Judy began to see the signs. There was the daytime wetting. Andy wet himself twice in school in the first week after the party. The wetting stopped thereafter, but there were other signs. There was a stiffness in his gait, indication of stress—it was a personal barometer. Then, there was his behavior in groups. He'd become withdrawn and unapproachable. Jo reported this. In the privacy of the house, his behavior was just the opposite, feverish, frenzied—he clung to any member of the family who happened to be nearby. He followed Judy from room to room. He never seemed to sit down. When he wasn't racing from floor to floor, he was muttering incomprehensibly to himself. His speech deteriorated. He returned to his early tendency to point and grunt.

Judy told herself it would pass. All children ran into situations that caused small traumas.

But the days became weeks and Andy failed to rally. Judy found that she didn't know how to cope with this youngest child. His reactions were just that little bit different. His perceptions of unspoken thoughts seemed strangely clear. He always knew when she was agitated. It agitated him. That made dealing with Andy's emotional problems treacherous and tiring.

Jack tried some normal roughhousing with all three boys. Andy became overexcited. He began choking. It brought back the terrifying memories of the years of programming.

* * *

232

Autumn into winter. The seasons were beginning to reassume their natural splendor. The Polikoffs took a long drive together to look at the leaves one November weekend, carpets of gold under bare outspread trees beneath paling skies. There was a hint of bitterness in the clean crisp air.

Judy found Andy crying one day, crouched on the steps, halfway down, halfway up, silent tears streaming down his cheeks.

"Nobody wants to play with me," he gulped, the tears falling to his lap. "Not Paul. Not Ricky. Not nobody."

There was a shrinking around her heart. She reached for him, tentatively, pulled him into her arms, and stroked his head, his neck, his stiff back. She kissed him gently, his tears on her lips.

"You have to try and understand that people have lots of silly things to do," she made her voice calm and light. "They get all mixed up in their own lives, doing so many things, they get so busy, silly silly people," she whispered, stroking him. "They don't have time for fun. It's such a shame. And they don't mean to make you sad, it's just that they're so busy thinking about all the things they have to do that they don't have any time left over to think about you."

"Not busy," Andy growled, chin coming up obstinately, reminding her forcibly of Todd. His face was red and soaking.

"Play. Not busy," he repeated angrily. "Pauly and Ricky with the ball. They say I can't catch good," his voice rose indignantly, but with a clear note of doubt. "I play good ball, don't I, Mommy?"

She nodded, stroking his hair. "Super ball," she murmured.

"I got my winner ribbon to prove it," he added, "and Todd was jealous." This with nervous triumph.

Todd was jealous. She didn't bother to deny it. It was true enough, all upside down and inside out.

"They hate me," said her youngest son, sniffing dismally. "They say, get out!"

She sat and petted him some more and kissed the top of his

head and thought, please God, I don't want to be a grown-up today.

Andy pulled back, finally, and looked into her face. She made herself look directly into his eyes because she'd found that Andy, when discussing himself, had an uncanny knack of knowing if she tried to lie or tell half-truths.

"It's probably true that some of the kids around here are jealous of you," she admitted slowly. "After all, they must see how much everybody's always loved you. Do you think all kids are loved as much as you?"

Andy didn't buy that. "Then where are they?" he asked defiantly.

She was truly bewildered. "Who?"

"All the ladies," Andy blurted. "The ones that loved me so much. Where are they? Why don't they love me anymore? Why did they go away?"

She stared at him, not knowing how to explain. The simple truth always seemed inadequate when explaining things to Andy, and she didn't know if this was his problem or hers alone.

"The volunteers?" she finally asked. "The ladies and men who came to help with the programming? They don't come anymore because Daddy and Mommy told them *not* to come anymore, and that was because Dr. Carr—you know Dr. Carr . . .?"

"Like Dr. Carr."

"Yes. Well. Dr. Carr told Daddy and Mommy that you didn't need all those people hanging around you anymore. Because you're better and you don't need a bunch of strangers around, playing with you like you were a little baby. Because you're a big boy now, who goes to school, and only needs his own family, just like every other big boy.

"Isn't it enough for Mommy and Daddy and Todd and Scott and Grandmom Polikoff and Grandmom and Grandpop Sokoloff and Uncle Ned and your school friends to love you?"

Andy took some time to digest this. There was little that was rapid-motion about Andy.

"What I think," he said laboriously, "is that I don't want to live here anymore. So why don't we just move?" Andy asked with a child's practicality. "That way I could make new friends someplace else, where nobody'd know I got brain damage."

NAME: Andy Polikoff
BIRTHDATE: 12/10/73
AGE: 4 years 11 months
TESTED: 11/9/78

TESTS USED: Stanford-Binet

TEST RESULTS:
Andy achieved a Stanford-Binet IQ of 90. He was distractible throughout the testing, showed signs of hyperactivity, talked constantly, and could not seem to keep his mind on the tasks assigned. Attempts at administering drawing tasks were abandoned as Andy was unable to perform adequately. It was considered that while Andy is intellectually average, he possesses significant attention and concentration difficulties, poor perceptual-motor skill development, hyperactivity, and memory problems to interfere with his learning abilities. Remedial school instruction and psychotherapeutic intervention are recommended.

IV
TOGETHER AGAIN

25

Prewinter darkened the house. Judy felt the nights drawing in, and planned her meals accordingly. No extravagances, not yet, no expensive cuts of meat—she'd grown far too careful for waste of any sort—but the chicken she had roasting was plump and prime and she hadn't scrimped, there was more than enough. She'd planned two vegetable dishes instead of one, and even allowed herself the pleasure of baking a fat apple pie for dessert.

The genuine joy she took in these things was part of a gradual lifting of her spirits, a lessening of fright, a general loosening up. It meant trying not to worry over every penny, every problem, every transient expression on the faces of her children.

Todd came drifting in before dinner one evening. With him was his best friend, Alan.

"Mom?"

She was standing in the kitchen doorway, having just checked on her dinner's progress.

"Can I eat out with Alan?"

Of course he couldn't eat out with Alan. That should have been obvious. Eating out was not yet part of their budget. Except for emergencies. Emergencies affecting Andy? She pushed the memory of Halloween aside, on the verge of a flat refusal, when she got a good glimpse of Todd's face. There was a narrow smirk on his lips. Todd expected to be turned down, in front of Alan.

That made her angry. Todd knew all about the shortage of money, Todd had known such things for a very long time, it

239

was an enormous, pervasive fact of life in their family. But suddenly, she recognized that it didn't matter what Todd knew about their finances or about what they could or could not afford. Todd was only seven, though she tended to forget his age in light of his attitude, which stank.

She found her voice.

"Sure. You can eat out with Alan." It was ripped from her prudent guts, but she had the satisfaction of seeing Todd's sharp surprise. "Where are you guys going?" she asked as nonchalantly as she could, praying for nothing more expensive or elaborate than hamburgers.

"Tony's," Alan said helpfully.

Pizza, then, or pizza steaks. More expensive than hamburgers but less, all in all, than the fishhouse or anything else.

Andy chose that inopportune moment to make a crashing descent from upstairs, Rocky at his heels.

"Tony's?" he screamed.

It was impossible for him to have heard them unless he'd been lurking on the stairs.

"For pizza?"

He jumped in near hysteria from foot to foot, an abbreviated war dance that set Judy's teeth on edge. The dog, overstimulated by all the noise and movement, began to bark hysterically.

"You gonna bring back pizza?" Andy threw both arms around Todd, who stared at him in desperate dismay.

"Are you?" He punched Todd in the chest with small fists that really hurt.

Todd tried to take a step backward, and nearly fell.

"Nah," Alan was saying calmly enough. "Not pizza. Just pizza steaks. And not here. At Tony's."

"I love pizza steaks at Tony's!" howled Andy, who'd never been there in his life. He disengaged from Todd, to Todd's enormous relief, only to dance wildly around the room, driving the dog into a total frenzy. A sudden dash brought him back to grab onto Todd's shrinking leg, his fingers catching in the cloth of Todd's jeans, nearly denuding Todd where he stood.

240

It should have been funny. It was only terrible.

"Can I go eat with you?"

With this question, everything stopped. Everything.

Todd, shaken, unnerved by this display, swallowed, tried to free his leg, glanced toward his mother for help. He realized his friend was watching this mad scene. He was a focus, suddenly—and didn't want to be.

The dog quieted as abruptly as its master. They all—dog, brother, mother, friend—stood waiting.

"This is grown-up stuff," Todd heard Alan saying gently.

"I'm almost growed up," Andy announced indignantly, the utter stillness of his body producing an undefined tension in the room. "Can I? I wanna go to Tony's!"

"No."

It was soft yet sharp and explosive, too, and came from Todd's deepest soul. It was a prayer to God more than a simple negative. It was too much unfairness, really it was. The episode with Scott in the kitchen had remained an ugly festering anguish. He'd hated being bullied like that, but the anger was the least important thing, for it had passed. What was forever was Scott. And Scott hadn't come near Todd, hadn't looked at him, hadn't spoken to him, not one small word, in all the months since August.

It was a nauseating memory because he knew Scott was right, he'd known it then. He'd known it even before the confrontation in the kitchen. He'd known it the second Andy fell. He was mortally ashamed when he saw the blood. Ashamed of having done this stupid thing for the amusement of his friends. And their comments, etched on his brain, made the memory worse. Comments he hadn't been able to deny because, after all, he'd instigated the voicing of them or they'd never have dared come to life.

Retard! That was Joey Goldberg's voice, Joey, who didn't have the right to call anybody else retarded, since he was the biggest jerk in the neighborhood himself.

Christ, Todd! That was Steve Levinson. We don't know how

you stand it, it must be rough, having to drag around a retard everywhere you go!

All the bitter unhappiness he'd harbored for so long was confronting him here, at the worst of times, in front of his friend Alan, who was *not* a jerk. In front of his mother, who'd shocked him by her swift acquiescence to his wish to eat out. A tiny portion of his outrage had been dissipated by the easy granting of the wish. He hadn't tried to understand that—he was very young still. And now this surprise, this treat, was being threatened too. Andy was the last person in the world he needed tagging after him.

But Andy was tugging at him again, and Todd's mind reeled. His ego, once bolstered by malice, inflated by his lifelong absorption with playing one role after another, was turning shaky with self-loathing, due not only to Scott's long anger but also, and in large part, to his own growing sense of family loyalty.

He avoided what he was sure would be his mother's glaring eye and dropped to one knee before the child.

"Look, Mom's already made dinner. Can't you smell it?"

It made his own request to eat out less than defensible but he disregarded that fact. She hadn't said anything, had she? She'd let him go, hadn't she? She owed him. Didn't she? An awful lot more than a dumb dinner out.

"Look," he repeated, "you eat dinner here, with Mom and Dad and Scott. Alan and me—we'll have our pizza steaks, which you'd hate anyway," which was undoubtedly true, yet somehow irrelevant, "and then later, after everybody's finished dinner, we'll come home, you'll be hungry all over again," which was also undeniably true, and he tried desperately hard to smile, "and we'll go down to Bill's, you and me and Alan, and get you an ice cream soda, the way you like it, with lots of whipped cream and a big cherry on top."

Todd hadn't the slightest idea where this additional money would come from, even if he'd really intended coming back for Andy, which he didn't. He simply assumed that his mother would cough up whatever was needed to keep Andy happy.

But Andy was shoving away from him so violently that he stumbled back.

"You won't come back!" Andy hissed. "Later you'll say you just forgot, or you thought *I* forgot, or you thought I wouldn't really want to go, or you thought I was already asleep, but it won't be true, you'll lie, you always lie, you'll just go and do it without me! Like Pauly and Ricky! Like everybody!"

It was said with such venom that Todd was appalled, but the next words were soft and gulping.

"You hate me!" With that, Andy began to cry, great choking sobs that brought not only Jack down from the bedroom where he'd been changing his clothes, but Scott in from the front porch.

Surrounded thus by his family, observed by his dearest friend, Todd felt the full force of ignominious defeat. He was aware of his mother waiting with great patience, silent. Of Jack, not commenting either. Of Alan, his very best friend, shifting from foot to foot, embarrassed and confused and wishing himself out of this mess. Of his helplessly sobbing baby brother. He would have liked to throttle Andy. Somebody should have murdered him at birth. He would gladly do it now, himself, if he could have a second's privacy.

Most of all, Todd was aware of Scott, standing by the front door, watching everything. Shadows of August. Numb, numb hurting. You shouldn't be able to hurt if you were numb, but you could, that was a fact, he'd been numb for years and he hadn't stopped hurting. There was hurt now, in his heart, it tore at him wickedly, amplified by Andy's searing gasps. He reached blindly to clasp Andy tight, squeezing his own eyes shut to defy a suspicious burning, stroking the child's shuddering back, and rubbing his cheek against Andy's hair, not for Andy but for his own comfort. Finally, the younger boy quieted. There was a last dismal hiccoughing sigh. He could feel Andy shivering in his arms.

"Hey," Todd said, his throat dry. "Cut it out, man." Hoarse and soft, meant only for Andy, not for this unwieldy crowd. "I wouldn't do that. I wouldn't lie."

But he had lied in the past and he'd meant to lie tonight. He just hadn't known that Andy understood lies. That was what he'd always told himself. He'd assumed, grim and lonely in his soul, that his parents and Scott would make up for his own uncaring behavior by over-loving Andy.

"I won't ever say I'll come back and get you and then forget or back out. Not ever again," he amended, while one part of his brain recognized the insincerity of such a blanket promise. "And I don't hate you. Why would you say I hate you?"

Memories, stirring and stabbing. He thought of the Friends' Picnic and the winner's ribbon. His own fury. His mother's rage. His father, taking him aside when they got home and talking to him, being disappointed in him.

Andy was sniffing wetly, rubbing his own cheek, shuffling. Todd knew defeat when he was soaking in it. He sighed and brushed his brother's tears away with his fingertips.

"If it's that important to you to go and waste a pizza steak—because you won't like a pizza steak and you won't eat a pizza steak—but if it's that important to you then you'll have to ask Mom for the money. I'm not gonna ask her. It was bad enough for me to ask her for myself."

Todd didn't look at Judy. He didn't see the softening on her face, the terrible love in her eyes. It wouldn't have mattered anyway, not just then, what mattered was that he had to get out of here fast, or else he'd die right in front of Alan.

To that end, his own immediate escape, he would have done anything. Confessed to anything. Spread-eagled himself on the living room rug for them all to kick and spit on. He'd have done all that and more too if it would have made Scott look at him without such loathing, if it could somehow have erased this entire scene and put him and Alan back outside, never having asked about eating out together in the first place.

244

"But Alan and me," he heard himself saying, "we talk about grown-up stuff. If you get bored, you just have to sit there and be quiet anyway. And you have to promise me you won't be a little pest, talking loud and running around and annoying everybody at Tony's."

It was highly unlikely that Andy could or would sit still and be quiet for ten seconds, let alone the time required to down a pizza steak. He hadn't been able to compose himself for weeks, ever since it became necessary to block out the voices and expressions of other people in the aftermath of the party rejection. But in the end Andy's behavior at Tony's was a minor thing. What mattered to Todd was that he simply could not breathe, that he was stifling, that all the self-protective acts of his life were falling apart to leave him just—Todd Polikoff.

And this because of the silent shadow of Scott, standing by the door, knowing him, judging him. Not forgiving him.

Andy had thrown himself back into Todd's arms, rubbing against him contentedly. Over his head, Todd looked helplessly at his older brother and saw the look on Scott's face: silent, openly derisive.

It made Todd physically ill. Crouched there, with his least important brother clutched to his heart, he stared at the brother who meant everything in the world to him and thought melodramatic thoughts about stepping in front of a speeding truck, or cutting his own throat. Then Judy said something to Jack, and Jack was holding out money to him, and he stood, a little dizzy, tearing his gaze from Scott's face, pocketing the bills without looking at them, then glancing tentatively at his mother.

There was a smile deep in his mother's eyes. It was like a hug. It made him feel uncharacteristically warm, stroked, loved, for that terrible moment.

He had to pass Scott on the way out. He had to come so close it was necessary to pull back to avoid touching him. Scott didn't budge, forcing the tortured proximity.

245

The street seemed smaller, the sidewalk too narrow, his legs the wrong length for walking. It was Alan who took Andy's hand as they crossed the street, but only because Todd felt so disoriented.

It was very late—just how late he didn't know. He lay curled on his side, facing the wall, as he'd grown accustomed to sleeping, back to the rest of the room, and to Andy. It gave him the illusion of privacy.

Nothing, of course, not his very best act, not his most colorful waking dreams, could drown out the sound of Andy's labored breathing. Andy always sounded just that way, as if he had a terminal head cold. He breathed through his mouth even when he was awake—something to do with not being able to fully control all the muscles of his mouth yet.

Developmental.

Todd had learned that useful word when he was four years old. He knew all the big words by then. He knew all Andy's problems. Like the breathing problems that had dogged Andy throughout his short life. Too many of Todd's nightmares involved Andy's breathing problems. Too great a proportion of Todd's waking life involved considerations of Andy, period!

He'd been forcing himself to do a lot of thinking about Andy recently. It seemed necessary since he suspected that Andy constituted a stick-like-glue component of his life. But the deepest thought, the really hurtful introspection, had started in the past few months of his estrangement from Scott.

He'd made a Herculean effort to understand his feelings about his younger brother. About the very real barrier, so great he could almost touch it, between himself and Andy. It was the barrier, he'd come to believe, between normal and not normal. Because that was another thing he'd carefully considered. That his mother was wrong. It didn't matter at all what she *wanted* the world to think because Andy *wasn't* normal. Not like she meant it to be. Andy never would be normal that way because

246

brain damage didn't just go away and Andy was brain-damaged and being brain-damaged wasn't normal.

What Todd didn't yet know was what that meant—being forever *not* completely normal. And he was starting to question whether he, himself, was completely normal. Because he'd been having long, unprofitable silent talks with himself ever since it stopped being possible to talk to Scott about his problems. And it didn't seem to him that talking to himself could be considered perfectly normal.

He lay quite still now in his bed. Inside his head, it wasn't nearly so quiet.

The house settled around him. Across the room, Andy tossed and wheezed. Todd thought he heard his father say something to his mother. It was possible his mother laughed—he wasn't sure. He shut these sounds out by the simple expedient of delving deep inside himself, but whenever he'd come up with a satisfactory analysis he'd get drowsy and lose the thread, or else get off on a tangent and forget just where he'd started, then the whole argument would go dead.

And it was desperately important to him to know why he couldn't bear Andy. At any other time in his life he would have gone straight across to Scott's room, no matter what the hour, and plagued Scott for answers. Now, he couldn't ask Scott anything at all, because Scott had decided to hate him. Scott had decided to love Andy.

He felt the threat of hot stinging tears in his eyes and opened them very wide to forestall their rolling down his cheeks. For a very long time now he hadn't permitted the tears, not even in private. If you cried it made you soft, and made it easier to cry the next time. It made you vulnerable. He couldn't afford to be vulnerable. Anyway, what did it matter who hated you or loved you? What mattered was to understand yourself.

All his nice rationalizations were being ruined, and he was being forced to face his own little meannesses as the nasty facts of life got clearer every day. Facts of life gleaned from the neighborhood, from the world outside the house, from those same people who'd volunteered to help Andy. They were the ones who shook Todd to the core, the ones who wouldn't let their little brats out to play with Andy after school, who wouldn't invite him to their kids' parties, who never had him over for supper.

They'd helped Andy. They were Andy's army. Now they were rejecting him.

If the rest of the world had been fairer to Andy now, maybe it wouldn't have been so difficult, so painfully miserable for *him* to have to be fair to Andy.

Todd was getting old enough to begin to wonder about people's strange contradictory behavior. And he was starting to suspect, ugly little thought, that so was Andy.

Which forced him, against his will, into a miserable position. It just wasn't his best role—defending champion. To stand tight against the world because rejection really hurt. Because it was wrong to throw away a little kid. Because it wasn't fair. Because Andy would understand they didn't want him around and it hurt Andy to know that, and Andy was his brother.

It wasn't fair. Andy was his brother. His friends had never been the same friends again, because he himself was forever after split between loyalty to them and to Andy. And that was the least fair thing of all. He didn't even *like* Andy.

He grimaced in the near dark. Scott had deserted him. He would have gladly died for Scott, he wondered if Scott knew that. The darkness wasn't dark enough, that was the trouble, there was a nightlight so the night was never complete. You could see yourself too clearly with the nightlight on, left lit in the futile hope that Andy might actually get himself up to the bathroom instead of soaking himself every single time he slept. The nightlight made the room dimly orange and Todd liked the light, but he never would have admitted it—nightlights were baby crutches big boys should certainly not want.

Andy was snoring loudly. Todd lay staring at the wall, at his own fingers, at his own sudden fist. It would probably mean

248

that Andy was dead if the room ever became *his* room, if the night ever came when there was no heavy breathing in the bed next to his.

He felt small and dismally alone, empty, yet weighted to the bed with a terrible weight. He hated himself—yes. He hated himself terribly. He felt unworthy and mean, and the world was getting heavier and heavier.

Feeling himself growing more and more upset, he tried to slip into fantasy. He considered the possibility of becoming a vegetable himself. On second thought, he decided it probably wasn't all it was cracked up to be. If you were sick enough, you were locked away, and couldn't eat pizza steaks or go see the Phillies or do much of anything. And Mom would look confused because she wouldn't know what she'd done wrong, and she'd start to cry and laugh, like that other time. And Dad would look scared, then crushed, then mad.

And Scott? Scott wouldn't look anything. Scott would say, no surprises here, another cop-out from Todd.

It was a bitter thought. He slept on it.

Saturday dawned. Andy, having soaked his bed twice during the night, awoke bright and refreshed at six A.M. His parents stood in immediate attendance.

Todd, normally fond of his bed on cold winter mornings, scrambled for the bathroom as soon as it was free, rejecting further sleep. Sleep would bring more dreams and the dreams had hurt tremendously. Even so, a quick splash in the sink did little to clear his head. He wandered to the door of Scott's room.

Andy was curled against Scott on the bed, Rocky lying on the floor nearby.

The scene made Todd vastly tired.

"Beat it, Andy." To his surprise, it was the dog that rose and sauntered languidly from the room at this command. Andy was less tractable. He squirmed from the protection of Scott's cradling arm, pushing away the book Scott had been reading to him, and came to his feet to glare aggressively at Todd.

Todd couldn't imagine a reason for this instant animosity. It was only last night that Andy had carried on in Tony's, jumping frantically around until half the people drifted out. Andy had no right at all to stand there glaring.

It occurred to Todd, suddenly and with force, that Andy manipulated people. That Andy was *able* to manipulate people.

"You can't make me," Andy announced flatly. "You can't make me go away. It's not your room!"

"Nothing is," Todd answered wearily.

Andy blinked, then dismissed this as unimportant.

"Well, it's not," he said, "and besides, Scott just got to where they're having this race and falling in the water and having a fight with big rubber sticks!"

Todd stared uncomprehendingly at his younger brother, laughed shortly, then rubbed a hand over his burning eyes. He had a terrible headache. He thought, I have to try to be friendly, to be his big brother, to stop imagining all these weird things and having these weird ideas. How could Andy manipulate anybody?

"Look," he said as reasonably as he could through a rising sense of malaise that made him weak, "I *have* to talk to Scott. It's important! Can't you understand that? Scott can finish reading to you about your race and water and rubber sticks later, can't he? It's the weekend. What's the hurry?"

To Todd's intense surprise, perhaps Scott's as well, Andy stood his ground, his voice shaking with rage.

"This *is* important! That's what's a hurry! It's more important than all your stuff with Scott. You always think what I want's not important! You always think it! This is more important than anything!"

This seemed hardly accurate, but Todd, already the perpetrator of too many unfair things, found himself in the impossible position of being unable to counter Andy's argument. He swallowed, not looking at Scott, who retained a heavy silence.

"Besides," Andy added boldly, "you always get Scott!"

250

Scott himself recognized the absurdity of this, and came to his feet, towering over both of them.

"What if nobody gets Scott?" he suggested quite pleasantly.

Two young faces turned toward him, ludicrously alike, unbearably distressed.

"I didn't sleep so good last night, and I want to take a shower," he said, turning to Andy. "I'll finish reading to you later, right before lunch maybe."

Petulant tears filled Andy's eyes and he stamped his foot and threw the book on the floor.

Scott pointed a finger at him. It reminded Todd, forcibly, of the finger Scott had stuck in his face in the kitchen that awful day in August.

"I don't like it when you act like a brat!" Scott announced grimly. "If later's not good enough, we don't have to read it at all. You're spoiled rotten, Andy!"

To Todd's amazement, Andy giggled. The tears dried up instantly.

"Rotten apples," Andy hooted, then burst out in wild laughter, and vanished in a whirlwind, going down the stairs in a series of crashes, bumps, and squeals with Rocky barking hysterically at his heels.

Scott glanced dispassionately at his remaining brother.

"You," he said coldly. "Disappear."

Todd flushed darkly as Scott turned his back and gathered clean clothes for his shower. He felt his lower lip threatening to quiver and brought himself under control with difficulty. Andy could take it when Scott griped. It didn't seem right that he, so much older, couldn't. He'd die if he didn't make it up with Scott.

"I said I have to talk to you." He delved desperately for a tough tone to give him some courage, but his voice came out plaintive and weak.

Scott glanced at him with contempt. "And I said I'm taking a shower. Maybe you're going deaf."

Todd watched him gather up his clean underwear, a clean

251

shirt, a pair of clean jeans from the closet. He realized, heart sinking fast, that Scott could simply walk right over him, unseeing, unhearing.

"I'm not going deaf, just nuts. I'm going nuts! All alone, thanks to you. Does that make you happy, Scott?"

But then he fell silent for Scott had frozen in his tracks, and for some reason that was terrifying—that Scott was actually listening to him saying something like that. Something he'd never meant to say out loud, only hint at.

But Scott only stood staring.

There was no end to the phenomenon that was Andy. Andy would always be brain-damaged, so it was safe to assume that he would get all the caring forever. All the love. All the extras. All of Todd's future life, droning on and on, would be exactly in step with the pattern so carefully learned and established.

Scott tossed his clothing on the night table and seemed about to speak. That was when Todd panicked.

"Never mind," he gasped, retreating rapidly into the hall, down the stairs, nearly tripping . . .

"Get back here!"

Scott's tone was so harsh that he obeyed it instantly. It made him feel like a jerk, though, coming meekly back into Scott's room, then watching helplessly as Scott closed the door.

"Sit down."

"Why?" Todd felt the danger of his own position, his self-control crumbling, his resistance slipping. "So you can tell me all over again how dumb I am, and how unfair I am to Andy? And how much you think I'm disgusting and how much you hate me? I don't need to hear again how much you hate me!"

His voice cracked several times during this small speech but the haze of fear lifted, he felt a little better, a little less sick in the pit of his stomach, a little farther from helpless tears, until Scott ruined it all by seizing him by the arm and half-dragging him from the door to the bed.

"You gonna beat me up?" Todd asked miserably.

252

Scott stood in front of him, legs spread. It made Todd very uncomfortable, Scott looming like that. He squirmed, discomfited, and the movement was very much like the squirming Andy did when he was scared to death.

Scott nearly grinned. The long estrangement from Todd hadn't been easy. Scott was genuinely fond of Todd.

"What's up?" he asked. His voice, if not exactly friendly, was at least interested.

"Up?" Todd repeated. He was developing this sloppy habit of repeating what people said when his mind went treacherously blank on him. He figured Scott would consider such mimicry flip, and he really didn't want Scott coming down heavy on him.

"I told you what's up," he said desperately.

"You said you think you're going nuts," Scott replied. "That's crazy." He apparently saw nothing funny, though, in this evaluation of Todd's statement. "What do you mean, you think you're going nuts?"

It was absolutely impossible to explain. He couldn't reveal all those things to Scott. All those dark thoughts, the half-dreams.

"I didn't mean it," he recanted. "After all, I'm just a kid. Only you think it's okay to push me around because Andy's more of a kid than me," this acidly, "and because you think, like everybody else, that Andy's the only one with problems around here."

Scott gave this some thought. He was silent for nearly a minute. It was a terrible lifetime for Todd—that minute.

"If you see yourself as such a poor little problem kid," Scott said finally, "then why do you spend all your time pretending you're independent and cool and don't need anybody or anything? Don't you know that makes people like me want to break your head in?"

It was one of those questions you couldn't possibly answer.

"I understood how you felt when the programming was going on," Scott said. "At least I thought I could understand

253

how a little kid must feel about all that. Nobody would have blamed you if you'd carried on a little for attention. But you didn't. You were putting on acts way back then, weren't you? But remember how awful everything was then?"

Todd flushed hotly.

"Would you really feel better if people were phony around you, like they're phony around Andy?' Scott asked him curiously.

Todd didn't reply. This question left him wondering.

"Like at the picnic, the winner's ribbon," Scott prodded him.

It was no use. There was no easy answer and Todd didn't think he wanted to lie to Scott about any of this.

"You're just seven," Scott said kindly, "and maybe you've got a rotten personality, but you were never stupid. Don't you want to try to figure all this out?"

Todd's back stiffened and the blood suffused his face. "Do you think I'd be sitting here letting you make a jerk out of me if I knew how to figure it out? And I don't have a rotten personality!"

Scott actually grinned a little. "All you have to do," he said gently, "is remember the way you felt through the two-and-a-half years of the programming."

That was easy. That was Todd's most pervasive memory. Mornings. All the months, then years of mornings. The mornings were the worst, waking and knowing it was starting all over again. Not just a bad dream. Real, in the house, filling it. The noise. The people. The confusion. The frustration of being unable to recall names, of being totally unable to associate names with faces. And it was deadly, this inability, for the fear was there, the deep-seated feeling that it was vital to know, vital to ingratiate himself, vital to be noticed, smiled at, loved.

But their eyes were on Andy. He passed through the rooms of his own house virtually unnoticed, and it frightened him. Nobody saw him. Nobody missed him.

They belonged, one and all, to the lump on the patterning table. They were a faceless, nameless army, assigned forever to

254

Andy. The memory lived harsh and full, undiminished by time.

Todd looked at Scott with glazed eyes.

"Strangers," he croaked.

"Strangers," Scott agreed. "Hanging in doorways, you could never get where you were going without saying 'excuse me' a thousand times. One afternoon I found this lady looking through my drawers. I never found out who she was, and I never saw her again either, and believe me, I looked for her. I finally decided she wasn't even one of the programmers. She'd just wandered in off the street and got lost in the general mess."

He noted the tiny grin on Todd's face.

"If you had a sense of humor," Scott said fairly, "which I didn't, and if you wanted to do a television series of your own, it would've had possibilities. Depending on whether or not it was the season for brain-damaged kids and their screwed-up families. *Pattern With the Polikoffs,* something like that. We would have been a hit. I don't see," he added calmly, watching his brother closely, "what there is about any of this to make you think you're going crazy."

Todd looked up into his eyes.

"You remember the kitchen?" Scott asked. "There were always women standing around, looking in pots, hunting through the refrigerator behind Mom's back, talking about their sisters and their cousins and weddings and funerals and their beauty parlor appointments and who was queer and who wasn't. There was never a time during the day, except meals maybe, when the house felt normal. And at night, there was always Andy, choking and yelling and having fits, most of that in the bedroom where you slept. It was a real mess," Scott summed up the programming neatly.

They were silent then, each remembering.

"Do you love Mom?"

Scott's question came out of left field and made Todd speechless with fright, for he wasn't sure he knew the right answer, and he didn't want to anger Scott.

255

Finally, he nodded dumbly.

"Don't just sit there and agree with me, you little ape," Scott said coldly. "Do you or don't you?"

Todd made an effort to give this matter the consideration Scott seemed to feel it deserved. He decided, after a bit, that he did, indeed, love their mother, though he wasn't totally sure why he should love this relative stranger.

"I love Mommy," he said, and it occurred to him that the rush of warmth he felt meant it was true. "And Daddy."

"Do you think they don't love you?"

But he couldn't answer this. His throat ached and he couldn't speak.

"Mom and Dad always loved you. Always. When you were a baby, before Andy, Mom was nuts for you. It made me sick!" Scott added, quite truthfully, but with a hint of mischief in his eyes. "Don't you think it killed a little part of Mom when she had to stop being with you and give all that time to Andy?"

Who do you love best, Mom? Scott, much older now, saw suddenly and clearly the impossibility of his own question. And something else. The reassurance he'd desperately needed and had failed to get from his mother. That same need was mirrored now on Todd's face.

He sighed. He felt like he'd been carrying the ball for an awfully long time.

"You weren't dumb even when you were little," Scott continued. "You must have seen how much Mom hated the whole mess, how much it all hurt her, how grateful she always had to be to everybody who came to the house. There must have been a lot of mornings when she didn't want to have to get up.

"And if you knew how rotten Mommy felt, if you saw how sick she looked, and if you understood that it was all wrapped up with Andy, then maybe you started hating Andy for all those reasons.

"Do you think that would mean you're crazy? If you hated somebody for hurting your mother like that, for ruining her whole life for her?"

Todd stared at Scott. He'd never thought about it that way at all, but it could have been like that, if Scott said so. He felt almost generous, having feelings like that, hating Andy because of what the programming was doing to their mother. And hadn't it really started something like that, all the little looks and comments he couldn't then comprehend, like bits of broken color without pattern, shards of pointed glass, stabbing and bleeding him until he felt he was insane?

Later though—and he had to admit this to himself—and not very much later, he hated Andy for himself.

He looked earnestly at Scott. "Is he better?" he asked, dreading the answer, knowing the truth without hearing it from Scott. "Is he better enough for Mommy to stop being sad?"

"Andy's better," Scott said. "He looks like every other kid his age. He's big and strong and cute, and he walks and talks and he thinks, too, and maybe that's the real surprise, the real miracle, because I don't think they really *knew*. I never believed they were really sure, the doctors or anybody else, if all that business with the patterning and the rest of the programming could make Andy normal in the way he thinks.

"So now he goes to school. He's with all the other kids his age who aren't any smarter than he is. And later, he'll go to kindergarten, and maybe he'll still be able to keep up. Maybe he won't ever fall back. And he's smart. Don't ever make the mistake of thinking Andy's not smart, Todd. Andy understands all the little mean things people do. He understands a lot of things better than me or you. He kind of 'feels' things out. And he's more than smart enough to know that everybody thinks he's a freak."

He said this in exactly the same tone of voice, and it took a second for it to sink in. When he saw Todd's eyes widen, he continued.

"How do you think that makes him feel?"

Todd sat quite still, then straightened his back bravely. "I don't care how it makes him feel."

Scott was silent for a moment. "No," he said finally, without

257

emotion. "I guess there's no reason for you to care."

But Todd was growing angry.

"I had to see it all my life," Todd grew a trifle shrill again, thinking of this, of his life, his total seven-plus years. "I don't want to have to see it anymore. I want somebody to see *me*. I don't want to always have to stand back so they can see Andy. I don't want to have to always make excuses for him!"

But he hadn't meant to say that. He hadn't meant Scott to know that. He hadn't even permitted himself to say that to himself when he was alone, in the dark.

"Hey, man," said Scott gently. "Andy's our brother, you know? That's not gonna change, is it? Unless he died," Scott added flatly. "Hating him as much as you do, do you think you could handle the guilt if he died?"

It was a detestable thing to ask. It was a hateful thing to think. You didn't talk about dying that way to seven-year-old kids. Todd felt like mentioning this to Scott, but he didn't think Scott would be interested.

"Everybody's gone, Todd," Scott said. "All the volunteers. Andy's got what everybody else gets, maybe less, because he's got a family but he used to have a lot more than a family, so what's left? He got used to all those programmers and then they were gone. He sees you have friends, and I have friends, and Mom and Dad have friends, but he doesn't have any friends. Everybody left him, Todd. Everybody went."

Todd closed his eyes and heard a dull buzzing in his ears and wanted to scream that this little talk was supposed to be about him, Todd, not more and more excuses about Andy.

"You have every right to feel cheated." Scott's voice pitied him softly.

Todd opened his eyes and found himself dangerously close to tears.

"I don't want to have to feel sorry for Andy forever," he whispered.

"But you will," Scott said, quite sure. It was an irrevocable judgment.

The tears spilled.

"And you're not nuts," Scott added, coming to the point at last. "You feel all those awful things because you got tossed out when you were just a little kid, when the programming started, and not because Mom wanted it that way, but because she had to have the space. Mom didn't mean to forget about you any more than she meant to forget about Dad or me, and if you've been thinking it was just you, think again! There wasn't room for anything but Andy. There wasn't room in the house, or inside her, for anything but the programming!"

It was a brutal statement. Todd's tears had stopped but the ache remained and he picked listlessly at the blanket.

"She went for years not seeing anything but that patterning table," Scott said. "I had this winter jacket, and the sleeves were all the way up my arms, and I couldn't zip it, it was too tight to close, and I froze all winter and it wasn't just that there wasn't money for a new jacket, it was that nobody even *saw* me freezing. If Mom had let herself see all those things, it would have driven her crazy. But I was too close to it all back then, that winter, all I knew was that nobody cared about *me*. If anybody had even *seen* how cold I was, it would have made me feel a little warmer, inside myself, and I wouldn't have felt like nothing would work except running away!"

Todd stared at him.

"They didn't have any choice," Scott said. "They did the best they could."

And that was that. And it would never be different. Because it was done. Chapters, already written.

"And I never said you were nuts," Scott informed his younger brother acidly. "I said you were turning into a little punk. And I meant it. And don't go getting that look on your face either," he warned, though Todd had no expression at all on his face except one of wandering misery. "Because it's not too late to give you that beating you've been begging for . . . What's your problem? You like getting beat up?"

Todd half-rose, only to find himself shoved down. He strug-

259

gled, still under Scott's hand, his fighting spirit bucking up.

"I'm not a punk, I'm not," he wailed. "Do *you* always act like you know you should?"

After a minute, the older boy sighed. The hand that gripped Todd's shoulder lightened up a bit.

"No. But you haven't even tried. After all, you have to have some loyalty to your own family, don't you? Even if you don't like them very much. Even if you're ashamed of them."

A dull flush, hot and miserable, suffused Todd from head to foot. His throat went painfully tight.

"I'm not ashamed of Andy."

"No?"

"No."

Scott studied him for long seconds. He wisely let it go. After all, Todd was only seven.

"You're not nuts," he reiterated firmly, for good measure. "You're not even really a punk. Not yet."

Todd opened his mouth, then shut it. Rage was warring with weary acceptance. Scott was close, if he was just a little younger he would have liked to snuggle up and feel Scott embrace him. And it was true, after all, that he'd never been exactly great with Andy.

"It's not nuts to want Andy off your back. Or to hate him sometimes, the way you'd start to hate anybody who was a pest. It's not nuts to feel bad inside, empty and alone and even sick, or to hate Mom and Dad, sometimes, for never having had the time to be just with you, all alone. It's not even nuts to hate yourself for thinking all that stuff. How else do you think you should feel after all this time, playing second string to somebody no better than yourself?"

Todd's face was terribly red. All the words stuck, all the tears stuck, balled up in a gummy mass of anguish, rage, and self-doubt.

"But you're old enough now to try to be better than that, Todd," Scott admonished. "You should at least want to like yourself."

"How do you know I think all those awful things?" Todd whispered, filled with awe by this God-image keeper-brother.

Scott smiled tiredly. He looked at Todd thoughtfully, then tousled his hair.

"Because I've felt all those things and thought every one of those thoughts myself over the past five years."

26

The day had been warm, warmer by far than might be expected for late November. Todd had gone out on his bike, alone, and ended up traveling farther than he'd intended, making him quite late coming home.

He was feeling better. The soft air had chilled as night approached, and cleared his head of years of junk. All things seemed remarkably sharper in perspective.

It was darkening as he pedaled sedately up the street. It was the first time he'd been so aware of his environment, his relationship to his setting, the things that made up his personality. It was the first prewinter he could carry lightly, the first day he could recall feeling like a healthy human being, whole, not fragmented, the old tight anguish relenting a little; and if he wasn't yet completely better inside his head, he was at least aware that he wanted to be happy. Happy with himself.

At the sidewalk near their car a stranger hunched over, doing something invisible and mysterious. It made Todd curious enough to stop, half-hidden, four cars back. This wasn't a street for strangers, it was a narrow neighborhood street where everyone knew everyone else.

Dusk deepened as he watched. It made a perfect atmosphere for imaginings. His skin crawled in delighted shivers as he conjured little plots, none of them really satisfactory, which was why he kept watching, wondering what the stranger was about.

The front doors of all the houses along the block were closed. It made him a genuine outsider, locked away from warm light. The feeling was pleasurable, part of his little mystery, a nice ending to his nice day. You couldn't face grave danger and triumph if your mother was waving from the window or if people you knew were walking down the block.

Lights showed through closed curtains all along the street. Night was coming. He could still make out the form, but not the features of the stranger, and as seconds passed he began to feel foolish. It was growing colder and he felt the chill through his jacket and it was fine to stand around, making up scarey stories, but he really could make up other great mysteries in the warmth of his own room or at the dinner table.

The figure straightened abruptly, dressed in clothes without color, bleached out by the darkening world all around. So swiftly that Todd didn't understand it, the stranger was pushing away from the curb moving off. Though Todd shrank back into shadow, the stranger never looked back, pedaling rapidly—that was it, pedaling a bike. And it was a boy. Todd wanted it to be a boy, because a boy was less threatening than a full-grown man, and it was suddenly necessary to make this story a lot less threatening because boy, man, ape, whatever, he was stealing Andy's brand new bike!

Todd froze there, unable to accept that somebody was stealing a little kid's bike. Not that it was a little bike, it was a good bike, full size, Andy was big and growing fast. There were training wheels on it. How could anybody steal such a thing?

Heart thumping, dreams of chase filling his head, he pushed off, leaning low over his handlebars, pedaling past the comfort of home, beyond parental advice. The figure was far out in front already. He noted this grimly, realizing that the thief had been removing the training wheels while he stood there watching, and the bike now sped effortlessly along the street.

Todd grit his teeth and cursed as fluently as his older brother. It was the final insult, stealing a bike from a brain-damaged kid.

In hot pursuit, he too sped along. He didn't feel tired, though he'd already ridden for hours. He hadn't eaten since breakfast, but breakfast was with Scott, and so it filled him and nourished him and still kept him alert.

He had to bring back Andy's bike.

He didn't know why. It didn't matter. He couldn't go home without that bike.

Night fell. Suddenly it was pitch dark, but for the street lights. There was a different smell here, a different feel, a sprawling, unending, view of empty lots.

The figure ahead became a reflector, guiding him, that single glaring light, and he stared without blinking, bent low, still pedaling fast.

It became hypnotic—watching that rear reflector light.

Broken bottles and trash lined the road. The row houses of his own neighborhood, each exactly alike, had vanished long since to be replaced by derelict buildings, single shacks, and the long row of low buildings to his right was a line of broken-down garages.

He felt his first true thrust of fear and slowed, and as if by mental command, the figure ahead slowed, too, turned, stopped. There was a scraping sound. A rasp. Todd crouched in terror on his bike, suddenly needing to urinate, up against a fence overgrown with dead weeds and stuffed with garbage, clenching every muscle in his body tight, held his breath and heard a groaning metal sound so close he nearly wet his pants.

He bowed then to expediency, leaning the bike carefully against the fence. He opened his fly and urinated into the night. Then, vastly relieved, he took a deep breath and crept forward toward the garages, keeping out of sight.

It was growing late—nearly nine o'clock, late for a little boy out alone on a bike. They'd combed the streets for Todd, not knowing where to look, for he'd taken off that morning for a ride and hadn't been back since.

Scott had been to every street in the neighborhood, to the houses of every one of Todd's past and present friends, to the schoolyard, the playground, the ball field, even to the dark grounds of the JYC. Jack had followed his own path in the car, cruising up and down adjoining blocks, straining to see through the dark.

Judy called every person she knew, while Andy clamored for attention, then threw a temper tantrum, and was finally sent screaming to his room.

Nothing. Nobody anywhere had seen Todd.

At nine-fifteen they were all back together, in the living room. They didn't ask each other questions. They didn't try to exchange comfort. It was too soon to call the police, and Judy had already called the hospitals.

At nine-thirty, the front doorbell rang twice. Judy went rigid in her chair. Scott rose and laid a strong hand on her shoulder. Jack went to the front door.

A stranger, middle-aged, white-haired, smiling tentatively, stood on the step. Beside him, flushed and triumphant, was Todd.

"You can't be serious!"

It was all Scott had said, and his eyes were half-amused as well as half-enraged. But it didn't matter, just as Scott calling him names or berating him had never mattered when he was little and they were friends. Scott was just upset, that was all, but Scott wasn't mad, he could see that for himself.

His mother crushed him to her heart, then held him away and looked into his eyes and that look was there, swimming in her tears, the look he'd dreamed and dreamed of, the love. And even after, right after, he wasn't shaken by her anger, he already knew the truth, she'd been so frightened and that was why she was angry at him—filled with fear, deadly fear—and that meant she loved him.

He shouldn't have followed a thief on his bike. He shouldn't have gone alone. He was only seven, he was a stupid baby to have thought it was possible to do such a thing alone. You didn't do things like that in real life. You could pretend you were brave in the dark, in your bed, safe and sound, with your family all around, but you didn't go and do things like that for real—nobody said exactly why not.

And you certainly didn't trail a thief successfully half across the city—well, not that far, but far enough, anyway. You didn't do that, successfully, to a hideout full of stolen loot, where three teenage boys, big and mean and with switchblade knives, sat around smoking and drinking and congratulating each other on the night's haul. You didn't do that because that was the stuff they made cowboy shows out of, or even worse, the stuff they made Disney films out of, and life wasn't a Disney movie or even very exciting, so that when you came home late and saw somebody stealing your brother's bike what you were supposed to do was go into the house and tell your parents, who would then call the police, who would then be able, almost certainly, to kiss off the bike.

He absorbed this in the three voices of his family—Scott, his mother, his father. Not that Scott actually said much of anything, Scott mostly stood there looking at him, an odd look to his eyes and mouth.

Todd listened to all this garbled talk, thinking it sounded silly, thinking how really tired he was, how hungry, and yet they stood around yelling at him for ten minutes or so. It startled him to hear his father shouting at the top of his lungs, and then his mother suddenly wrapped her arms around him again, kissing him, crying again, then his father swung him up into his arms as if he were a child, and he hooked his strong young legs around Jack's waist and hung there in comfort, and all that sort of ruined the effect the yelling was supposed to have had.

And upstairs, later, in his bedroom, undressing slowly and quietly so as not to wake Andy, he remembered waiting on the lot by the garages, waiting for the three teenage boys to leave their loot for the night, recalled opening the garage door in a fearful sweat—it wasn't even locked, but God, it creaked, though he lifted it slowly and carefully—remembered how easily he'd extricated Andy's bike from a wealth of other stolen bikes, thinking finally of the man who'd pulled up beside him as he walked along, trying to walk both bikes at once. This kind man, a total stranger, had listened to his garbled story and had smiled, then loaded both bikes, and Todd, right into his car and driven to the house. Todd, thinking of all this, of what he'd done that night, smiled a little, and then looked up to find Scott in his doorway.

And Scott came and stood over him, then handed him his pajama top, and started to say something and swallowed hard. Scott, his Scott. Who grimaced and knelt to look at him, level, equal. And finally smiled.

"You little idiot," said Scott. "I'm proud of you!"

27

"We tried."

The phone was slippery in Judy's hand, and Jack was close beside her. At the far end of the line, Alexander Thorpe made no comment. He knew how hard they'd tried to enroll Andy in public school for the coming September.

"The District Child Study Evaluation Team recommended a restricted environment. No mainstreaming because a facility exists that's specially for children like Andy. They've labeled him 'learning disabled.' He's been approved for a private school for learning disabled children. Are you listening to me?"

But she didn't give Thorpe a chance to say anything.

"Your last piece," she told him, terribly tired and sad. "Your finished portrait of Andy Polikoff."

"Don't cry."

"I'm not crying, Jack."

"It's okay."

"It's not."

"He knows he's brain-damaged, Judy. He'll handle it."

"They're condemning him to be less than normal all his life. They're labeling him again. It's not fair, Jack."

"There's nothing permanent about this placement. He'll start school in a restricted environment where he'll have more personal attention than he'd get in public school. Later, when we know more about his potential, we can see again about mainstreaming him. For now, for always," Jack looked at her, "he deserves his own chances, doesn't he?"

The question finally brought them back to a shared understanding. Judy looked up through a haze of tears to try and see exactly what Jack saw and, miraculously, did.

"To run," she whispered.

Jack smiled.

"To win."

It was after midnight. The boys were all in bed, presumably asleep. Jack was still downstairs, though she'd been waiting since 11:30 for him to follow her up to bed. When he finally turned out the living room light and climbed the stairs, she lost her nerve and fled to the bedroom window, staring blindly out, afraid to read his face.

The nightgown hadn't been worn in years, folded and forgotten at the back of her dresser drawer behind more practical things. Palest pale green, it wasn't sheer, it was a gown, not a

267

skimpy tease, yet a tease it was, very definitely a tease, low in the neck, high in the waist, and belted under her full breasts with a ribbon of emerald green. It fell full-length and clinging, and her hair was soft around her shoulders, deep chestnut red, gleaming in the lamplight from Jack's side of the bed.

He stopped short in the doorway to look at her, and when she didn't turn, didn't speak, he started to retreat.

"Jack."

He hesitated, then came slowly into the room. He looked like the recipient of some careless joke, like a badly used child, distant and remote. Judy felt that sudden, swift fright, the fright of so many other nights, and conquered it desperately.

"Do you still love me, Jack?"

He took his time about answering. Trust Jack. He'd never jumped from frying pan to fire without first considering the move carefully, in all his adult life. He was a slow, intense man. She hadn't known how intense. She'd thought he'd be easy to live with, obvious and gentle, and he was none of these things, except gentle. Perhaps. Gentle.

Finally, he looked at her. His eyes were opaque.

"You're my whole life," he said, and his voice was flat and harsh and a bit cold—strange.

Her throat tightened and she stared at him, helpless, willing him to come to her, to scale the barrier she couldn't cross herself, but he didn't cross the room, he only watched her in silence. Because *she* had turned away, and it had to be she who came back. He was grim about this. He'd thought about it. There was ice from groin to heart to brain about this. He would not yield on this, he could not afford to give in on this. He loved her, too deeply it seemed, he'd suffered too much, standing by her in silence for all those years, making no demands . . .

Should he have made some demands on her?

But this was futile thinking. It was late for such evaluations. He was gripped by a sudden calm. If she turned from him now, having his admission of love, it was over between them, the hot intensity of their love. He'd never leave her, he meant what he'd said, she was his life, the reason for everything, nothing mattered outside that fact, nothing ever had, but if she turned from him now, if she couldn't make the effort to break down this last barrier, this wall of her own creation, then his dreams of a normal life together would die. It had been too hard, being just her best friend.

She did not turn away. She made a small sound of anguish, of release, her face twisting with misery and panic, then faltered like a woman blinded, away from the window, around the bed, over to where he stood, waiting, and he took her back into the exultant clasp of his strong arms.

Postscript

The Polikoff case came to trial in civil court, in Philadelphia, in the fall of 1979. A settlement was reached after most of the testimony was heard, and before the summation speeches. This settlement was placed in trust for Andy.

No judgment of any kind was ever formulated.

No cause for Andy Polikoff's brain damage was ever proven.

At the time of this writing, a gentle normalcy has returned. All the people who gave financially to the Polikoffs have been gratefully repaid. There is no longer a single focus in the family. Each member has taken back his or her rightful place. The myriad threads of growth and change enjoy unlimited space to form the ordinary patterns of life.

This spring, Scott joined the Air Force. In his new absence, Todd and Andy have drawn closer together. Last summer was Andy's first overnight camp experience at Camp New Horizons—his first time away from the family. It was a huge success, an enormous step toward independence, not only for Andy, but for his parents.

And finally, within the next year, Andy will be mainstreamed. He'll have a new group of peers. New chances to run. To win.

But the greatest victory was won by them all. The family stayed strong.

Spring 1982
Philadelphia, Pennsylvania

271